THE
TIN MAN

The Ted McMinn Story

THE TIN MAN

The Ted McMinn Story

Ted McMinn

with Robin Hutchison

BLACK & WHITE PUBLISHING

First published 2008
by Black & White Publishing Ltd
29 Ocean Drive, Edinburgh EH6 6JL

1 3 5 7 9 10 8 6 4 2 08 09 10 11 12

ISBN: 978 1 84502 214 3

A CIP catalogue record for this book is available from the British Library.

Typeset by Ellipsis Books Limited, Glasgow
Printed and bound by MPG Books Ltd, Bodmin

ACKNOWLEDGEMENTS

I'd like to thank my wife Marian for her love and understanding. Without her I'd have been in the gutter a long time ago. My daughter Dayna and son Kevin have always been there for me even when I wasn't there for them. Their grandparents Tom and Isabelle did a great job in helping to bring them up. My brother Mitchell and his wife Stella have been a great support over the years, as have Marian's children Gavin and Leanne and her granddaughter Taylor.

Mention must also be made of Drew Busby, Jock Wallace and Arthur Cox, who taught me everything I learned on a football pitch and much of what I discovered off it. I talk to Arthur almost every week and dearly wish I could do the same with Jock.

I owe an enormous debt of gratitude to former Derby County physio Gordon Guthrie and Derbyshire Royal Infirmary surgeons Alex Cargill and John Rowles. The first two put me back together several times only for the last one to saw me in half. Along the way Dr Les Redlaff at Derby and my GP Dr Ed Doris helped pick up the pieces. Tom Crowley and the staff at the Derbyshire Royal Infirmary's Amputee Centre, along with the doctors and nurses on Ward 31 and Sarah and Liz at the Pulvertaft Hand

Clinic, gave me back my independence. All of them made sure I'm hale and hearty and walk on at least one of my own two feet today.

My good pals Clive and Angie Thompson, Kim Thompson and Matt Morgan, Dave and Dawn Clarke, Ian and Wendy Liddle, John Timmins and all those in Scotland and Aston on Trent, who stood by me through thick and thin will be friends for life.

I'm indebted to my old mate Bob Chipres, his family and the other friends I met in Seville, who made sure I survived in that fantastic Spanish city. Emma Benjafield translated what the Spanish media made of my attempts to do so.

Everyone at Black & White Publishing in Edinburgh deserves thanks for showing faith in the book when others didn't. In particular, Campbell Brown signed us up and gave us the space to get on with it, Alison McBride provided invaluable marketing support and Janne Møller researched a wealth of interesting photos.

Craig Whinning of the *Cumnock Chronicle* and Palmerston kit man Ian Black filled in the missing blanks in my memories of Glenafton and Queen of the South and Buffs historian Jim Cochrane reminded me of what I walked out on at Kilwinning Rangers.

The people who accompanied me on the bike ride and those that dug deep to sponsor us should be as proud of their achievements as I am. Newhall RSC made sure I wasn't saddle-sore for long.

Colin Tunnicliffe organised my testimonial better than a man with twice his hair and half his girth. Committee members Bill Williams, Alex Grant, Toby Sills, Paul Clouting and Iain King provided him with invaluable assistance and helped me

ACKNOWLEDGEMENTS

assemble two teams of fabulous players. They, along with all the staff at Derby County, gave up their Bank Holiday weekend to help me out. The Rangers and Derby supporters, and all those who couldn't get tickets, made it one of the most incredible days of my life. As the song says: Simply The Best!

Tunners also introduced me to my ghostwriter Rob Hutchison, who came up with the idea for this book to pay for his new kitchen. After the endless cups of coffee I've made him in mine, he now owes me a small fortune . . .

This book is dedicated to my Dad,
the late William Wallace McMinn, who brought me
into this world, and my wife Marian,
who kept me in it.

CONTENTS

THE TIN MAN

FOREWORD
BY FORMER ENGLAND CAPTAIN
MARK WRIGHT

Ted McMinn was always getting me into trouble. I still remember the day I sprinted sixty yards to stick up for him during a bust up at the Baseball Ground. He was writhing around in the mud after being floored by Trevor Putney of Norwich City. Putney was trying to get the ball out from under Ted's legs and wasn't being too choosy about how he did it. I charged across the pitch and knocked him over the advertising hoardings into the crowd as all hell broke loose among the players. The ref sent both of us for an early bath once the dust had settled and we were even spoken to by Derbyshire Police. Needless to say, there was nothing wrong with Mr McMinn, who was by this time hiding behind our physio Gordon Guthrie. I'd later discover he had a habit of doing this and I soon lost count of the number of times I had to step in to sort out a 'disagreement'.

None of us actually believed he was a professional footballer when he first joined the Rams. We all valued Arthur Cox's judgement and thought he must have been half decent to play in Spain. But he didn't half look ungainly with the hunched shoulders and the gangling gait. Fortunately, appearances can be deceptive. When he took to the pitch Ted was usually magnificent and he often ripped defences apart. Very few people could dribble the ball like he did and he was without doubt the best crosser of the ball I ever played with or against. I'm sure Paul Goddard and Dean Saunders wouldn't have scored half the goals they did for Derby had it not been for him.

Ted always gave 100 per cent too and that endeared him to the supporters of the clubs he represented. Had it not been for a series of bad injuries I'm sure he would have played for his country – he certainly had the talent. I wonder if Scotland might have fared any better at Italia '90 had he been available to Andy Roxburgh? Ted would have worn the dark blue jersey with pride. If there's a more passionate Scot out there I'd like to meet him (or maybe I wouldn't!). Whether it was a game of cards on the bus or a frame or two in the snooker club, it was always Scotland v England with Ted. Deano occasionally got a look in as the token Welshman, but it was the English Ted loved to beat. And he always managed to do it with a smile on his face.

Whether it was in the changing rooms or charging down the wing, the Tin Man always had a laugh and a joke with his colleagues and the paying public. Arthur knew he could lift the other players single-handedly. It was for that reason alone that I had no hesitation in recruiting him as my assistant when I got into management at Southport. I was a disciplinarian and wanted things done the right way. But if I was the bad cop, Ted was definitely the good one and he always managed to keep everyone's spirits up.

He certainly needed every last ounce of his famous sense of humour when it came to the terrible news about his leg. None of his old pals could believe it when he told us he had to have it amputated. He'd suffered with bad circulation and gout for years and, like all of us, probably had too many painkilling injections. But it was a real shock to everyone in football.

When I look back to certain times when I needed to come to Ted's rescue on and off a field, it's fair to say I never thought he'd be strong enough to cope. Yet his inner strength has amazed me and I've been hugely impressed by the way he's battled back. Typical of the man was the gruelling bike ride he did to raise money for the amputee unit at the Derbyshire Royal Infirmary, where he had his operation. Mind you, he spent so much time in there as a Derby player that it's only fair he put a bit back!

Ted being Ted, he's turned his disability to his advantage. He's such a bandit in the amputee golf tournaments he now plays in that he should tee off wearing a sombrero and a droopy moustache. The first one he entered was to raise money for The Murray Foundation at a golf course near Cumbernauld in Scotland. Ted entered the tournament from his home address in Derby and was horrified when he saw his name on the leader board next to the St George's Cross. I'd have swapped one of my England caps to see the look on his face! Still, it didn't stop him winning the tournament and quite a few more across Europe in the months that followed. I might have to take a trip down to the bookies before he enters the next one to see what price they'll give me!

FOREWORD
BY RANGERS ASSISTANT MANAGER
ALLY MCCOIST

Plenty of players could have done it, but very few would have got away it. Ted McMinn was one of the few. We were playing Ilves Tampere of Finland in a UEFA Cup game at Ibrox and he'd picked up the ball level with his own 18-yard box. He'd then gone on one of his mazy runs, gliding past four or five defenders. Robert Fleck and I burst into the box at the Copland Road end, while he beat the fullback and got to the byeline. But as he swung his left boot to cross the ball he clipped it with his right and fell flat on his arse. Tampere got a goal kick and 30,000 Rangers fans got the laugh of their lives. They then gave him a standing ovation and belted out his name as he went bright red and we tried not to wet ourselves. Two tickets to the Ted McMinn show please!

We knew it was going to be box office stuff from the minute he arrived from Queen of the South. Forget film star good looks, he was a big gangly thing with no two parts hanging the right way. But God he was fun. The Rangers fans were right royally entertained in the few short years he spent in Govan. The sad thing is they don't know the half of it. He'd have to write another book to cover all the fun that wee Durranty and I had with him off the park.

And that's not to say he played the fool all the time. He must have been horrible to play against. I still remember the times when he ripped the Celtic defence to shreds during Old Firm games. You almost felt sorry for big Roy Aitken and the boys, who were left tied in knots by his runs. But if he was a nightmare to play against, he was a centre forward's dream to play alongside. I'm sure I wouldn't have scored half the goals I did in the early days of my career had it not been for him and our great mate Davie Cooper.

The two of them were fantastic wide men and followed in a great tradition of Rangers wingers. Davie was all silky skills and deft touches, whilst Ted charged at people and beat them for sheer pace. The truth was he played the game like you used to in the playground, putting the ball round one side of a defender and running round the other. Had he been born a Brazilian and not in Castle Douglas we'd have been raving about him for years.

The sad thing is he never played football for his country. Players have to be lucky with knocks during their career and sadly Ted wasn't. Had he not picked up his terrible knee injury when he was at Derby, I'm sure he would have come with us to Italia '90. How different might it have been against Costa Rica if we'd had the Tin Man to put the fear of God into them? The Tartan Army would certainly have loved him. They appreciate the skilful players like all fans, but what they really love is a player who's as eccentric as them. And they broke the mould when they made McMinn.

Missing out on international football may have been heartbreaking, but of course the really tragedy came when he hung up his boots. I was devastated for him when I heard he was going to lose his leg. I phoned him up expecting it to be a difficult call. But he was his usual self, laughing and joking. I'd gone on to cheer him up and he'd made me feel better! His optimism and humour was unbelievable. Apart from his skill, I'm sure that's the real reason why fans have always warmed to him.

His testimonial game at Pride Park will live long in the memory of everyone who was privileged enough to have been there. Along with the rest of the Nine-in-a-Row side, I was lucky enough to play in the game. I still remember the thousands of Bluenoses that turned out for him that day and showed why they're the best fans in the world. For them and us it was a coming together of the Rangers family to pay tribute to one of our own. Wherever blue is worn, Ted McMinn will always be one of the club's favourite sons.

PREFACE

I'm told that many of the great comedians suffer from depression. After making people laugh for hours on end they come off stage drained like an empty bottle. What the audience sees is a mask; a cheerful entertainer, whose job it is to make them laugh. But when they've gone home and the mask slips, the laughter is replaced by darker thoughts.

My mask slipped about an hour after the last visitor left Ward 31 of the Derbyshire Royal Infirmary. I'd been at my jovial best before that as a steady stream of visitors had come to wish me all the best. I'd greeted their grapes and good wishes with a stoical smile. Some stayed for five minutes, others for an hour. Most wanted to reminisce about my career and in particular my debut against Manchester United. Outwardly I grinned and inwardly I grimaced. There was nothing I wanted to talk about less.

Twelve hours previously my right leg had been amputated four inches below the knee. One of the tools of my trade was now gone. Under a general anaesthetic and the bright lights of an operating theatre, half of what had given me a career as a professional footballer had been sawn off.

At least I wasn't alone. My wife Marian was asleep on a

chair with her head on my bed, finally getting some rest. She was exhausted after weeks of worry and a day that had pushed her to the emotional limits. The pale white room was quiet in the ghostly glow of the low-level lighting. What had once resembled a Saturday afternoon on Sauchiehall Street was now still. The only noise I could hear was the beep of the monitors tracking my progress and administering the morphine when the agony got too much. Doctors had also given me tablets for phantom pains, but from time to time I got a sharp twinge in a foot that was no longer there. I desperately needed the toilet too after the endless cups of tea. But I wasn't about to wake Marian up for help, as she'd been on the go from 6 a.m. that morning.

Instead my thoughts drifted off to the future and what my life was going to be like when I got out. How was I going to cope in the big bad world as an amputee? After being prompted all day, my thoughts also drifted back to my past and the things I'd said and done. I felt sorry for myself at first and cursed my rotten luck. Why had I contracted this infection that had left me where I was? Why was it me who was now disabled and couldn't even get out of bed to go to the toilet? What the hell had I done to deserve this?

As I lay there staring at the whitewashed walls, I couldn't help but feel that the answer to the last question was 'quite a lot'. I'd often raised a smile and been the entertainer. But there were too many times when what I'd said and done had left other people masking the pain.

1

SEAGULL SURPRISE

If the last contact I'd had with my mother, Evelyn McMinn, had been seeing her outside our flat, suitcase packed, I'd probably have forgotten about her abandoning my brothers and I. But unfortunately she left it for fourteen years and then decided she wanted to be part of my life again. I think the fact that I'd just signed for Glasgow Rangers might have had something to do with it.

Things were going pretty well at the time. I woke up every day in Govan's Bellahouston Hotel with a large room-service breakfast waiting to be devoured. After a hot shower, I pulled on my gear and walked across the road to the Albion training ground, where we were put through our paces. The banter came thick and fast as we honed our passing and shooting and ran off our pre-pasta diet of pies and pints. I was surrounded by seasoned pros and dreamed of establishing myself as a first-team regular like them. I also dreamed of swapping the royal blue of Rangers for the dark blue of Scotland and running out at Hampden. With each passing day the darker days of my childhood were becoming a fading memory. Then it all came flooding back.

I don't know how my mum thought I'd react when I found

her letter stuffed in my pigeonhole, alongside the usual bundle of dockets, fan mail and autograph requests. She began by apologising for not keeping in touch and said it would now be nice to meet up. Maybe we could arrange to go for a drink, or have a chat about the old days? It had been such a long time after all, and hadn't the years just fairly flown by?

Well not for my dad, William Wallace McMinn, they hadn't. Not for a man who'd often have to work an eighteen-hour shift to put food on the table and clothe his four young boys. They'd positively dragged. We weren't alone in being dirt poor, but sharing the experience didn't lessen the load. Things on Dumfries' Lochside estate were in seriously short supply. Our clothes were handed down, darned and then darned again. Warmth was self-generated or enjoyed on the rare occasions we were allowed to put the heating on. Toys were envied and jealously guarded and love didn't come easy from a father too tired after a hard day's graft to lift his head to speak. Not that my mum, who now fancied a drink with her successful son, appeared to care very much.

She'd chosen to get out when she could. Dad may have seen it coming, but he didn't let on to us. The first we heard of it was an almighty row when she returned one evening from the town-centre bar where she worked. Mitchell, Martyn, Dean and I had all been sleeping. Mitchell being the oldest at eleven had his own box room. Martyn, seven, Dean, three and I as a six-year-old were tucked up in the other tiny bedroom that had just enough space for our three single beds. Despite the paper-thin walls, none of us could make out what they were arguing about as one by one we sat up to listen. We all snuck out onto the landing and took up position on the top stairs in our vests and Y-fronts. Four little boys sat in the dark, quietly crying.

Then the living room door burst open and Dad stormed out of the flat as we scampered back to our rooms, pretending we'd been asleep all along.

He was quiet the following morning when he finally returned and busied himself about the flat. 'Get out you lot and play. Stop getting under my feet,' he growled. Later on, my brother told me to go to the corner shop to buy sausage rolls for lunch. On my way I saw my mum standing across the road with her belongings at her feet, waiting impatiently for a lift. I stopped and waved but she didn't look in my direction. I made my purchases and hurried back only to find that she'd left. It felt like a black and white movie with her stood on a platform as the train rolled in, and gone once the steam had cleared.

Whether courtesy of British Rail or not, she came back. But it was only for a week. Having persuaded a pal on the estate to give him mum's new address, Dad convinced her that she'd be better back home with her family. After a few days of pretending everything was normal she was off again, this time for good. He made one last attempt to track her down one night when we were bundled into the back of his Vauxhall Viva and driven to Edinburgh. The windscreen wipers struggled to cope in the driving rain as he peered in vain down one close after another, hoping one would yield his errant wife. I think even dad knew that the scrap of paper he clung to as we splashed through the sodden streets was all that was left of his marriage. Sitting in the back, tired and confused, I vowed I'd visit Scotland's capital again in happier times. But if my mother didn't want to come with me, then that was her lookout.

I'm sure she had her reasons. The company of one of her regulars was probably one of them. But she was gone and we had to make do without her. Dad took it hard, much harder than us in truth. He had time off work and Mitchell later claimed he was very close to having a nervous breakdown. But what was a nervous breakdown on a housing scheme in 1960s Scotland? You just got on with whatever life threw at you. And so, as the only one-parent family at Lochside's St Ninians Primary School, did we.

Kids were cruel of course, they always are. We were always the scruffiest and the smelliest, as far as they were concerned. They were probably right. But there was little point dwelling on the fact we could only afford to put the hot water on for a bath on Sundays so we didn't. We were clothed, after a fashion, and we still got a card and a present on our birthdays or at Christmas time, even if it was a board game with half the pieces missing. The festive season was always a nightmare for Dad. From September onwards he'd shovel up any spare shifts that were going at the ICI plant where he worked as a fitter to make sure we didn't have to do without. I got a bike one year. It had seen better days so we deliberately got it dirty to pretend it was new. The baldy tyres with bulges out of the sides were a bit of a giveaway though.

Our diet was on the threadbare side of thin as well. We'd eat whatever and whenever we could and often did without. With Dad working all hours we regularly got by on crisps and lemonade. We were entitled to free school meals, of course, but as my attendance was patchy I didn't take advantage as often as I might. There was rarely anything in the fridge apart from on a Friday when Dad would come home with eggs, bread, beans and some chopped pork. But it was lucky to survive the weekend. A treat was a sausage supper divided between two of us, each chip jealously counted. As well as scrumping for apples and brambling, we developed a knack of stealing seagull eggs. We'd take them to our short-sighted granny Peggy McMinn, who'd poach, fry and scramble them and provide us with much needed protein. But her use of a fertilised batch to cook a sponge cake one day put us off our thievery for good.

If we were the scourge of the seagulls, Peggy was the peril of Dumfries' driving instructors. She finally passed her test at the age of sixty-five after literally dozens of attempts. The problem was her dislike of junctions, at which she always thought she had the right of way. Car after car would scatter pedestrians as another large cross went on the examiner's clipboard. Sadly she was no better once she'd passed her test and we used to dread the annual trips to nearby Balcary beach in her Hillman Imp. Getting there wasn't too bad, but the return journey to Dumfries involved a number of busy junctions. As others cowered behind the couch watching Dr Who, we'd cower behind the leatherette car seats as quarry wagons thundered past or slammed on their brakes. The trips came to an end one Christmas when she took Dean for a drive and knocked out his two front teeth ploughing into a tree. Sadly the end came for her soon afterwards, as a vicious cancer robbed the cuddly wee woman of her dignity and then her life.

Dad would accompany us on our trips to the beach and escape the squabbling for a short time by swimming hundreds of yards out to sea. The four of us would hunt in rock pools for crabs, shrimps and mussels and cook our catch over a fire in a can filled with salt water. We'd sometimes trap flounders or other small fish and treated the diarrhoea that usually followed as a hazard of the job.

In the absence of a mother, neighbours were kind to us. We'd often be called in for a sandwich or a cup of tea as we waited for dad to get home from work. But if we went to bed hungry there was always his piece box to raid during the night. He must have lost count of the number of times he opened the little metal tin for his ten o'clock and discovered half the sandwiches had already been eaten.

Football was my release, as it was for many. As a toddler I'd never be without my teddy bear and earned the nickname that still sticks to this day. And after Ted had stuck, hardly anyone called me Kevin. But after going to school at St Ninians Primary my teddy was quickly exchanged for a ball that I'd boot at a wall for hours on end. Despite being small, I was soon asked to join in kickabouts with the older boys. I even persuaded Dad to buy me some boots. Adidas ones modelled by German legend Franz Beckenbauer were all the rage at the time. Less sought after, but more affordable, was Woolworths' Winfield brand that came with an extra stripe. Ever resourceful, I coloured it in with a black felt-tip pen and strolled about like the Kaiser himself.

Even from these early days I was fast on my feet, could dribble with the ball and was usually skilful enough to evade the tackles that came thick and fast. Sundays would always see large-scale games between rival housing estates, where no quarter was given and none asked. Around thirty youngsters on each side would gather in the hope that one of the older boys would pick us in the starting eleven. As often as not, my name was chosen and I took my chances among the flying boots. It was rare that I didn't return to the flat covered in cuts and bruises, yet the respect I'd earned from my peers always eased the pain.

When I wasn't playing football I did my best to watch it. I fell in love with my local team, Queen of the South, after my first visit as an eight-year-old. My friend Stuart Jardine and I had snuck into their Palmerston Park ground through a hole in the fence at the Terregles Street end. We later discovered that we could get in for free at half-time when they threw open the gates. If dad had given me the 50p admission fee it meant I could buy a meat pie from the hut at the back of the terrace. The woman who worked there sometimes took pity on us and gave us a pie for free if she had some left at the end of the game. That saved us even more money and we were eventually able to put it towards a seat on the supporters' bus, which left the town for every away game. A long-haired lad called Rocky, who wore a Wrangler denim jacket, would always be on it. If a good crowd turned out the bus would be half full. We looked on enviously as three or four packed coaches made their way up to Ibrox or Parkhead.

The games were the highlight of my week and removed me temporarily from my drab existence. As I had little time or aptitude for lessons, football was also the one part of school I enjoyed. Fortunately a teacher called Mr Bodell encouraged me, and I found myself picked for the St Ninians team when I was two years younger than the other players. We played all the schools round our way and were successful more times than not. As I was better than most of those in the team and never got the ball back when I gave it to them, I developed a selfish game that involved very little passing. Given free rein at centre forward, I charged at the opposition and often came away from matches with a hatful of goals.

Dad encouraged me to play but would never come to parents' evenings at Maxwelltown High School, which I went to after St Ninians. He was too embarrassed being the only single parent. Teachers were largely sympathetic and turned a blind eye to my truancy because of it. The one positive thing they could note was my enthusiasm for sport, even if they didn't think I could do anything with it. I regularly told careers advisors that I wanted to be a professional footballer and was greeted each time with the same sigh and shake of the head. But the teaching profession's lack of belief was not the only thing threatening my dream: I'd also developed chronic asthma.

My condition divided the medical establishment. Some put it down to living in a damp flat, which we never got round to papering. Others said it was caused by the anxiety of my mother's departure. There were even some who suggested it was directly linked to a fractured skull I'd suffered hitting a dry-stone wall in a sledging accident as a nine-year-old. It was just another thing to be ashamed about, as far as I was concerned. I didn't have a mum and now I had asthma. What else could go wrong? If anyone got the flu, I got it twice as bad. Winter after winter echoed to the sound of my coughing and wheezing.

Luckily the asthma rarely affected my football. I can only remember once having an attack on the pitch, when I was playing for the District team. I'd forgotten my puffer and the combination of a biting-cold wind and over-exertion brought it on. The condition was news to my pals who didn't know I had it, and they were seriously concerned when I collapsed and couldn't get my breath. I was struck by an even worse attack a few days later and was taken to hospital, where I was put in an oxygen tent and monitored. I emerged five days later to be told I'd have it for life and there was nothing they could do.

Even when I was playing professional football I only used my inhaler in a toilet cubicle after flushing the handle to disguise the noise. A lot of players have pre-match rituals and quite a few are sick with nerves before games. I'd take my inhaler and then throw up, which rather defeated the point! But I got used to it being part and parcel of my life. When I see kids with asthma now I'm pleased there's less of a stigma about it. Giles Barnes at Derby is an asthmatic and I often see him using his inhaler. It's great that he doesn't feel the need to hide it.

Unfortunately, my asthma couldn't be hidden from the British Army. Like my brother Mitchell, who became a cook in the forces when he left school, I thought the profession could be my ticket out of Dumfries. Remarkably enough I passed the entrance requirements when, as a fifteen-year-old fresh out of school, I went to see the recruitment sergeant. But the medical was a step too far for my wheezing chest and they turned me down. I returned to Lochside where a pal told me there was a job going as a labourer at Robinson's Sawmill. After the briefest of interviews I signed on the dotted line. I stacked wood and helped customers with their orders and was finally presented with the princely sum of £18 on completion of my first week. It was a job that somebody with no brains could do, and that suited me down to the ground. I was a manual worker who enjoyed his football on a Saturday.

Not that I was getting a game at the time. Having left the school team with a reasonable reputation I was asked to play for Dumfries High School Former Pupils by their manager George Murdoch. George was one of those guys who seemed to do everything at the club. He picked the team, washed their kit, lined the pitch and did his best to look after the finances. He did everything in fact, apart from pick me. The standard was a reasonable one for amateur level, but most people including George thought the physical demands were beyond me. Malnourished and asthmatic, I was still short of the muscles required to hold my own. I'd train as hard as I could on a Wednesday but, come Saturday, I was always on the bench.

Then one weekend a teacher called Mr Fife got stuck in Stranraer on a broken-down bus. I knew something was up when I overheard the captain and George having a heated debate over his replacement. 'But we don't have anyone else,' exclaimed George. 'Well fine,' replied the skipper, 'but *you* can tell his dad that he's got a broken leg when it gets snapped in half by the first tackle.' With worried looks all round I was handed Mr Fife's jersey and told to stay out of trouble on the right wing. The ball didn't come to me very often, but when it did, I managed to skin the fullback and cross it for our centre forward. By half-time we were 3-0 up and cruising. Mr Fife had turned up by then, but George was more than happy with his replacement. We ran out 5-1 winners. I kept the shirt the following week and never looked back. The following season we won the league at a canter and lifted every cup we entered. Growing physically, and in terms of confidence, I began to feel more at home in my surroundings.

Old George eventually gave way to a new manager, Glen Graham. Glen had played for Ayrshire Junior side Glenafton in his younger days and knew a thing or two about the game. He was now employed as a prison warder at Dumfries Young Offenders Institution and ran their Sunday League side, who competed against other prisons across Scotland. Each team was allowed two non-prison warders and Glen asked me if I'd like to come and play. Fortunately I'd never had cause to see the inside of a prison and the stark reality of life behind the wire came as something of a surprise to a naive eighteen-year-old. Many of the inmates were in for gang related offences and they presented quite an intimidating audience watching on the side-lines. It was even worse at Shotts and Barlinnie, where you were ill-advised to wade into the spectators to retrieve the ball.

SEAGULL SURPRISE

Under Glen's watchful eye my game developed and I began to pay less attention to my surroundings. After a season in charge he suggested our centre forward Stuart Cochrane and I should consider making the step up to Juniors. Glen still had good contacts at that level, particularly at his old club Glenafton. Handily, they were due to have trials for prospective new players at their ground in New Cumnock and, after a quick phone-call from Glen, we were booked in.

2

DIAL M FOR McMINN

Legend has it that the hills and glens overlooking Glenafton's Loch Park provided refuge for Scottish hero William Wallace during the country's Wars of Independence. My father, who was named after the great patriot, was my hero when I was a child. Not only did he work all the hours God sent to provide for my brothers and I, he always got me to where I needed to be during the early days of my career. If a change of shift prevented him from giving me a lift, he'd pay someone else to drop me off. Alternatively, he'd make sure the family Volkswagen had enough petrol in it so that my older brother Martyn could act as chauffeur. The problem for me was that Martyn always drove as if the Hammer of the Scots himself was hot on our heels. While none of us were pure as the driven snow, Martyn was definitely the black sheep of the family. He learned to drive at the age of thirteen in other people's cars and was banned from the road before he was legally old enough to be on it. But as often as not my father turned a blind eye to his misdemeanours when handing over the keys to the Golf.

For much of the 1980s the A67 that runs between Dumfries and New Cumnock was a bad road. Its uneven cambers and dangerous bends accounted for the lives of too many motorists.

Martyn, who fancied himself as a rally driver, looked upon this as a challenge. Having hotfooted it out of Dumfries and negotiated the thirty-eight miles of winding road that lay between, we'd regularly screech to a halt in a cloud of smoke outside Loch Park. Martyn would then grasp his watch with a look of disgust or, often as not, punch the air and shout 'Ya beauty, two minutes off my personal best!' Fortunately for Stuart Cochrane and I, it was Dad who took us there for the first time for our trial in July 1982. We made the trip at a more leisurely pace accompanied not by the skirl of the pipes, but by the theme tune from the hit series 'Fame' that was never off the radio that summer. This was my big chance to make people remember my name!

Loch Park then was much as it is now. Three quarters of the ground consisted of grassed banks and there was a white rail to separate supporters from the pitch. They've since added a new clubhouse and a corrugated iron stand, but neither of them was there in our day. It could have been Hampden to Cocky and I, who were impressed by the fact that they had advertising hoardings. The pitch was also fantastic and appeared to justify its reputation as being one of the best playing surfaces in Junior football. We changed in silence with the other twenty youngsters who'd been offered a trial by manager Tommy McGinn. We then played two forty-five-minute halves with frequent changes made to both sides.

It wasn't the first trial I'd had, having been asked by Queen of the South to attend several bounce games whilst playing for Dumfries High School Former Pupils. On every occasion I'd blown it after nerves got the better of me or I'd convinced myself I wasn't good enough. Glenafton was different. Having a friend with me probably helped and for the first time I felt at ease. I felt we both did okay but only three people were to be told they'd made the grade. Remarkably, Cocky and I were two of them. Club Secretary Alex Jess gave us £30 each to sign amateur contracts and paid us £10 a game. I'd moved on to £20 a week at the sawmill by now but felt like a king when the money was handed over.

Dad kept my feet on the ground by demanding that I hand over some of the cash in dig money. After landing the job at the sawmill he'd started taking £5 a week off me, which he now increased to £15. I'd put the cash on his bedside table every Friday night. Martyn, who was working as a mechanic at a garage in Dumfries, had a similar arrangement. Both of us bought our own food and still guarded it as jealously as we had done when we were kids. There were fewer mouths to feed by then as Mitchell was away with the merchant navy and Dean had joined the King's Own Scottish Borderers and was stationed at Peebles.

Cocky and I made our debuts against local rivals Auchinleck Talbot in a sectional game of the Jackie Scarlett Cup. Talbot would go on and dominate the game at Junior level in the next few years, becoming the first team to ever win the Scottish Junior Cup three seasons in a row. They had the makings of a decent side when we took them on. But we weren't intimidated and got into them straight away. Tommy played me on the right wing, with fellow Dumfries High School Former Pupil player Alex Beagrie beside me in midfield.

It wasn't long before I was booted up in the air as the older heads tried to rough up the youngsters. A guy called John McMillan was eventually given his marching orders after several over-zealous tackles and the Talbot players accused me of getting him sent off. The decision changed the face of the match and we eventually ran out 2-1 winners. It had been a bit of a baptism of fire and I had the bruises to show for the first game I was ever paid to play in. But I felt very comfortable in my new surroundings and was confident I could prosper.

Attendances at Junior games in those days were much bigger than they are now. Where Glens will pull in crowds of two or three hundred, we used to regularly play in front of 800 to 1,000 spectators. I developed an affinity with the home crowd, who liked my style of play. I managed to score a couple of league goals and set up my fair share for my colleagues too, picking up the odd man of the match award along the way.

Supporters used to describe me as eccentric. I had few if any tricks but I was always keen to take players on. This usually meant running full pelt at the fullbacks with my arms flailing beside me. My job was to beat them any way I could before putting in a cross for Cocky or one of the other forwards. The most frequent thing I heard from fans, which stuck throughout my career, was that they never knew what I was going to do next. Whilst happy to go along with the compliment, I've always found that odd. If you asked any footballer if they planned out every move in their head beforehand, you'd surely get very few who said yes.

Still, I must have been doing something right. Within just two weeks of making my debut at Loch Park the phone began to ring. Scouts had started filing good reports and there were a number of senior clubs who were keen to take a look at me. Glens quickly put me on a professional contract, as they didn't want me leaving on the cheap. I got £200 for signing the deal and was now on £30 a match.

The problem for people trying to get hold of me was, like most people who lived in Lochside, we didn't have a phone.

We didn't tell them that of course, as we liked to kid on we had all the mod cons. Instead, we regularly gave out the number of the public phone box on the street. So did half the estate unfortunately, and most evenings were spent with a crowd of neighbours standing outside the box arguing whose turn it was to make a call. Clubs who got in touch must have thought I lived in a big house as they waited on the end of the line for someone to run to our flat to get me!

Kilmarnock were the first to dial the McMinn hotline when they asked me up to play in a reserve game against Celtic at Rugby Park at the end of August. Cocky was asked along too and we both had reasonable games, me up against a young Tommy Burns in midfield. The pitch was a bowling green and I was delighted to be asked back the following week. After another ninety minutes the manager Jim Clunie said he wanted to sign me and offered an amateur contract of £80 a week. I'd train on the Tuesday and the Thursday and play for the reserves on the Saturday. It was a big opportunity, but I turned it down.

Looking back, I think it was the travel that didn't appeal. Kilmarnock was a long drive or the best part of two hours on a train that stopped at every lamp post. It was bad enough going to Glenafton three times a week with my maniac brother at the wheel. I'd often get back form training at midnight and have to be up at 6 a.m. the next morning to go to work. I was young and keen and could play every night. But I also felt like I'd be burning myself out.

I didn't have long to dwell on my decision as Ayr United got in touch the following week. Dad drove me there this time and I had a reasonable game. Assistant manager George Caldwell said he liked the look of me and was keen to offer a contract. However the decision would have to be made by manager Willie McLean. The third brother of Scotland's famous football family was away on other business. But he'd be in attendance at Broomfield the following week where Ayr were set to take on Airdrie.

McLean was there all right and took an immediate dislike to me in the dressing room. He eyed my scrawny legs with scepticism and was even less impressed by my choice of boots. I'd been weaned off the four stripe Winfields by now and was sporting a white pair of Alan Ball's, which I'd bought in the sale at Woolies. One of them had a hole in the toe and McLean told me I couldn't represent the mighty Ayr United in such shoddy footwear. Instead, he handed me a brand-new pair of moulded Adidas World Cups. They were the nicest boots I'd ever seen. The snag was they were a size eight and I was a size ten and they began to cut off the circulation in my toes as soon as I put them on. I hobbled through the game and did little of note. At the end McLean took great pleasure in retrieving the boots and informing me that I wasn't good enough. Little did he know that his loss might soon be his brother's gain.

The Kilmarnock deal was still on the table and members of the Glenafton committee were keen to make a few quid for the club by moving me on. The pound signs flashed in their eyes when the next man to call the phone box was Rangers' assistant manager Tommy McLean. Manager John Greig had not seen me play, but he'd heard good reports from his network in the South West. The club had arranged for a number of youngsters including me to take part in all day training session.

I was sick with nerves and got off to a particularly bad start in the warm-up. I'd never done proper training drills before and was so unused to the commands barked at us that I spent most of the session doing press-ups as punishment. During the game that followed, in which the reserves and trialists took on the first team who'd play that Saturday, I marked Jim Bett and didn't get near him. I hardly got a kick of the ball as the touch-and-go game touched and went. Quite simply, I wasn't anywhere near the same level as anyone else on the pitch, in terms of fitness or skill. After being thanked for coming, I was given the big thumbs down by Tommy and travelled back to Dumfries feeling flat as a pancake.

Rangers might not have wanted me, but Queen of the South did. Word had got round at Palmerston Park that I'd been having trials and, after letting me go in the past, they were keen that I didn't slip through the net again. Rather than use the phone, Chairman Willie Harkness and his brother Sammy called round in person. I'd supported Queens throughout my childhood and I was excited by their interest. The brothers were tremendous servants of the club, with Willie in particular devoting much of his life to the cause. He first got involved as a ballboy before making his debut as a player in 1938. He went on to take charge of the club and also became chairman of the SFA, leading the national team to the 1978 and 1982 World Cups. And here he was at my door, desperate to sign me.

Manager Drew Busby was even more complimentary the following morning when he said there would be no need for a trial. He hadn't personally seen me play, but everything he'd heard was good. I'd be straight into the first team on Saturday. The Glenafton committee weren't quite as enthusiastic when they heard what was on the table. Kilmarnock hadn't given up hope of signing me and a sum of £5,000 was being talked about. Queens were prepared to offer £325 up front along with a £1,000 worth of lottery style scratch cards. It was a pretty meagre

DIAL M FOR McMINN

offer even by the standards of the day. But when Glens realised my heart was set on joining my local club they knew they couldn't stand in my way. Willie even got me to take the box of scratch cards up to Loch Park on my final visit to pick up my papers. I don't think Glens were too impressed when they later realised the licence had expired on the cards.

Drew threw me straight in for my debut away at East Stirling on 3 November 1982. I was nervous as hell on the bus on the way up to Falkirk, but we managed to win 2-1 and I didn't feel out of my depth. The game was a little faster if anything, yet there wasn't too much of a change from Junior football. Drew, who played centre forward as well as managing the team, put me on the wing hoping I'd provide him with plenty of scoring opportunities. He was a rampaging centre forward in the style of Steve Bull and used to batter defenders if they got in his way. Most of his goals seemed to be bullet headers or thumping drives. I managed to get on the score sheet just two weeks after my debut, when I scored in our 3-2 win at Stenhousemuir. It gave me a great lift and proved I could cut it at that level.

The problem was I tweaked my hamstring in the process. I knew I hadn't torn it, as I was able to walk about without too much agony. But Drew insisted I got it seen to quickly before it got worse. He sent me up to Edinburgh to an old boy who'd looked after his injuries when he'd played at Hearts. The guy was 110 if he was a day, but he had powerful, healing hands and would patiently massage my legs as I perched on his dining-room table.

The hamstring kept me in and out that season and I ended up making only twenty-two appearances. When it got too much for the old healer, the club doctor would inject it with cortisone on a Friday night before a game. The back of my leg would then go numb and I'd go to the cinema to relax. I found it most comfortable to drape my leg over the seat in front. But the cortisone made my leg jump up and down and if I held it too high it almost caught in the projectionist's beam. God knows what people thought I was up to, jerking about on the back row.

The hamstring was much better by the start of the 1982/83 season, when I became a regular in the team. But as my fitness improved, morale declined. Most of our players lived in the Glasgow area and, to save them petrol money, they trained separately from the Dumfries boys, on Tuesday and Thursday nights. The fact that we only got together on match days meant that we never really bonded. The Glasgow boys also resented the fact the locals – Cocky and I, George Cloy, Graeme Robertson and Rowan Alexander – were popular with the supporters, and there was often friction when we were selected instead of them.

Fellow winger Jimmy Robertson seemed particularly bitter, having considered himself to be 'Mr Queen of the South' for a number of years. He was always having a dig at me for one thing or another, and was particularly fond of taking the mickey out of my appearance. After doing so during a pre-match get together at a local hotel, I stood up at the table and gave him both barrels. The pent-up anger combined with my comparative youth was all too much for me and I found myself bursting into tears and storming out. Drew later admonished me for my outburst and told me I had to grow up. But he also put his arm round me and told me I was headed for much better things than Jimmy Robertson.

Both the team and I were lucky to have Drew, who was the glue that bound us together. Despite our differences, we began the season playing good, positive football. We quickly climbed up the league thanks to a number of decent victories, including a 2-0 win over Stenhousemuir in which I managed to score again by cutting inside the fullback and hitting a shot with my left foot. This time it was made all the sweeter as I scored at the Portland Drive Terrace, the traditional home end where I'd stood as a boy.

I also scored against Albion Rovers a couple of months later, in what was the worst ground I ever played in during my career. We battered them 4-1 after clambering out of their decrepit changing rooms and over the dog track that ran round the pitch. There were about 100 spectators huddled under a corrugated roof and another 200 people gathered on a high point outside the ground. I don't know if the club had been expecting the 200 to be inside because they grossly miscalculated the number of meat pies they were hoping to sell. As a consequence we were all given as many as we could carry after the game and I spent the rest of the week eating them for my lunch at work. Those pies must have had a secret ingredient as they propelled us up the league. By the morning of 14 April we were second top to Forfar and looking a very decent bet for promotion. Then we choked.

If we'd won even a couple of our last five games we'd have probably got up, but we somehow managed to lose all but one of them. Clydebank started the rot on the 14th itself with a 2-0 victory, before we went down 6-3 to Arbroath, 3-0 to Forfar, drew 0-0 with Stranraer and lost our final game of the season 3-1 to Stirling Albion. Drew was absolutely furious and laid into us afterwards, picking up a teacup and launching it at the wall. The crockery sailed over my shoulder and smashed into a thousand pieces in the shower cubicle behind me. He was so upset that we didn't dare complain when everybody subsequently cut their feet. My abiding memory of the season will always be standing under that lukewarm shower, as blood and wasted opportunities swirled down the drain. It was the final straw for the board who responded to the disappointment of the fans by giving Drew Busby the boot.

His replacement was Nobby Clark. There were high hopes for Clark, who'd played in the successful Queens team of the previous decade, and wasn't to be confused with the Bay City Roller of the same name. The fixture list at the start of the 1983/84 season had a rock-and-roll feel about it however, when we were drawn out of the hat against the mighty Glasgow Rangers in the first round of the Scottish League Cup.

Unlike nowadays, when top-flight sides rest their best players in the early rounds of cup competitions, Rangers put out a full-strength side for the first of the two legs up at Ibrox. They beat us 4-0 and coasted through the match. But it was great to play at such a fantastic ground, even if only 8,000 spectators turned up to watch. There were almost as many at Palmerston in the return leg, where they stuck another four past us. We managed to get one back this time, although my main contribution to the match was a late tackle, which annoyed their giant goal-keeper Peter McCloy. But I relished my first taste of the big time. Little did I know that there was a lot more to come in just a few short weeks.

3

SIRLOIN STEAK, COOKED

Sunday 21 October 1984 dawned much the same as any other day that autumn. I dragged myself down to the corner shop, aching from the previous day's game, to pick up a bacon roll and the morning papers. There was further speculation on the back pages that my days in Dumfries were numbered. The rumour this time was that English giants Liverpool and Newcastle United were both keen to sign me. It was only a matter of time before I made the big-money move across the border, by all accounts.

I was getting used to being linked with other clubs and I found it less unsettling than some players. Week in, week out, the directors' box would be full of scouts and I got used to being told that yet another team was running the rule over me, whatever that meant. Liverpool's chief scout Geoff Twentyman had certainly checked me out along with the club's former manager Bob Paisley. And Arthur Cox would later tell me that Newcastle had me watched by no fewer than seven members of staff. The Mountie always gets his man in the end, it would seem.

Fortunately, I'd always had a very honest relationship with Queens Chairman Willie Harkness and his brother Sammy. As custodians of a Scottish Second Division club, they were realistic about the financial rewards a lucrative transfer fee could provide and promised they'd never stand in my way. But I was a little surprised to see them that Sunday evening when they turned up unannounced at the flat. Dad was working a late shift again and little Dean was dispatched to answer the door. He returned to inform us that two men in suits were outside and, as he hadn't been in trouble with the police, it must have been one of us. I approached with caution and was relieved to find Willie and Sammy shifting nervously on the balls of their feet.

Still embarrassed by the state of the flat, I didn't invite them in. But it wasn't hospitality they were after. Willie opened up: 'Hi Ted, just wondered if you'd be all right to take a wee trip to Glasgow in the morning?'

I thought about it for a second or two and said no. 'I've got my work at the sawmill I'm afraid. Why, what's it about?'

'I shouldn't worry about your work son,' came the reply, 'because you're signing for Rangers. I'll come up to Glasgow with you. See you at Palmerston at 8 o'clock. Put a tie on and don't be late.'

The whole conversation lasted less than thirty seconds then they were back down the stairwell and out into the street. It wasn't so much a request as a command. I was signing for the biggest team in Scotland whether I liked it or not.

I was still concerned about getting time off work at short notice when Dad finally got in. He told me not to be so daft and to concentrate on getting a good night's sleep. In the morning he tied my tie for me, as he had been doing for years. I'd never quite developed the knack of putting one on and used to creep into his bedroom early in the morning to ask if he'd do it for me. Half asleep, he'd sit up in bed in the pitch dark and tie it round his own neck over his pyjama top before handing it over to me and going back to sleep. This time I put on a white shirt, a pair of Burton's trousers, white socks and black patent shoes. Fashion wouldn't arrive in Dumfries for some years to come!

A nervous tension hung over the car as we made the journey up the M74 past Moffat, Lesmahagow, Larkhall and Hamilton. The four of us, Willie, Sammy, Dad and I, were lost in our own thoughts. I'd been to Ibrox before when Tommy MacLean had me up for a trial. But I'd been turned down flat back then. The boot was on the other foot now. As we pulled to a halt outside the ground, the huge main stand loomed up over dad's battered Golf. We'd have looked far more respectable arriving in Willie's Mercedes, but Dad had insisted on driving. The imposing red brick facade with its arched windows and blue and gold club crest on each gable end couldn't have been more different to Palmerston. Taking deep breaths, we all went through the main entrance and were greeted by Club Secretary Campbell Ogilvie. He led us up the famous marble staircase and through what felt like acres of wood panelling, before we made our way to the trophy room. The victories that delivered each silver cup, gilded shield and polished plate were then explained in great detail to us as we tried to take it all in.

Afterwards, Dad and I were led out into the Directors' Box to catch our breath. We spent a minute or two gazing out at the vast green pitch and banks of endless terracing as the paperwork was prepared downstairs. The stadium was empty but for a handful of ground staff marking out the lines and mowing the grass. Dad was the first to break the silence. 'This is every father's dream Kevin,' he said with tears appearing in the corner of his eyes. 'I'm very proud of you.' He'd never been a football fan himself, but his old man had been a Rangers supporter. He was well aware of what it meant. It was the most emotional that I'd seen him since mum left. But this time he was happy. I smiled at him and we shared an unforgettable moment together as father and son.

When it was time to sign the contract, Rangers Chairman John Paton leant over me dressed immaculately in club blazer and tie. I put my name to three copies of the document. I was told I had a five-year contract and would be picking up £250 a week in wages. That would be topped up by a £30 supplement if I played for the first team and an extra £10 a point. The club would put me up in the Bellahouston Hotel across the road until I settled in and I was to report for training on Friday, following the team's return from the UEFA Cup tie against Inter Milan.

There was also the small matter of a £10,000 signing on fee that was to be matched by a grateful Queen of the South, whose immediate financial future had been secured by the £100,000 transfer fee. I floated out of Ibrox in a trance, wondering all the way back to Dumfries what a sawmill worker earning £20 a week was going to spend £20,000 on. And, perhaps more importantly, where he was going to put it given that he didn't even have a bank account.

Finances were still on my mind the following morning when I went into tell the lads at the sawmill that I was leaving. I hadn't phoned in sick the previous day and was expecting a rollicking. But they owed me my wages from the previous week so I couldn't just tell them to stick their job. After clocking in, I tapped on the door of the office and was glared at by all and sundry. The owner Jack Robinson wasn't best pleased.

'Where were you yesterday?' he moaned. 'You can't just come

and go as you please you know. If you were sick you should have let us know.'

'Aye, I'm sorry I should have,' I mumbled by way of reply. 'It's just that I've signed for Rangers and I'm not going to be coming to work any more I'm afraid.'

Silence descended as the rest of the office took in the news. Jack's son Stuart, a chip off the old block in more ways than one, then came out with the immortal line: 'What the fuck do you want to go to Berwick for son?'

The lads on the shop floor were quicker to catch on. They'd kicked me round the yard wearing steel toecapped boots during our lunchtime games and were delighted that I was escaping after five long years. They were also pleased that I could now get them in to Ibrox for free and began demanding complimentary tickets.

My transfer to Rangers was the back page news in the *Dumfries & Galloway Standard* and merited a small mention in the nationals too. It was never going to be the main story as Maurice Johnston had signed for Celtic from Watford that week, for a fee four times that of my own. There was also renewed speculation that another promising youngster, East Fife's Gordon Durie, was moving to Hibernian. Rangers had also been ordered to pay a £2,000 fine after trouble flared in Dublin during the game against Bohemians in the previous round of the UEFA Cup. One paper carried an article on the story accompanied by a photograph of me holding a large 'Welcome to Ibrox' sign above my head on the pitch. Another had a picture of Jock Wallace and I after he'd told reporters that he'd spent so much on a twenty-two-year-old Second Division midfielder because he 'believed in buying good players'. Why he was clenching his fist under my chin in the photo remains a mystery.

I vividly remember my first day's training at Ibrox. I'd checked into the Bellahouston the night before and swiftly ordered the most expensive thing on the menu, safe in the knowledge that the club would pick up the tab. I was about to start eating three square meals a day for the first time in my life. The hotel restaurant's specials board was going to get a hammering, whether I could pronounce what was on it or not. I went to bed early, but through a combination of indigestion and nerves, I couldn't sleep. I was now a full-time professional footballer at one of the biggest teams in Britain. I was living the dream. But I was also the new kid on the block and I had serious doubts that I could cut the mustard.

Jock Wallace's assistant manager Alex Totten introduced me to the players the following morning. The apprentices and the reserves were wary, concerned no doubt that I'd be taking their place. Few if any of the first-team recognised me as I shyly shook their hands. To a man you could see them saying to themselves 'Ted who?' I felt like a supporter meeting his heroes and had to stop myself asking Davie Cooper if he wouldn't mind signing my autograph book. Goalkeeper Peter McCloy broke the spell. Big Peter remembered me from the previous season's League Cup tie. I'd gone in late on the man they called the Girvan Lighthouse and offered him a bit of lip for good measure. 'Aye,' he recalled gripping my hand tightly, 'You're the cheeky wee bastard who shoulder charged me at Palmerston.' It wasn't the most promising start.

Training was light, as it always was on a Friday. Free kicks and corners were the order of the day. After a fifteen-minute warm-up we went through the set piece routines and ended with an eleven-a-side match. I did my best to keep up but felt woefully off the pace. Physically, I was skin and bone, weighing in at ten stone wet through. I could just about keep up when we did laps of the pitch, but large numbers of press-ups and sit-ups were beyond my scrawny muscles. Mentally, I was still adjusting to the fact I wouldn't be getting up at 6 a.m. to do a nine-hour shift at Robinson's Sawmill. Jock Wallace must have seen some potential. But I felt like a hopelessly unfit hillbilly who needed to shape up fast.

Fortunately Alex Totten took me under his wing. I'd turned up at training with one pair of boots. They were £40 Adidas ones that had cost me a week's wages, including the £15 boot allowance I'd been given at the start of the season by Queens. But they'd seen better days. All the other players had at least three pairs and I was swiftly handed new ones at the end of training. As soon as I'd been given them, they were handed to one of the apprentices to break in so I didn't get blisters. I was amazed that such a practice went on and was in a daze when McCloy tapped me on the shoulder.

In those days, the first team all got changed in the home dressing room whilst the reserves and the youth players had to make do with the smaller room allocated to the visitors. Having signed a five-year deal, I fully expected to be in the second team for months. But as I looked at the team-sheet for the following day's game against St Mirren, there in black and white, on the subs' bench, was quite clearly one 'T McMinn'. My boots were shabby and the goalie thought I was a prat, but I'd arrived!

Hiding behind big Peter I made my way into the cavernous changing rooms, quickly finding an unoccupied peg in the corner. I was about to dive into the large communal bath when Totten approached with a clipboard. 'Right Ted, pre-match meal. You're the new boy. What would you like?' I wasn't used to having a choice and looked round anxiously as twelve pairs of eyes honed in on me.

'I really don't mind,' I mumbled, looking at the floor. 'Whatever the other boys are having.'

'Well do you want a steak?' he asked.

'Aye that'd be great Alex, thanks very much.' A week ago I'd been a part-time footballer who worked in a sawmill. Seven days later I was on the verge of my debut for Glasgow Rangers. Not only that, they had steak as their pre-match meal.

'Is that a sirloin, rump or fillet, Ted, and how do you normally have it?'

'A sirloin,' I replied hesitantly, 'and, er, cooked maybe?'

'Aye, I know that son, but are we talking rare, medium or well done?' he snapped, as some of the players began to snigger.

'Oh, I always have it well done,' I said blushing and trying to remember what I'd heard said on television. Totten ticked his list.

'Mushrooms?'

'Yes please, boss.'

'Tomatoes?'

'Aye, that'd be great.'

'Onion rings?'

'Oh lovely, yes.'

'Chips?'

'Definitely. I love chips.'

'What kind of chips do you like?'

'What kind of chips do you get?'

'Well, fat ones or skinny ones.'

'Oh fat ones for me, that'll be grand.'

'And finally Ted, are you a tomato ketchup man or HP Sauce?'

SIRLOIN STEAK, COOKED

'Always ketchup for me please, boss,' I beamed, sitting back to savour the forthcoming feast.

But my contentment was short-lived as the changing room door was flung against the wall. In strode big Jock, rain glistening on his square spectacles. The waiter quickly turned traitor.

'Listen to this gaffer,' said Totten, as the whole room began to laugh. 'You'll never guess what the new boy wants for his pre-match. He's having a sirloin steak and he'd like it well done, if that's ok with you? He wants mushrooms, tomatoes, onion rings and chips. But he doesn't want ordinary chips he wants big fat ones. And he doesn't want HP sauce he wants ketchup. He's very strict about that – says it's his favourite!'

Jock went redder than anything Heinz could produce, stared me in the eye and growled, 'Listen son, I don't know what it was like at Queens, but when you play for me you'll have scrambled eggs on fucking toast like everyone else!'

As introductions went, it was hardly the most promising. But it was a taste of things to come with Big Jock. He was six feet four inches and sixteen stone of intimidation, every inch the soldier who'd made his mark in the jungles of Malaysia. When he listened, he eyed you with a cold stare. When he spoke, he growled. His network of scouts thought there was enough raw potential in me to mould a decent player. That mould had been formed a long time ago by the club's founding fathers, as far as Jock was concerned. 'Character' was his favourite word and would be trotted out at every opportunity. It was what was expected of you when you put on the blue jersey. He knew every detail of that jersey's history and was steeped in its traditions. Had he been a stick of rock he'd have read Rangers Football Club from top to bottom.

My debut at Love Street the following day was less explosive than my pre-match meal order. For the first time in my career I was pleased to be on the bench. It gave me a feel for it without throwing me in at the deep end. The game was never in doubt and we went 2-0 up thanks to goals from Ian Redford and Iain Ferguson. I was minding my own business with twenty minutes to go when Jock told me to warm-up. As I jogged up and down the touchline I could hear folk asking one another who I was.

New signings are paraded in front of the cameras these days and fame is instant. Back then, nobody knew me from Adam. Thankfully, I got a good reception from the 14,000-strong crowd when I came on and replaced Ferguson. I was petrified I was going to make a mistake. Luckily, my first touch was good and the game didn't pass me by as I'd feared. But I was relieved when the final whistle came. I'd done nothing of note and hadn't exactly set the heather on fire. Yet I was off the mark as a Rangers player – and it was a damn sight better than working in a sawmill.

My first Old Firm game was a much livelier affair predictably, even if it was only for the reserves. No sooner had I got in the first team than I was out of it again, fortunately through no fault of my own. The team were in the League Cup final at Hampden and I was cup-tied having turned out for Queens earlier in the season. There was no point going away to the team hotel at Turnberry with the lads, so I knuckled down to take on our greatest rivals. It was an early kick-off on the Saturday at Ibrox and came hot on the heels of a full match I got against Dundee on the Wednesday night. It was early days and people were still finding out my strengths and weaknesses and whether I wanted the ball to my feet or over the top. Alex Totten gave me plenty to do in training and was keen that I developed my technique, but I was obviously doing enough to keep my place.

Reserve-team football it might have been, but there was no

less at stake to the 10,000 plus supporters packed into the main stand. They got right behind the team and let us know exactly what was required. We had a talented side containing some of the club's emerging talent, including Derek Ferguson and Ian Durrant, and were confident about getting a result. I had a couple of decent touches early doors and was feeling good.

About half an hour in I played a one-two on the halfway line with Ferguson and turned blind into what felt like a double-decker bus. Hoops centre half Paul McGugan was never a dirty player, but he wasn't known for his delicacy either. He'd caught me above the right knee and I went down like a ton of bricks. The leg immediately began to swell up as I tried to run off what I thought was a dead leg. But it was stiffening by the second. Eventually I had to come off as worried medical staff began muttering about a blood clot. Moments later I was on the way to Ross Hall Hospital by ambulance. After much debate I was given the all-clear and told I could go home in the morning after the bruising had come out. I wasn't badly injured but I was black and blue and had been given my first taste of the Old Firm. It was no place, I concluded, for delicate one-two's.

I watched the final from the comfort of my sofa the following afternoon, with a can of lager and an ice pack strapped to my leg. Iain Ferguson grabbed the winner in front of nearly 45,000 at Hampden as the club retained the trophy they'd won against Celtic the previous season. I was more than a little envious sitting alone in my hotel room as the players cavorted around in front of the massed ranks at the Mount Florida end. Silverware had been a distant dream at Palmerston. Cups were what other teams in higher divisions won. I had to pinch myself as I took it all in. This was my club and these were my pals. And next year, that was going to be me.

4

WELCOME TO THE GOLDFISH BOWL

I spent the months after the Cup Final bedding in at Ibrox and adjusting to my surroundings. Getting used to the idea of being a full-time footballer took some doing. I still had to pinch myself when I went across the road to training. There was a definite hierarchy in the squad, with the senior players like Davie Cooper most certainly top of the tree. Coops was a fantastic guy and always had time to pass on bits of advice to a fellow winger learning the trade. He was also the undisputed king of the heady tennis court that was the focus of our attention before training.

The court was basically an old volleyball net that was strung up outside the changing room. But the players used to spend hours trying to beat each other with headers and volleys. The apprentices and the new boys like me used to look on with envy as the likes of Coops, Ally McCoist, Craig Paterson and John McClelland slugged it out. Plenty of money changed hands on the side and you weren't allowed a piece of the action unless invited. I was quite content to watch the experts.

Jock Wallace was keener to get me involved, even if he did have concerns about my appearance. He became obsessed about my skinny frame and would shake his head at our Friday morning weigh-ins, when I regularly tipped the scales two stone lighter than the others. His solution was to get Alex Totten to give me extra training sessions and to tell me to eat two portions of steak a day at the Bellahouston.

It paid off when I got a run in the side starting with a substitute appearance in our 2-1 defeat at home to Aberdeen in mid-November 1984. I was only on the pitch for twenty minutes, but I kept Jim Leighton busy with a couple of fierce shots and was disappointed not to get the equaliser. On the Tuesday night we took on Australia in a friendly and it was sad that only 4,000 spectators turned up to watch Super Cooper and me rip them apart.

These performances earned rave reviews in the papers and journalists were falling over themselves to describe my 'eccentric' style of play. I considered myself to be an orthodox winger and couldn't understand what the fuss was about. It was flattering to be compared to South African star Don Kitchenbrand, even if I didn't endear myself to older Gers fans when I told Rodger Baillie of the *Daily Record* that I'd never heard of him.

But others went way over the top in their apparent praise. Jock MacVicar in the *Daily Express* said I'd be more at home on a basketball court, whilst others described me as an 'oddball hero', 'a true tanner ba' man' and 'master of the unpredictable'. The most original was our very own *Rangers News*, who weighed in with a tongue-twister of their own when they described me as 'perpetual motion personified'. That had all the players scratching their heads.

Over the years there's been a great deal of talk about my two nicknames – and most of it is rubbish. I was christened Kevin and was always referred to as that by my dad and brothers. Terry Butcher said in his book that I changed my name to Ted because Kevin was a Catholic name. Now I love Terry to bits, but he's got that one wrong. I'd been known as Ted since I was knee-high to a grasshopper on account of my first companion being a cuddly toy. When I joined Rangers I signed my name Kevin on the autograph cards that were sold in the club shop as I thought it was the done thing to do. But there was some confusion as to what I should be called in the programme. Jock told me to stick to one or the other and I chose Ted because I'd never liked Kevin. It had nothing to do with religion. I made the mistake of telling a couple of the newspapers this and every time I went out Celtic fans would shout 'All right Kevin' to wind me up. As often as not I'd greet them with a two-fingered salute.

I've heard people say that Butcher also christened me The Tin Man when he came to Ibrox. It's true he mistook me for a centre half when we met during a pre-season friendly at White Hart Lane and couldn't believe I was a winger. But I'm not sure he can claim credit for it in all honesty. However, the name was quickly picked up by the papers, whoever was responsible for coining it. I suppose I did run a bit differently to others, but when you're largely self-taught like I was then it's inevitable that you have certain quirks. Throughout my career I just tried to entertain people. The supporters paid good money to come and watch us and it was up to us to turn on the style.

Scottish football at the time was full of hammer throwers and jobbing professionals. Davie Cooper was the one true exception. I was nowhere near as skilful as he was but I tried to emulate him by running at the opposition. I certainly didn't model myself on a character in *The Wizard of Oz*. It's a bit difficult when you've never seen the bloody film. But hey, I didn't have to think too long about the title of this book – so it's not all bad!

A week after losing to Alex Ferguson's Dons we put Morton to the sword at Cappielow and then secured successive 1-1 draws against Dundee United and Hearts. We then beat St Mirren again before I sat out December's Old Firm game with a niggle. A goal from Coops earned us a draw at Parkhead. Next up, between Christmas and New Year, was a trip to Boghead. Dumbarton's old ground stood on the shores of one of Scotland's loveliest beauty spots. But as its name suggested it was no thing of beauty itself. Things weren't helped by the howling gale that greeted our arrival on 29 December.

Jock's plan to counter the conditions was to play Coops and I on either wing. We could then get the ball into the middle for Iain Ferguson to head home. I forget the name of the guy that played fullback against me that day, but from the moment we lined up I could see he wasn't up for it. His fear was all the encouragement I needed. Every time I got the ball I skinned him and cross after cross rained into their box. Coops and I were having a field day.

Five minutes before half-time and 1-0 up thanks to Ferguson, we got a corner. The wind was so fierce that Big Peter McCloy had already sent several kick-outs one bounce over Dumbarton's crossbar. In order to keep the ball in play, I reckoned that I'd have to start it off towards the halfway line. As I was working this out the corner flag blew over and I had to screw it back in place before I could take the kick. More in hope than expectation, I then blasted it as hard as I could with my right foot. The wind took it high into the air before hurling it past their bewildered keeper Gordon Arthur and into the top corner of the net.

It was quite obviously a complete fluke but it was my first goal for Rangers and I was claiming it. I started with a dance round the recently replaced corner flag, much to the amusement of the travelling fans in the 8,000-strong crowd. I then took the plaudits of my teammates who'd come over to celebrate before running down the touchline to high-five the supporters. I was still pressing the flesh when Hughie Burns called over: 'Get back on the pitch Ted, the referee's waiting to re-start the match and Jock's going bananas!' Sure enough, Jock's face looked like a beetroot and you'd have thought I'd put the ball in my own net. But it didn't stop me celebrating with fans on the other side of the park a few minutes later when the ref blew for the interval. I was still milking the applause when Jock's voice boomed out from the tunnel: 'Get fucking in here Ted, you've only scored a bloody goal!'

We ran out 4-2 winners in the end and the great minds in the media began asking if I'd done enough to justify a place in the starting line-up against Celtic three days later. Fortunately for me, Jock quickly calmed down and didn't hold my over-enthusiastic goal celebrations against me. On the morning of New Year's Eve I was told I'd be playing the following day. I was tucked up in my hotel bed by 10 p.m. that night. Try as I might, sleep just wouldn't come. It may have had something to do with the Rangers fans, who decided to see in the New Year of 1985 outside my window. But I didn't begrudge them their boozy sing-song. If anything, it reinforced just how much the forthcoming match meant to them and their opposite numbers in green and white.

There were plenty of supporters in evidence the following morning when I made my way across the road. Despite there being three hours to go before kick-off, hundreds of people were milling around. All of them wanted to wish me well and many said they were looking forward to me ripping the Celtic defence to shreds. Sadly their show of support did little to calm me down and by the time I got through the throng I was a nervous wreck. As I got changed, senior players told me to enjoy the occasion and to take in the unique atmosphere. This was what being a Rangers player was all about. I tried to focus on the job in hand and went through my usual routine. I took my time getting changed before going to the bathroom with my inhaler. Flushing the toilet as usual, I took a deep breath and subsequently lost my breakfast. I then emerged with blood-shot eyes as the noise from above began to filter into the changing rooms. My legs felt like jelly.

I don't know how it is now, but in our day no words were exchanged between the teams as we lined up in the tunnel. The handshakes and messages of good luck that were customary with other teams no longer applied. Instead, we eyeballed our opponents and fixed them with the meanest stares we could muster. In my case it was the experienced Danny McGrain, who looked like a bearded Hannibal Lecter when he emerged from the away dressing room. The referee called us together and we ran out into the daylight to be confronted by a wall of noise as the two halves of Scotland's most divided city vented their spleen.

If the truth be told, I was massively out of my comfort zone. Any one of the 45,000-plus crowd could have done a better job than me that day. Had a hole emerged on the pitch I would gladly have jumped into it. Nothing went right. From my first touch to my last I was hopeless. The best run I made all afternoon was when Jock took me off just after half-time. We ended up losing 2-1 despite Davie Cooper scoring, and the disappointment on people's faces at the end is still etched on my memory. We, and I in particular, had badly let them down. But I learned from my experience. In fact, the game probably taught me how to handle pressure and how to perform more than any other in my career. And luckily enough for me, I was never to taste defeat in that fixture again.

I wish the same could have been said for the team that winter. We followed up our Old Firm reverse with a 2-2 draw at Dens Park before Hibernian beat us 2-1 at Ibrox. My form was indifferent to say the least and I was dropped to the bench for the away trip to Aberdeen. The Dons were the real power in the land that season and would go on to win the league by seven points from Celtic, losing just four games in the process. On a heavily-sanded pitch we were taken apart. Frank McDougall scored his first hat-trick for the Pittodrie club despite the linesman's ludicrous attempt to chalk his third off for offside. I came on when we were 4-0 down and could do little to prevent the demolition. Despite Robert Prytz grabbing a consolation from Davie Cooper's tapped free kick, we went down 5-1 in the end. With Celtic not playing that day, the Dons went eight points clear at the top of the table. It was a miserable journey back to Glasgow with the fans letting us know what they thought as they passed the team bus.

Fame in the Old Firm goldfish bowl came at a high price for many of the players. I was no exception. Staying at the Bellahouston was great and I was still getting to know the sights of the city with the other lads. But as often as not I'd go back to Dumfries to see my family and my old pals if I had a day off. Those whose sympathies lay in the blue half of Glasgow welcomed me with open arms. The area boasted few players that had made it at senior level and they were proud of my achievements. But there were others who I'd known all my life who now crossed the road because I wore a Rangers badge on my jersey. Others went further and I began getting involved in punch-ups in the pub. They'd be fine after a few pints but then things would get out of hand. I was never a fighter, but I'd stand my ground if people began insulting my family. Fortunately the local police were helpful more times than not. I'd played football with many of the officers during my amateur days and they were happy to take me home in the back of the van. Dad was less impressed, however, and it got to the stage where he told me to stay up in Glasgow to keep out of trouble. The final straw was when his windows got put in after we'd beaten Celtic. He didn't need that sort of thing at his age.

It's hard to be told by your own family that going back home is more trouble than it's worth. But that was life as an Old Firm player at the time. You were far less cosseted and protected than they are now. There were no high walls on posh estates to hide behind and no fancy cars with blacked out windows. You may have been a professional footballer, but you were the same as everyone else. You drank in the same pubs and got carry-outs from the same fish and chip shops. If they wanted to tell you what they thought of you to your face, they could. The pressure of the big city was too hot to handle for me. I found it very difficult being the centre of attention every hour of every day. Wherever I went I was getting baited. There were always people waiting for you to step out of line. They just wanted a piece of you. Half of them wanted to get you into the toilet and give you a good going over and the other half made sure nobody got near you. It wasn't a way of life I was used to.

But the hurly-burly of the social scene had its amusing side too. I still remember jumping into a taxi outside Ibrox during my first few weeks at the club and asking the driver to take us to the best nightclub in town. We thought nothing of the rosary beads hanging from his rear view mirror or the picture of the Pope on his dashboard. We weren't too concerned either that the place on the Clyde where he dropped us off had people in fancy dress outside. It was Halloween after all.

The bouncers were very friendly and the place looked nice enough from what we could make out in the semi-darkness. We ordered our drinks at the bar as the Village People's YMCA was given a spin on the turntable. A couple of the boys went off to check out the talent as the manager came over to chew the fat. I was just mulling over his kind offer of free membership when the pushing and shoving started on the dance-floor. And before I could have another sip of beer I was frogmarched out of the place by my pale-faced pals. We then spent a good ten minutes making sure nobody would breathe a word about our short stay in Glasgow's premier gay club.

Rangers' answer to the social minefield was to get the players married off as soon as possible. Jock in particular preferred the players to be settled down. I think his time in the army with the King's Own Scottish Borderers had instilled the need for discipline and strong moral fibre. Cruising nightclubs of any description was not for him and it wouldn't be for his players either.

During my teenage years I'd had little time for girlfriends. Every spare moment was taken up with football and honing my technique. Joining Queen's and having my picture in the local paper changed all that. I began getting recognised around town. Guys would buy me a beer and girls would come up to talk to me in the pub. It was nothing like it is today with the so-called WAG culture and I was hardly beating them off with a stick. But it was nice to be in demand, particularly from the female of the species.

My first serious girlfriend was Jackie Gallagher. She and her family lived a few hundred yards from our flat in Lochside. I used to pass the clothes shop where she worked on the way to Palmerston and finally plucked up the courage to ask her out when I saw her in the pub one night. She was a tall, well-built girl with dark hair and we started going steady. She was also a good Roman Catholic and a regular churchgoer. What with her bible classes and me spending most of my time playing football, we didn't have much time to get up to no good. But had we decided to do so, her intimidating brothers were always waiting in the wings to protect her dignity.

Jackie's religion had no impact until I moved to Glasgow. I was aware of the sectarian split in the community growing up in Dumfries. There were separate schools of course and the Old Firm had as many supporters in our part of the world as it did in others. But there was never the same tension that existed in other parts of the West of Scotland. Signing for Rangers gave things a sharper focus. I was immediately made aware of the club's traditions and gently reminded of where 'we' and 'they' stood in the great scheme of things. Of course, none of this came from the club itself but you couldn't help picking up on the various nudges, winks and comments you heard. Jackie and her Celtic-supporting brothers were aware of it too. But it didn't stop her accepting an invite to Ibrox for my first reserve game against Dundee. She'd travelled up from Dumfries with my pal Graham Dalglish. As I was stretching in the tunnel prior to kick off, I caught sight of her leaning over the barrier and waving. I also caught sight of the gold crucifix that was swinging from her neck and prayed none of the other players or supporters had seen it.

It would be wrong to say we split up soon after that simply because she was a Catholic. That was not the case. But I have to admit I felt from that moment onwards that our relationship would struggle to last. I was desperate to take my chance at Ibrox and fit in with the other lads. My early experiences had already taught me that I was hopelessly out of touch. I knew nothing of posh food, designer clothes or the Glasgow high life and felt like a country bumpkin. I didn't care a damn what religion people followed – and still don't – but as an impressionable youngster I didn't want to rock the boat. I'd heard rumours that other players who were dating or married to Catholics had had a hard time.

Why would I want to put her or myself through something similar? It's hardly something I'm proud of, but we split up. Rightly or wrongly, that's just how it was. I'm glad things have changed now and most people have moved on. But Scotland was a very different place then, for all of us.

I was hardly living the life of a good Christian – Catholic or Protestant – at the time. As well as Jackie Gallagher, I'd also begun seeing a girl called Jackie McCalley. The second Jackie was also from Dumfries and lived on Summerville Road, a stone's throw from Palmerston. She was around five feet nine inches tall with a slim figure and straight blonde hair. She also had fewer inhibitions than her namesake, which suited me down to the ground. The two of us would meet up in Glasgow or when I was back home and she'd often stay over at the Bellahouston. It seemed to me as a naive twenty-two-year-old that I had the best of both worlds. I was living rent-free at hotel opposite the ground, could go out with my pals and team-mates whenever I chose and also had female company on tap.

Things were to change when my stay at the Bellahouston came to an end. The club suggested it was time I moved into my own accommodation. I was also getting tired of hotel life and had well and truly exhausted the room-service menu. As chance would have it, the girlfriend of team mate Robert Prytz was selling her flat in Shawlands so she could move in with him. It was a typical one-bedroom affair in a tenement block on Deanston Drive. It was also just three miles and a short cab ride from Ibrox every morning. I had a quick look round and handed over the £18,500 asking money which I'd been itching to spend since I'd pocketed it as a signing-on fee. The bachelor lifestyle suited me down to the ground. If I wasn't out playing snooker with the boys after training I'd return to the flat and lounge about in front of the television. I survived on carry-outs and sandwiches and became a regular at a pub called The Village on nearby Kilmarnock Road. Jackie would come up at weekends, tidy the place up and make sure I had enough clean clothes for the week.

I needed more than nicely ironed shirts on my first foreign trip for the club, which came in March 1985. I didn't own a passport, as they're not generally required when your holidays are spent on the beaches of the Solway Firth. The furthest I'd travelled up until then had been an away trip to Aberdeen the previous month, where I'd sat on the bench and watched us getting gubbed 5-1. I'd also been to exotic locations like Tannadice in my short footballing career. But it was Arabs of another type that Jock had us taking on when he announced we were off to Iraq. We had a window in our diaries between games against Dumbarton and St Mirren after Dundee had put us out of the Scottish Cup for the second season running. I'm still not entirely sure why the club thought a trip to the Middle-Eastern state would be the best way of filling it. But I'm guessing money changed hands somewhere down the line. Jock, who I'd later discover had a thing about sandy places and was used to arduous overseas trips, thought it would be a great way of keeping match fit.

My grasp of foreign affairs isn't much better now than it was then. But I think I'd know if the country I was flying into is at war these days. It didn't occur to me that Iraq had been fighting with its neighbour Iran for the best part of five years until I saw the lines of soldiers guarding the airport in Baghdad. I'd spent the flight from Glasgow in a state of high excitement after Club Secretary Campbell Ogilvie had dished out £200 spending money to each player. The bus drive to the hotel rein-forced just how much money that was when we saw the poverty on the war-torn streets. I thought I'd had a tough upbringing until I saw the children begging at the side of the road.

All was quickly forgotten I'm ashamed to say, when we headed for the hotel bar. As one of the youngsters I was entrusted with getting the first drink of the evening. The shelves looked a little empty as I stood in front of the moustachioed manager. But he seemed happy enough when I put in my order for eighteen beers for the boys. He returned some minutes later with a tray full of Skol lager cans, before casually informing me that the bill came to £180. Needless to say, it was the only round of the night and I retired to bed soon after to ponder the old adage about a fool and his money being easily parted.

There were plenty of moustaches on show the next day when we lined up against Iraq in Baghdad's Al Shaab Stadium. In fact all of our opponents seemed to sport one. There were plenty in the crowd too which was made up almost entirely of off-duty soldiers back on leave from the front. We'd heard from their colleagues the night before, as we lay awake listening to the dull crump of shellfire on the battlefield. We'd just got to sleep when the loudspeakers began blaring out from the mosques near our hotel.

Despite our sleepless night, the bumpy pitch and the intense heat we managed a 1-1 draw. It was no disgrace against a side that would win that year's Pan Arab Championship before qualifying for the 1986 World Cup in Mexico. Two days later, our opponents proved they were no mugs when they beat us 4-1. Our consolation came courtesy of Prytzy, who hailed from an even colder country than us. The heat hit us hard again when we travelled to nearby Amman in Jordan to take on Kuwait. The game took place on an Astro Turf pitch that shimmered in the sun. I usually played with a bright red face, but I knew something was wrong when I started going dizzy at half-time. My apprehensions were confirmed when I began vomiting up blood and I was quickly diagnosed as having sunstroke. It was either that or I was still coming to terms with the price of the lager.

Our Middle-Eastern break didn't have the desired affect unfortunately. The team lost three games on the bounce on our return to Scotland against St Mirren, Dundee and Aberdeen. We limped to a fourth place finish that season despite also going down in our last two games of the campaign against Dundee United and Hibernian. The one bright spot on the horizon was Ally McCoist.

John Greig had finally signed the boy from Bellshill the previous June at the third attempt. His form, not unlike my own, had been so up and down that Greigy's successor had suggested a transfer back to Sunderland might be easy to arrange. But he eventually repaid Jock with ten goals in the last nine matches of the season. Ally was mustard in the eighteen-yard box and nearly always popped up in the right place at the right time. He was easily the most naturally gifted centre forward I ever played with. He had an infectious personality and was the life and soul of the dressing room, even when things weren't going well. But as I was soon to find out to my cost, his high jinks sometimes came at a price.

5

MATCHES AND DISPATCHES

Before I could start preparations for my first full season at Ibrox, I had a wedding to attend to first. Jackie had moved into my flat in Shawlands in the spring of 1985 and the new-found domesticity helped bring a bit of stability to my life. I don't remember an awful lot about my proposal other than the fact I did the deed when we were putting up the decorations the previous Christmas Eve. In the years that have followed I'm sure she's chosen to recall even less.

In particular, she won't want to be reminded of the cheesy picture of the two of us and a large blue and white cuddly toy that appeared in the *Daily Record* with the picture caption: 'Jackie . . . and two lucky Teddy Bears!' The news was met with approval by Jock and the powers that be up the marble staircase. There was also general excitement in the media with photographers falling over themselves to take the pictures of the big day. We didn't have matching thrones and we hadn't negotiated a multi-million pound image rights deal but our humble wedding was as close as it came to celebrity in Glasgow that summer.

The wedding was a topsy-turvy affair, typified by us becoming the first couple in history to go on honeymoon before our wedding. Pre-season training and my lack of planning was the problem. Jock wanted us back in during the first week of July and, with the nuptials pencilled in for Wednesday 27 June, there was nothing else we could do. After a week round a hotel pool in Tenerife we presented ourselves complete with sunburn and minor food poisoning at the gates of the church. The venue we'd chosen was the Crichton Royal in Dumfries. Its impressive red sandstone walls, stained glass and marble floor looked suitably impressive for a Premier Division footballer. The church also shared its grounds with a Victorian mental hospital, which would later seem quite appropriate.

People have subsequently asked me if I loved Jackie. It's a simple enough question but one I certainly couldn't have answered at the time. How do you know if you love someone when you've not loved anyone before? I hadn't seen my mother since I was a six-year-old and the only female company I'd kept was that of my classmates and my granny. I'd been going steady with Jackie Gallagher when I was at Queen's. But it was as much because it was the done thing to do as anything else. Jackie McCalley was a nice enough girl and she certainly deserved someone better equipped emotionally than me. The truth is I probably knew it at the time too. As I stood there in my kilt at the altar, beetroot-faced beside my best man and old school friend Raymond Marshall, I was gripped with an enormous sense of foreboding.

I would have dreaded what was round the corner too, had I known what pre-season under Jock Wallace was all about. I breezed into Ibrox a freshly married man and was only too happy to tuck into a big breakfast. Davie Cooper insisted it was the most important meal of the day and shovelled extra bacon rashers onto my plate. I should have realised something unpleasant was about to happen when the team bus made its way out of Govan, along the M8 and twenty miles past Edinburgh in almost total silence.

We emerged at Gullane on the East Lothian coast with the wind whipping the North Sea spray into our faces. After a brief jog along the freezing beach, we stopped at the foot of a giant dune. Jock then put in a line of poles and sent us up the steep-sided sand to do a 'minimum of thirty' shuttles. As a group of press photographers began snapping away, Coops turned and grinned: 'Welcome to Murder Hill, bacon boy.' Much to Jock's delight, my fry up and I soon parted company and it wasn't long before the seagulls were recycling it. He took great pleasure in directing the photographers to record the torture as I knelt on all fours throwing up. And then it was back to pounding remorselessly up and down the slope, as he stood at the bottom screaming at us to go faster. On more than one occasion he even stopped proceedings to rake the sand back into place and make it harder. He'd only have enjoyed it more had he been allowed to prod us with a bayonet. After what felt like weeks of torture, Jock eventually called it a day. I innocently asked where the showers were and he glared at me. 'If you want a fucking shower son,' he growled, 'get stripped and get in the fucking sea.'

Hard as it was to stomach, our pre-season punishment seemed to do the trick. We beat Dundee United on the opening day of the campaign before recording back-to-back 3-1 wins over both Edinburgh clubs. A draw with Celtic at Parkhead was then followed by victories against St Mirren and Clydebank. The problem for me was that I wasn't getting a game. I'd picked up a couple of minor knocks and niggles in training. My form was also in and out too, and I couldn't produce the goods consistently. I had nobody to blame but myself. You often hear players moaning about not being picked these days and many are persuaded to move clubs by their agents after just a couple of weeks in the reserves. I didn't have an agent of course and, sitting on a five year contract, was happy to bide my time. It was all a learning curve as far as I was concerned.

I was on the bench for my first taste of European football when we took on Osasuna in the UEFA Cup. We won 1-0 at home in torrential rain. Nicky Walker could hardly bounce the ball as the turf was so sodden. Our goal came from skipper Craig Patterson's diving header after he emerged from a ruck of players to nod a Hughie Burns free-kick into the goal at the Copland Road end. Late in the second half Jock angered the restless crowd when he hauled off Bobby Williamson and a bemused Davie Cooper. The whistles and the boos stopped when substitute Derek Johnstone and I almost combined to grab a second from a corner a few minutes later. Big DJ's bullet header went just wide of their left hand post. I really should have doubled our lead when an Ally McCoist flick put me in behind the Spanish fullback but my right-foot strike was cleared off the line. Johnstone then put another header over the bar before not-so-Super Ally took a complete air shot after my chipped cross had found him free on the penalty spot.

My indifferent form was matched by that of the team. We surrendered our 1-0 advantage against Osasuna, going down 2-0 in the away leg, before spending October and November losing as many games as we won. We reached the League Cup semi-final with wins over Clyde, Forfar and Hamilton but Hibs edged us out 2-1 in another two-leg affair. The season was going nowhere fast. Jock's answer was to take our minds off things with another foreign trip. We headed off again to exotic climes at the end of November. But rather than another trip to a war zone, we stopped off on the holiday island of Malta. We were to have few battles on the pitch but the locals were certainly up for a fight.

We ran out 4-1 winners against a team called Hamrun Spartans in our first match thanks to goals from Ally McCoist and youngster Scott Nisbet. Most of the boys treated it as a stroll in the park, but I always enjoyed the challenge of playing against overseas players and gave it my best shot. It didn't stop me going out for a few pints afterwards however, as I was just as keen to soak up the local culture. We were staying in the resort of St Paul's in the north west of the island, about ten miles from the capital Valletta. It's a busy little place in the summer months, but it was quiet as the grave out of season. As we moved from one empty bar to another it was clear the boys were getting restless. There was precious little talent to ogle and none of the atmosphere of the pubs and clubs back home. Fortunately, we had court jester Derek Ferguson to keep us amused.

Fergie had just broken into the first team and was impressing colleagues and opponents alike with his skill and vision. He certainly spotted an opening on the way back to the hotel when he noticed that most of the locals left the windows of their cars wound down. The first I knew of it was when a beige-coloured saloon rolled slowly past me with nobody at the wheel. Derek had let the handbrake off and was giggling away with Ian Durrant and Stuart Munro as it picked up speed on the gentle incline. Their laughter soon stopped as they realised the car was headed for the quayside at a great rate of knots. And they didn't hang around to hear the bubbles coming up when it mounted the kerb and plunged straight into the harbour. In fact, they were halfway back to the hotel before it came to rest under twenty feet of sea water.

Funnily enough, we'd been spotted. It wasn't hard given that we were all wearing club tracksuits at the time. We emerged at breakfast fairly sheepishly the next morning to find two members of the local constabulary breaking the news to our ashen-faced manager. The big man finished his breakfast in silence and then convened a team meeting in the hotel bar. As we all stood staring at our shoes, he said that it had come to his attention that a car had ended up in the sea the previous evening. He wasn't interested in conducting a witch-hunt as he knew none of us would own up. But the owner was understandably annoyed by the loss of his vehicle and wanted compensation. He suggested we had a whip-round and sort it out between us. We duly did so, putting in a fiver each and ended up collecting £75.

The incident would have been front-page news nowadays, with the aggrieved car owner telling all and sundry that overpaid louts had ruined his life and livelihood. We managed to keep it quiet and the story never leaked out. Jock wasn't interested in blowing it out of all proportion and knew the guy would be only too pleased to get a few quid for his motor. I also suspect he was just relieved that none of us had been in it during its brief interlude as a submarine.

The incident didn't stop us hammering Valletta 7-0 in the last game of the trip and we returned to Scotland on the crest of a wave. But we were soon to realise that cars weren't going to be the only thing to end up in the drink. Our title ambitions were looking decidedly seasick too. The rot probably set in when we were hammered 3-0 at home by Aberdeen in late September. I remember watching from the bench as fans spilled onto the pitch to show their disgust at our performance and the referee's decision to send two men off. The ref was forced to stop the match briefly until order was restored. But it was clear all was not well on or off the park.

Fortunately for me, Rangers fans are a remarkably resilient breed. The ones that enjoyed the good times during the Nine-in-a-Row years seem to have wiped from their memories the dark days of the mid-80s. I still get people stopping me in the street or when I'm on holiday, telling me I was one of their favourite players. They say they used to love watching me running at opponents and making a fool of fullbacks. But I have to admit that for much of the 1985-86 season the only thing fans were doing was tearing their hair out.

The highlights, few though they were, came as usual against Celtic. Following the draw at the end of August it was honours even as we headed into the fixture on 22 March. We'd stuffed them 3-0 at Ibrox in November and they'd roared back with a 2-0 win at Parkhead on New Year's Day. It was hugely impor-tant for both teams to secure the bragging rights in the decider. I'd had a good run of games since the turn of the year and was playing quite well. I was no longer nervous about the prospect of taking on Celtic and was looking forward to the challenge. On another bog of a pitch we found ourselves 2-0 down after just thirty minutes. Mo Johnston bundled home the opener at the Copland Road end with a right foot shot before Brian McClair doubled their lead in almost identical circumstances. The Celtic fans went mental at their end as three sides of the ground looked on in stunned silence.

Willie McStay and I had been having a real ding-dong battle on the wing and both had been booked for our troubles. Not long after their second goal, I collected the ball in front of the away end to prevent it going out for a goal kick. Out of the corner of my eye I saw Willie coming at me like a raging bull. There was no way he was going to stop. As his two feet left the ground I saw a gap between his legs as wide as the Clyde and poked the ball through it.

Willie clattered into me, scissoring my legs with his own and I was thrown into the air like a rodeo rider. I landed in a heap on the other side and immediately clutched my leg. As I lay there in the mud, Willie added insult to injury by putting his face next to mine and calling me a dirty orange bastard. Despite the pain, I looked up and replied: 'Aye Willie, that's as maybe, but you'll be in the shower before me you thick prick.' Sure enough, the ref had little alternative and sent the big defender off. As I was getting treatment from the physio, coins and lighters began raining onto the pitch from the Celtic end. The ref had retreated to a safe distance and suggested we did too, but it was clear I couldn't go on and would have to be substituted. I felt like a busker as I limped slowly back to the dug-out. There was enough loose change to keep the electricity meter going for a month.

I was receiving treatment on the bench when Cammy Fraser's bullet header got us back into the match. The Gers supporters nearly lifted the roof off the place as they roared us on to get the equaliser. But shortly after half-time Tommy Burns made it 3-1 when Johnston's through ball split our defence. Ally McCoist wasn't to be beaten and produced a fine solo goal before being half-strangled by Hugh Burns in the celebrations.

Hughie started off the move that led to the leveller when he fed Dave McPherson down the left. His cross was half-cleared and Robert Fleck smashed a shot that took a wicked deflection past Pat Bonner. Much badge-kissing ensued as Ibrox threatened to self-combust. We all thought we were in seventh heaven when Cammy Fraser helped on a looping header from Dave McKinnon to get his second of the game and make it 4-3. But Murdo MacLeod got a deserved equaliser when he thumped an unstoppable right-footer past Nicky Walker. If it wasn't the best Old Firm game of all time it was certainly up there with the best. I tell my kids that I played a major role in the game. But the reality is I deliberately tempted one of their fullbacks into getting himself sent off and left the field myself when we were 2-0 down. Major role indeed!

From the start of October to the end of April we won just seven Premier Division games out of a possible twenty-seven. All but one of the victories came at Ibrox and three of them were two wins over Motherwell and another over Clydebank, who finished second bottom and bottom respectively. Hard as it is to believe now, when the team runs out in front of crowds of 50,000 plus every week, our 4-2 win over the Bankies on 7 December was watched by as few as 12,731 people. Hearts, who would go on to lose the title to Celtic on goal difference on the last day of the season, beat us three times out of four in the league and also dumped us out of the Scottish Cup in a five goal thriller. Long before Scotland was gripped by the excitement of the final day, Jock was under immense pressure.

Looking back we should have anticipated his dismissal. We ended up finishing fifth in the championship and it was the only season in the club's history in which we failed to average at least one point per match. Ironically, it wasn't a league or a cup game that spelt the end, but a humble friendly against Tottenham. We took on the Londoners at Ibrox in the first week in April and lost 2-0 going on twenty. To a man we were rubbish that night and were quite rightly booed off the park. We trudged off knowing something had to give. The John Lawrence organisation had just bought a majority shareholding in the club and put their man, David Holmes, in place as chief executive. He wanted to create an impression on the place and didn't take long to do so.

We had the day off after the Spurs game and I'd pencilled in a long lie. I was woken up shortly after 9 a.m. by the telephone. It was Davie Cooper. He didn't say hello and didn't bother with the pleasantries. 'Have you heard the news Ted?' he said. 'They've sacked Jock.' A radio bulletin later confirmed the story. I was gutted. Big Jock had been my mentor. He was a hero of mine. He'd been the one to take a gamble on me and was the reason I was now a professional footballer. I owed him a huge debt of gratitude.

Unfortunately, the feeling wasn't shared among all of the players. The ones that weren't getting a game were delighted that he'd gone. As far as they were concerned, the new regime brought renewed hope. The painful truth for players and fans alike was that the team simply wasn't good enough to compete. Jock probably went to his grave regretting the day he agreed to take charge of the club for a second time. But it was a very sad day indeed when he was shown the door. These things are never easy and things had to change. But they were quick to forget the achievements of his first reign.

Into the vacuum left by the departure of his huge personality seeped a huge amount of uncertainty. The new man would have different ideas and would need to bring in new signings. Would I be part of those plans? I had just over three years left to run on my contract and was playing reasonably well. I was certainly no worse than anyone else. But the doubts were starting to creep in. As the phone began to ring again with journalists looking for a quote, I couldn't help but feel that my days at Ibrox might be numbered.

Three of the four games were away from home and we lost 2-1 at Clydebank and St Mirren with no discernable change in our fortunes. But we then kept our hopes of playing European football the following season alive with a 1-1 draw at Pittodrie. I scored one of the most memorable goals of my career when I picked up the ball inside my own half, beat two defenders and hit an unstoppable left-footer past Bryan Gunn in the Aberdeen goal. It was so memorable that Ian Burns in *The People* newspaper described it as being scored by 'Big Ken McMinn.'

I didn't meet Souness until pre-season training in July. He was exactly the same in real life as he came across on the television. There was a grit and determination in him and a constant, pent-up aggression. He told us he was a born winner who wouldn't stand for second best and that our years of under-achievement were now over. Starting with training, things were going to change. Large bowls of pasta appeared at mealtimes along with huge quantities of vegetables. Red meat was swapped for lean chicken and late night sausage suppers were frowned upon. We would stay over together in a hotel the night before a game, whether we were playing home or away.

We expected the continental touch to include more ball work, but we hardly saw one for weeks. In fact all we seemed to do was sprints against the clock, with either Souness or Walter timing our every move. We were no longer allowed to turn up for training wearing jeans or a tracksuit either. If you look like Rag Arse Rovers you'll play like them, he reasoned, so collar and tie it was for all of us. A long list of dos and don'ts appeared on the changing room wall including a complete ban on golf amid fears we would pick up injuries. Here was a guy who'd had a hugely successful career and picked up tips from some of the world's best coaches. Who were we to argue with his methods, even if Ally McCoist had just spent a small fortune renewing his subs at East Kilbride Golf Course!

One of the first things he did was take us away to a spa hotel in the middle of Germany's Black Forest. We were congratulating ourselves on having avoided another trip to Gullane when we realised the hotel didn't have a drop of alcohol in it. Not only that, it was miles from the nearest village so there was no chance of sneaking off for a cheeky pint or two. During our ten-day stay we trained in the morning and then got an early night or played an amateur team. It was hard going, for the complete lack of anything to do as much as the physical side of things. On the final day we played FC Cologne and went down 2-0. Souness, for once, didn't seem overly concerned. He said it was time we let our hair down and ordered a fleet of taxis to take us out for a beer. By the time we got changed and were taken to the nearest hostelry it was well after 10 p.m. The barman looked none too pleased to see us and was reluctant to serve us. We managed to persuade him in the end but as we were halfway down our first drink he began switching off the lights and asked us to leave. A beaming Souness greeted us back at the hotel and asked us if we'd had a good night. He'd known all along how long it would take us to get there and when the bar shut. He could be a mean bastard sometimes!

The German theme continued when we got back to Ibrox. We played Tottenham Hotspur in a pre-season friendly at White Hart Lane and emerged with a draw before taking on Bayern Munich. In front of a large crowd and despite the presence of our new signings, England internationals Chris Woods and Terry Butcher, we surrendered 2-0, conceding late goals to bad defensive errors when we ran out of steam. Souness was livid and laid into us in the changing rooms. As he was ranting and raving he kicked over a large plastic drinks container full of orange juice drenching coach Don Mackay from head to toe. Not realising what he'd done, he continued his tirade as the sticky liquid dripped off Don's scarlet face and freshly laundered suit. We couldn't contain our giggles and enraged him even more until it looked like he was going to brain one of us before he'd finished. If this was him after a pre-season friendly, what was he going to be like when it really mattered? We didn't have to wait long to find out.

Hibernian away was the first league game of the season and we made our way through to Edinburgh on a sweltering hot August day. Souness was keen that we didn't let the occasion or the heat get to us and urged discipline and caution in his team talk. As the sun beat down on Easter Road's famous sloping pitch we conceded an early goal. Souness was then bundled off the ball in the centre-circle and a number of hefty tackles flew in from both sides. As the referee tried to restore order, Souness flicked an innocuous looking kick at George McCluskey with his right foot and opened up a large gash on the inside of his right knee. All hell broke loose and both sets of players began pushing and shoving one another. Chris Woods ran fifty yards to join in the action and had to be dragged away by Terry Butcher, whilst new boy Colin West banjoed Mark Fulton whilst nobody was looking.

Souness, who had already picked up a yellow card, was given his marching orders and left the pitch with the jeers of the Hibs fans ringing in his ears. The game never really recovered and turned into a running battle, with just about every player booked before the ninety minutes was up. Ally McCoist equalised from the penalty spot but we let in another goal in the second half and lost 2-1. We felt flat. It was an ignominious return to his hometown for Souness and a dreadful start for the new regime. In fairness to him, he held up his hands in the dressing room and apologised for letting us down. He was, he said, totally out of order. But it was the first and last time he ever said sorry.

Our first home game was against Falkirk and we laboured to a 1-0 win thanks to another McCoist penalty. Souness needed to act and did so by dropping me from the team. I hadn't played badly and was more than a little fed up that I'd taken the blame. It looked to have done the trick when we went 2-0 up in the next game against Dundee United. But two second-half goals from Gallacher and Redford helped them go top of the league and left us languishing in seventh place. It was clear the team would take time to gel.

We were all delighted with the new signings as it showed a clear signal of intent from the club. Woods and Butcher were terrific players and it was great to see quality Englishmen coming to play in Scotland rather than the other way round. But their arrival blew away the wage structure that had been in place for years and left a great deal of uncertainty in the dressing room. I don't care what line of work you're involved in, when guys are on vastly different wages for doing the same job there will always be conflict. Souness's iron discipline was meant to keep the whole thing in order. But it led to a nervous tension in the first few weeks. Other than the new guys, nobody was quite sure where they stood or what the future held.

A number of the established players sorted out a pay rise not long after Souness arrived. Nobody really knew what everyone was on, but it was assumed the new imports were on much bigger wages. Never being the most confident guy in the world, it took me weeks to pluck up the courage. Ironically, it was Souness who prompted me to do so before training one day.

As usual he was dressed immaculately in one of his Italian designer suits and he looked me up and down as I walked into the changing rooms. My suit had seen better days and the plastic heel was hanging off one of my shoes, but I thought I looked ok.

'Where did you get that lot,' he enquired, in a disparaging voice.

'Well the suit's from Burton's and the shoes are Clarks,' I replied.

'How much were they?' he asked.

'I think the shoes were £9.99.'

He scoffed and showed me the Armani label on his suit. Fair enough I thought, if you want me to dress better you'll have to pay me more.

I told Walter that I wanted to speak to him afterwards and a meeting was arranged. I climbed the marble staircase with butterflies in my stomach and was ushered into the manager's office. He had my contract out in front of him and didn't seem at all surprised I was looking for more money. I'd told myself I'd ask for another £30 a week and managed to blurt it out. I was still on the contract I signed in the autumn of 1984: £250 a week, plus £30 appearance money and a tenner per point.

To my surprise, he agreed straight away and said Campbell Ogilvie would sort out a new contract for me by the following morning. I left wishing I'd asked for £50 instead, but happily signed the new terms the next day. It wasn't until I got my docket at the end of the week that I realised there was no change in my take-home pay. I queried it with Campbell who looked a little embarrassed. 'Did you not read the contract?'

he asked. I hadn't. 'You've got an extra £30 on your basic, but you're no longer getting any appearance money.' Of course, I should have checked the contract before signing it but I also think they should have pointed out that other changes had been made to the new deal. I felt like I'd had the wool pulled over my eyes and all for a measly thirty quid.

Financially naive I might have been, but I was back in the first team for the first Old Firm clash of the season. Ian Durrant scored in a 1-0 win after being played in by Davie Cooper. In a brilliant bit of ball control, Coops beat one man inside before sending a reverse pass outside again with his left boot. Durrant then slotted it past Pat Bonner to send Ibrox wild. Despite a great deal of pressure from the reigning champions, we hung on for the win. After an indifferent start it was just the tonic the fans and the players needed. It was also a great boost ahead of our League Cup quarter final against Dundee. I'd missed the first game of the competition against Stenhousemuir and was on the bench when we scraped past East Fife on penalties following a 0-0 draw. But I was back in for the Dark Blues' visit to Govan and got the last goal of the game in a 3-1 victory.

We managed to win our next two games in the league as well, against Motherwell at Fir Park and at home to Clydebank. Coops and Dave McPherson did the damage in the former, whilst I added a fourth to complement Fleckie's hat-trick at Ibrox in the latter. The victories set us up for our first taste of European football that season, when we were drawn against Ilves Tampere in the UEFA Cup. The Finnish club were more famous for their ice hockey team and looked like a poor side in the first leg at Ibrox. We won 4-0 again with Fleckie repeating his hat-trick feat of three days previous and Ally McCoist adding the fourth this time. I started on the bench but came on for

Souness when he decided to go for the jugular with me on one wing and Coops on the other. Between us we were making mincemeat of their fullbacks and it was entertaining stuff for the Ibrox crowd.

They had plenty to cheer halfway through the second half when I endured the single most embarrassing moment in my football career. I'd gone on a mazy run after picking up the ball in our half and had beaten several of their players. I pushed it past the final opponent and got to the byeline to put my cross in, having spied Fleckie on the penalty spot. As I went to chip the ball with my left foot I unknowingly scuffed it with my right and took the most almighty air shot. I landed in a heap as the ball trickled out for a goal kick. I lay on the ground hoping it would swallow me up, not knowing what the crowd's reaction would be to a moment of high farce. But when I finally plucked up the courage to lift my head I heard the stands roaring with laughter at my misfortune. Thousands of voices then began singing 'There's only one Ted McMinn' as I trotted back to the halfway line with a face like a tomato. The gaffe would have been more at home on a public park, which is where we played Tampere in the second leg. We contrived to lose 2-0 in front of a crowd of just over 2,000, but still managed to get through 4-2 on aggregate.

The win against Dundee in the quarter-final of the League Cup set us up against their city neighbours Dundee United. I was a bag of nerves before the game as usual but ended up playing a blinder. I set up our first goal by tying their fullback Dave Beaumont in knots before crossing for Coisty to stab home at the near post. Then during the second half Stuart Munro stuck a ball over the top and I ran through to nutmeg goalkeeper Billy Thomson with an angled left foot drive. For reasons best known to himself, my dad celebrated by staying sat in his seat whilst everyone around him went mad. Later on in the game I remember going over on my ankle on an uneven patch of ground and felt a sharp twinge in my left foot. I ran it off and thought nothing else of it. What pain remained was dulled by the 'Hagar the Horrible' man of the match of the award and a barrel of lager from the sponsors. I was chuffed to bits that I was now just ninety minutes away from winning my first Cup Final.

I went out for a few more beers with some mates that evening after completing an interview for the Saint and Greavsie programme on STV. Former Tottenham player Jimmy Greaves, who made up one half of the duo, was becoming as famous for his brightly coloured shirts as his catchphrase 'It's a funny old game, Saint'. After appearing on the show earlier that season I'd told him I was a big fan of the garish designs and he posted the one he was wearing up to me from London. It was a bright green number with black polka dots on and a *Daily Record* photographer persuaded me to wear it with a pair of shorts and flip-flops for a photo. It was the first and last green jersey to grace the Main stand and I looked a real prat in it on the back page of the paper the next day.

The day after the semi-final I had some decorating to do in my flat. By the time we reported back to Ibrox on Friday I was getting a lot of pain from my foot. Souness spotted I was in trouble and immediately pulled me out of training. We had a massive game against Aberdeen the following day and he wanted everyone who'd played in the semi-final to be fit. I was left in the hands of new physio Phil Boersma who'd replaced outgoing sponge man Bob Findlay that week.

Phil was a mate of Souness from their playing days at Anfield and was a really nice guy. But in all honesty he didn't appear to know a hell of a lot about physiotherapy. After scratching his head for a few minutes, he got out the ultrasound machine. He would subsequently use it to treat everything from a dislocated shoulder to an ingrowing toenail. He rubbed the machine's pads on the top of my swollen foot for half an hour or so then told me to get a taxi home and rest up overnight.

By the next day I was in agony but Souness was having none of it. I reported early and told him I wasn't going to be able to play. I remember the sneer on his face as he accused me of bottling it. 'You just don't want to play against Willie Miller and Big Eck do you?' he said.

'Of course I fucking do,' I replied, 'but I can't play if I'm injured.' Souness laughed and told Phil to give me an injection. The club doctor was sent for and a cortisone needle was jabbed straight into the bone. As blood shot out of my foot, numbness began to spread down to my toes. In what he would later describe as mind games, Souness then sent me out onto the pitch to warm up telling me the pre-match atmosphere would take my mind off the pain. At 2.45 p.m. it was no better, so another needle was stuck into my foot. I put my sock back on and it began to fill with blood. Souness was adamant I was playing so I limped out with the rest of the lads looking white as a sheet.

I don't know how I got through the first half. I tried to kick the ball as much as I could with my right foot. But every time I was tackled on my left, pain shot up my leg. It was like running around with a six-inch nail stuck in my boot. At half-time I was put up on the physio's couch for a third time and had yet another cortisone injection. Souness turned his back on me as he barked out orders to the lads. He was not making any substitutions. But with just a few minutes of the second period gone,

I squared the ball for him and he rifled it into the Aberdeen net. Amid his celebrations he signalled to the bench to take me off.

A car was waiting take me to Ross Hall Hospital and I jumped in the back still in my kit. When we got there a doctor removed my blood-soaked sock and X-rayed my foot. As he pulled the result up on the screen it was clear there was large gap in one of my metatarsal bones; I had been running round with a broken foot. The doc cleaned me up and then put on an old-fashioned plaster of Paris cast. I began to panic and asked him how long it would have to be on for and he told me four weeks. Maths had never been my strong point at school but even I knew that I was going to miss the Cup Final.

As a private ambulance returned me to Ibrox, sorrow turned to anger as it slowly dawned on me that Souness had pushed me into playing against my better judgement. Of course his mind as usual would have been focused on picking up a couple of poxy points. The bastard should have realised that I really was crocked to begin with but he didn't seem to give a toss. I hobbled into a near-empty Ibrox and handed over my X-ray and medical notes to Phil. He held them up to the light and may as well have been looking at a copy of *Playboy* for all the sense it seemed to make to him.

Souness then joined us and I told him I was out of action for at least four weeks. As he turned to go I saw him making the same mental calculation I had. But all he'd say was 'that's too bad'. A taxi took me back to the flat in Shawlands as the last of the post-match punters staggered out of the pubs near the ground. The following day would be my twenty-fourth birthday. But as I sat in the back with the tears rolling down my cheeks, I didn't feel I had an awful lot to celebrate.

7

A QUICK DRINK AFTER WORK

Depression affects footballers far more than they let on. The man in the street thinks it's all sweetness and light, with telephone-number salaries and a floozy on each arm. They often remind you how they'd happily swap places with you. The highs are indeed very high and it's hard to beat the buzz of scoring a winning goal in front of thousands of supporters. But the long periods of inactivity give many a fan's favourite too much time to think. Injuries are the worst of it. When you're ready, there are long stints in the gym with fellow convalescents. And friends and family try their best to keep your spirits up. But you miss the camaraderie of the training ground and the regular activity in the lead up to match days. As often as not you sit on your backside piling on the pounds, becoming increasingly bitter about your bad luck.

Sat on mine with a broken foot, I was determined not to fall into the trap. Despite being told to rest up I gritted my teeth and hobbled into Ibrox every day on an old pair of wooden crutches. I couldn't join in with the rest of the lads but I kept my upper-body strength up by doing weights. Souness believed I'd picked up the injury falling off a ladder when I was decorating my flat. The papers picked up on the story and my old photographer pal at the *Record* persuaded me to pose up a ladder with a paintbrush in hand. The lads cracked up when they saw me and I got pelters from McCoist and Co. Souness was less impressed, so I did my best to appease him. For fourteen days on the bounce I did my sit-ups and my pecs, my triceps and my biceps, before carefully easing into the bath with my foot keeping dry on the side.

By the fifteenth day I was sick to the back teeth with the whole palaver and had had enough. I wasn't going to miss this bloody Cup Final. Without giving it another minute's thought and without consulting with the medical men I plunged my foot into the warm water and began to pick at the plaster. Within ten minutes I had the whole thing off, leaving a mess of white plaster and bandages on the bottom of the bath. My calf muscle had shrunk slightly with the lack of exercise but my foot didn't look too bad. I was pleased as punch. I hobbled through to the physio's room to consult with the oracle Phil Boersma. He asked me how it felt and I told him it was ok. When Souness came in after training he was surprised to see me. But he took one look at my foot and without speaking to me told Phil he had two weeks to get me fit.

Achieving that was easier said than done. I wasn't allowed to join in with the rest of the lads as there was to be no physical contact. That meant I couldn't really use the Albion training ground, which meant I was stuck at Ibrox. Phil got me doing some gentle jogging on the red blaize at the side of the pitch and I built up the speed slowly and surely.

He also had me hopping up and down the terracing of the East Enclosure like Skippy the bush kangaroo. I must have looked like an idiot bouncing all over the place. But I wanted to play so badly that I didn't care.

There was a dull ache on the top of my foot and I spent every session trying not to grimace. Every time I turned or changed direction I was hit with a sharp stabbing pain. The foot swelled up so much that I had to put an ice pack on it after every training session. But the days ticked by and my hopes were raised as I felt myself getting closer to an adequate level of fitness. The problem was, having not played for over three weeks, I'd lost my match fitness. Souness's answer was to name me as a substitute for the mid-week visit of Portuguese side Boavista in the UEFA Cup. It was three days before the Cup Final against Celtic.

Injury wasn't the only issue. Since busting my foot, Robert Fleck had been winning plaudits playing in my position. But against Boavista he didn't have one of his better days and was hauled off just before half time. I was thrown on in his place and was delighted to be back on the pitch again. Goals from Dave McPherson and Ally McCoist helped us win the game 2-1 and I had no adverse effects from my foot. It still ached and I couldn't run flat out. But I'd got through forty-five minutes without breaking down. Souness asked me how I was and I told him I was fit as a fiddle. I'd love to think he respected me for going through the pain barrier to make the Cup Final. But deep down I think he thought I was thick. He never struck me as the sort of person who'd put his body on the line for the cause. Other people's bodies were fine, but not his own.

Be that as it may, my name was on the team sheet when the Cup Final squad was announced. Fleckie was up there too but as a sub. He was very unlucky given how well he'd been playing. As was customary, the whole squad went through to Turnberry for a couple of days in a hotel before the game, training down the road at Troon's ground. We arsed about in our club tracksuits and played a bit of crazy golf in a desperate bid to fill time before the big day. But it was difficult to keep yourself occupied in the days before PSPs and iPods. Souness certainly saw to it that we didn't get near the bar.

The foot was well on the way to being healed, yet I still felt woefully short of match fitness. Celtic must have sussed out that I was going to play and replaced Derek Whyte with Murdo MacLeod. I'd run poor Whytey ragged in the 1-0 win at Ibrox in August and they feared a repeat performance. Murdo was a bugger to play against. He was hard as nails and never let you settle into a game. He was also one of those fullbacks who liked to let you know he was there early on in proceedings – football speak for giving you a right good kicking in the first five minutes.

The trip to Hampden seemed to take forever despite our police escort, as we weaved slowly through the match-day traffic and large crowds. We tried to play cards and McCoist and Durrant went through their usual repertoire of gags. But the truth is most of us were bricking it. There was an uneasy silence on the bus like there had been when we went through to Gullane for pre-season training. This time it wasn't the dread of impending physical punishment but fear of not doing ourselves justice and letting down the supporters to whom we knew it meant so much.

We were constantly reminded of it as we neared the ground. Going down one street you'd be greeted with clenched fists and shouts of encouragement from lads in blue shirts. Going down another and you'd have nothing but spit and abuse from others with hooped scarves. My mouth was as dry as the bottom of a budgie's cage. By the time we got into the cavernous changing rooms under the old South Stand we were wound up like coiled springs. There was no need for much of a team talk from Souness.

The match wasn't a classic and will probably only be remembered for being bad-tempered. Old Firm matches are always high octane affairs, but this one was particularly passionate. The ref hardly had his yellow card in his pocket and Mo Johnston got himself sent off for headbutting Stuart Munro. He then endeared himself to thousands of Bluenoses by crossing himself in front of them as he walked off. Jack-in-a-box Ian Durrant grabbed the opening goal with a smart volley in the second half, before Brian McClair equalised for them fifteen minutes later. With just five minutes to go big Roy Aitken dragged Terry Butcher down in the box like a nymphomaniac trying to get someone into bed and a penalty was awarded.

The only man to take it was Davie Cooper, who'd recently held his nerve to take Scotland to the World Cup Finals in similar circumstances against Wales. Sure enough, up stepped Coops and side-footed it past a despairing Packy Bonner. An ocean of Gers fans packed under the corrugated-iron roof at the Mount Florida end went mental.

My contribution was far from stunning and I was taken off with ten minutes to go. But I was really happy just to have made the starting eleven and delighted to be winning my first Cup Final with the club. After collecting the silverware from the dignitaries on the balcony we took it over to the fans, scooping up the scarves and daft hats that rained down on us. It was the best feeling in the world celebrating with your own, knowing the terracing behind you was completely empty.

Losers don't hang about at Hampden. The supporters were the ones who deserved their day in the sun after being starved of success for far too many years. They'd come back in their numbers that season and backed the new regime to the hilt. Their first bit of silverware was a sweet moment to savour. As I sat in the changing room looking at my medal afterwards, surrounded by scarves and empty champagne bottles, I had to pinch myself. Almost two years ago to the day I'd been living with my brothers in my dad's council flat, working long shifts in a sawmill and earning next to nothing. I felt tremendously lucky to be a Rangers player, and one who'd just won a Cup Final at that. It was one of those days when it was just great to be alive.

I was never one to turn down a party but it never occurred to me that there'd be an official reception back at Ibrox. My first reaction was to ring up my mates and go out on the razzle. And so as the rest of the team sipped champagne with the directors, I was throwing lager down my neck in Glasgow. We later heard that the team had headed for a nightclub called Panama Jacks down by the Clyde. It was no good to me as I'd been barred from there a few months previously after a case of mistaken identity.

It happened the night of the first Old Firm game of the season. As often as not on those nights, the club was heaving with supporters of the victorious team. A number of my mates had a drunken sing-song to remind the few Celtic supporters who were out that we'd won. Before I knew it I'd been accused of singing sectarian songs and was being thrown down the stairs by an over-zealous bouncer. It wasn't my style and I was annoyed at copping the flack. I later found out that a number of the players including Chris Woods, Terry Butcher and their wives took some stick in there after the final and had to leave. I can't say I was surprised.

A QUICK DRINK AFTER WORK

Saturday nights out in Glasgow could be a nightmare. After settling in Shawlands I fell in with some pals who drank in a pub called The Village. They were all staunch Rangers supporters and were a great set of lads. There were none of these hangers-on that you get these days and nobody was going to sell a story to the tabloids. They acted as unofficial minders and always watched my back for me when we went out on the tiles. On more than one occasion I was escorted to the toilets during a night out and would return a few minutes later to be told an 'unwelcome element' had been asked, or rather told, to leave. As often as not there'd be a few broken glasses or even a pool of blood on the spot where we'd all been standing. You didn't ask too many questions!

Most of the lads at Ibrox had their groups of non-footballing friends who served the same purpose. It sounds self-indulgent now, like we were big-time Charlies, but we never asked for it. There was just an unwritten rule that they'd provide it. They were the reason we could go out in town without having to look over our shoulders. I don't know how the young Old Firm players do it now. I suspect a lot of them get a taste of it early on and can't be bothered with the hassle after that. I'm sure they'll all now be advised about their conduct too and what you can and can't get away with in the glare of the media spotlight. We had none of that. We were naive and probably a bit too arrogant. But our view was that nobody was going stop us going out for a pint after the game.

In many respects I wish someone had, particularly when it came to one Thursday night in October 1986. The rule was that you didn't go out for a drink forty-eight hours before a game. But after training Coisty asked Ian Durrant and I if we wanted to go to a pub he knew in East Kilbride. The manager was a pal of his and needed a couple of celebrities to break a charity bottle for him. We'd be pictured in the paper and the money would be handed over to a good cause. We knew we shouldn't be out but we didn't see how it could cause any harm. We turned up at the place, did what we had to do then had a couple of quiet shandies. It was always good fun being out with those two as they were a great laugh. One thing led to another and we decided to have a few more drinks before heading to a local nightclub.

Almost as soon as we got in there we knew we'd made a mistake. We quickly became the centre of attention with Rangers fans falling over themselves to get our autographs. Unfortunately there were a number of Celtic supporters in there too, who were less pleased by our presence. A couple came over and began to give us a bit of abuse. Had we been a bit more grown-up and a bit more sober, we'd have put down our pints and left quietly. We had no business being there on a Thursday and were only going to get ourselves into trouble with Souness if any of this leaked out. As it was, we were full of drink and chose to stand our ground until the management of the place stepped in to cool things down. Coisty, being on home territory, was particularly keen to give as good as he got until the blokes giving us grief were kicked out.

We thought the problem had been solved until we got outside and realised that the same crowd were waiting for us. I was about to suggest we forgot all about it when Coisty leant over my shoulder and landed a haymaker on one of the guys knocking out a couple of his teeth. As blood began to dribble out of his mouth his mates came forward and a scuffle broke out. The red mist came down and I chased after the guy who'd taken the smack in the mouth. He got a head start on me as I dealt with one of his pals but I quickly gained ground on him as we sprinted over a main road and past a row of shops. Just as I was about to grab him he dived into a building and slammed the door in my face. I hammered on the glass and told him what I was going to do with him when I got hold of him. A bloody, gap-toothed grin then began to spread across his face as he slowly pointed at the sign above the door. I looked up and quickly realised that I'd only gone and chased the bloke into a police station.

I neglected to mention this minor detail to my two companions after returning empty-handed to the nightclub. The guy was quick on his toes and had just got away, I told them. We knew we were in a spot of bother but were hoping nothing would come of it. How wrong we were. After a night on Coisty's couch we all went in to training the next day in his car wearing the same clothes we'd had on the day before. We pulled into the car park and before we'd even switched the ignition off, goalkeeping coach Peter McCloy yanked open the door. 'The gaffer wants a quiet word boys,' he smiled.

We climbed the marble staircase like naughty schoolboys on the way to the headmaster's office. Souness sat scowling behind his desk and we soon realised we weren't going to get away with a couple of sides of lines. He asked us one by one if we'd been out the previous night and one by one we lied. He then asked us again. 'Before you consider your answers, you might like to know that the boy is pressing charges and has already been in touch with the police,' he spat. At this point Coisty slowly slipped his bruised and bleeding hand in his pocket and we all began to blurt out our pathetic excuses.

Souness's reaction was to fine us two weeks wages and to tell us to train on our own. Jogging round an empty Ibrox gave us time to think up our excuses and it was a good job too. We got showered and changed and were greeted by the club's solicitors. Durrant and Coisty were taken to the police station and for some reason I was given until the Monday to present my side of the story. Before the weekend was out we were all charged with assault and breach of the peace. The victim had claimed all three of us had hit him and was determined to take us to court.

Souness was understandably furious and told the press we'd been carpeted for a 'breach of team discipline'. He later tried to pick us off one by one and winkle out who'd done what. I'm sure he thought I was the main culprit but I could hardly tell him different. I wasn't going to break rank or point the finger at one of my pals. We were all out when we shouldn't have been and I was the one stupid enough to chase the guy into the police station. Coisty was the one who'd thrown the punch and taken us there in the first place. But when the team sheet went up after training it wasn't the club's leading goal-scorer who was dropped to the bench. It was me.

If things weren't great in my professional life, they were hardly a bed of roses in my personal one either. I'd been living with Jackie for over a year now since we got married the previous summer. But things were on the slide big style. I wasn't used to living with a woman and found it difficult to cope with someone else's feelings. There were the obvious benefits of living with an attractive young woman. But the steady supply soon dried up. We argued like cat and dog over the smallest things and as often as not she'd storm back to her parents in Dumfries.

I bitterly resented the loss of my freedom too. It got to the stage where I'd have to ask permission to go out for a pint, even if it was just across the road with my mates. I'd face the third degree and be asked what time I'd be back, knowing full well she'd spend her time watching the clock on the wall until I returned. Looking back, I was probably very selfish. I'd moved her up from Dumfries because of my career and she had few friends and little to do. But I couldn't help feeling like a caged animal.

Football was a welcome distraction. Following the bust-up in the nightclub I sat on the bench for our goalless draw against Hibs. I then got the number ten shirt back as we humped Falkirk 4-0 and our Cup conquerors Hamilton Accies 2-0. McCoist and Fleck in particular were on fire. Between the middle of December and the start of February, wee Fleckie hit ten goals in nine games, including a hat-trick against Clydebank. I'd done nothing wrong in the two games and we'd won comfortably, but Souness dropped me for the next game against Dundee United, which was the day after Boxing Day. We won that 2-0, again thanks to Fleckie and Coisty and their good form kept me out of the New Year's Day game against Celtic at home.

Despite not even getting a seat on the bench, I enjoyed our 2-0 victory, with the deadly duo combining once more. Souness had us all back to the hotel afterwards and told everyone to bring their wives and girlfriends for a party. Jackie and I had had one of our falling-outs and I was stuck on my jack jones as the other couples enjoyed themselves. We were under strict instructions not to leave the hotel to avoid any trouble in Glasgow. But I was fed up with being the club gooseberry. I left it until midnight, phoned up a couple of pals and got a taxi into town.

I'd love to say I sneaked out a back entrance without Souness ever finding out. But I was so pissed off that I walked out the front door in my club blazer. We ended up in a nightclub called the Savoy and I drowned my sorrows with a right good bevvy. I eventually crawled into bed, blitzed out of my mind, at three or four in the morning, still swigging a bottle of champagne. Incredibly, when I eventually surfaced the next morning the heat was on someone else for a change.

Unbeknown to me Fleckie and Stuart Munro had also broken the curfew after finding the club function a touch tame. They'd persuaded a waitress to take them into town and had partied the night away at another nightclub. They'd even arrived back three hours after me after hitching a lift on a bin lorry. Word got back to Souness that players had been out in town. He didn't know who it was then. But like a member of the Gestapo he began drawing up a list of suspects and started getting people in for interrogation. The thumbscrews came out a couple of days later.

After beating Motherwell thanks to a Graham Roberts goal, we thumped the league's whipping boys Clydebank 5-0 at Ibrox. The lads were in high spirits and began making plans for a big night out. Before we'd so much as pencilled in our first port of call, Souness ordered everyone to be ready for a team meeting in fifteen minutes. I half expected what was coming, but his chilling words have stayed with me to this day.

'Two players broke curfew after the Celtic game and have been fined a thousand pounds,' he began. 'But there was another player who broke curfew too. I'm going to give that player an opportunity to own up.' Everyone looked at one another in silence, hoping a guilty look or a red face would identify the culprit. I didn't move a muscle. He didn't have anything on me as far as I was aware. What was the point of turning myself in when I was in enough bother as it was? 'Right, well, if they haven't got the bollocks to admit it, I'll tell you,' he continued, turning to me. 'It was you Ted, wasn't it? You broke the fucking curfew because you're a fucking joke. Well, you're fined too and I'm suspending you for two weeks.'

Having spent the last thirty seconds looking at my shoes, I got up to leave. He pushed me back down in the seat. 'Where the fuck do you think you're going pal?' he raged. 'Do you think I'm finished with you yet? Sit down until I tell you to move. You're a fucking disgrace and you think you can go out on the piss whenever you want. Well you *can* go out whenever you want from now on because you're finished. You'll never play for this fucking club again.'

8

ORANGE SQUASH

After publicly humiliating me in front of my peers, Souness went upstairs to spread the news to a wider audience via his post-match press conference. He told reporters I'd been suspended for two weeks but refused to go into details. I packed my kitbag and trudged disconsolately out of Ibrox, the sympathy of my teammates ringing in my ears. I sulked in the flat for all of five minutes, jumped in a taxi and went out drinking with my pals. I should perhaps have reflected on events and used my time productively. But I just wanted to get blitzed. After a tour of my usual haunts I passed a newspaper stand outside Central Station whilst in search of a late night fish supper. Predictably, pride of place on the back of the first editions was the dramatic news that I'd been suspended. Less predictable was the suggestion that it might have been due to a domestic dispute with Jackie.

I can see where they got the idea. After the sports boys filed their copy from Ibrox, news hounds were dispatched to the flat to see if they could glean any additional info to flesh out the story. Jackie answered the door in a pair of dark glasses, which she'd taken to wearing after watching the soap opera *Dallas*. In the dimly lit stairwell the reporters deduced that I'd been giving Shawlands' answer to Sue Ellen Ewing a good hiding. In the absence of any confirmation from her or any other sources they couldn't go the whole hog and accuse me. But the implication was that our marriage was on the rocks because I was a wife beater.

I've always shrugged off hangovers pretty quickly, but I had a lot to have a sore head about the next morning. The telephone woke me. It was assistant manager Walter Smith playing good cop to Souness' bad cop. He told me to hang in there, see out my suspension and knuckle down on my return. Worse things happened at sea apparently. Well not as far as I was concerned. I thanked him for throwing me a life jacket but told him that I was abandoning ship. For once it wasn't just the drink talking. A certain Jock Wallace had been making enquiries about me. My old gaffer had bounced back from his dismissal at Ibrox and was now managing Spanish First Division side Seville. Sitting in his apartment, he'd watched my performances in our two UEFA Cup games against Borussia Monchengladbach on Spanish television. He'd also flown over to Glasgow for the New Year's Day Old Firm game, prompting speculation in the media. The *Daily Record* said directors had given him permission to 'buy British' and he was running the rule over Robert Fleck and me. Fleckie was going nowhere, but I was open to offers.

As I was mulling over a move, the phone rang again. It was the *Evening Times'* Chick Young. He said he'd never had me down as a wife beater and wondered if I wanted to give him my version of events. I had nothing to lose and was keen to take back a bit of control, so I gave him his exclusive. In return for the story Chick bought me a plane ticket to Seville. As the story hit the streets on Monday 12 January, I was jetting out to meet up with my old mentor. Following the Skol Cup Final a few months earlier I'd done an interview with a journalist called Peter Black. In an explanation of my so-called eccentric style I told him that the day I stopped enjoying the game would be the day I 'quit playing'. Well, I wasn't quitting the game altogether, but I was quitting my beloved Glasgow Rangers because the manager no longer wanted me. As we headed south, 40,000 feet above Europe, I couldn't help but notice that Chick had bought me a one-way ticket.

There was a strange symmetry to my signing for Seville. I'd been a sawmill worker and part-time footballer with Queen of the South on the Sunday night and a Rangers player on the Monday morning. In just as big a step, I was a Rangers player on the Sunday night and was embarking on a new life in a new country on the Monday morning. It turned out that the two clubs had been negotiating a deal for weeks. Jock had offered £200,000 after I'd played well in Europe. The bid had initially been rejected by Rangers, who were holding out for double the amount. But after the carry-on in East Kilbride and the curfew-breaking incident, Souness bit their hand off. Seville's board was understandably concerned that they were signing a bad apple and made sure Jock went through everything with a fine-tooth comb. I assured him that I'd just been a silly boy and that nothing would come of the court case. It was good enough for him and I signed on the dotted line.

Despite the fact the world and his wife knew I was signing, Jock wanted to keep it hush-hush for some reason. He met me at the airport in his Opel saloon car and as we approached his apartment on the drive back to Seville he told me get under a blanket in the back seat. His place was always surrounded by press photographers who wanted to get a picture of him. As he drove through the automatic gates they snapped away as usual until he'd parked up outside. He then got out and gave them a wave, went into the apartment and waited for them to disperse.

Well over an hour later I was allowed out of the car and ushered up the stairs where his wife Daphne had a cold beer waiting for me. It was all a bit cloak-and-dagger for my liking but Jock assured me they had a different way of doing things over in Spain. I had a medical in secret at the hospital the next morning after repeating the back-seat blanket routine. But it appeared that a last minute hitch might sink the deal. Rangers and the Scottish Football Association were refusing to release any papers until the money was in the bank. Seville President Luis Cuervas had a reputation as being a bit of a wheeler-dealer by all accounts and they didn't want to take any chances. After days of delays the dirty deed was finally done and I emerged from hiding like a Scottish Scarlet Pimpernel.

Jock used the free time to fill me in on the dos and don'ts of Spanish football and what I could expect. Unlike today when you can watch games from the Primera Liga every week on television, no pictures were beamed back to Britain. But the game was really taking off after years in the doldrums. John Toshack was in charge of Real Sociedad and Terry Venables was the boss of Barcelona. Fellow Scot Steve Archibald was at Barca with El Tel, who would also sign Gary Lineker and Mark Hughes. Former Liverpool colleagues Michael Robinson and Sammy Lee were to team up at Osasuna.

Jock said it was an exciting time to play in the league but warned me to expect a very physical challenge. The game was much slower than the harum-scarum of Scottish football but the defenders took no prisoners in the tackle. The greatest difference with back home, however, was that we only got paid annually. Our entire year's salary was handed over in a single cheque at the end of the season. In the meantime we got by on a living allowance of around £400 a month. I was beginning to understand why Rangers were reluctant to release the paperwork.

I missed our 2-1 home win over Mallorca with the delay in signing, so my first game was away to Cádiz. Despite the proximity on the map, it was a four-hour coach ride and we set off at 8 a.m. for a 5 p.m. kick-off. I rode shotgun with Jock on the bus as we made the journey to the coast but I was thrown in with the players when we reached the hotel. Not one of them spoke a word of English and my Spanish did not yet extend beyond 'cerveza'.

Sadly, there were none of those to be had when we sat down for lunch. I was presented with a large menu but asked if I could have a simple omelette. The other players, who were chattering away like sparrows, all began tucking into large bowls of soup before an enormous tomato salad was laid in front of them. The waiters then brought out bloody steaks served with mashed potato for everyone and followed that up with a fish course. I was finally handed a sorry-looking omelette as they helped themselves to a large fruit platter. I was absolutely starving by this time, but there was no way I could have launched into that little lot. I knew my pre-match ritual would have me throwing up whatever I ate and I'd still have my head down the toilet at half-time if I'd eaten even half of what they did! It occurred to me that diet, never mind climate, was the reason the pace of the game was much slower.

By the time we waddled onto the pitch it was still stinking hot and I had visions of the sunstroke I'd suffered in the Middle East. But there were so many delays for injuries I had plenty of time to get fluids on board. The main problem I faced was that I gave away free kicks almost every time I tackled. The ref frowned on anything that looked like you were showing your studs. Players would crumple at your feet as soon as you made contact with them and I was introduced for the first time to the imaginary yellow card, waved at the ref by the players every time they hit the dirt.

They were no shrinking violets themselves. Jock had warned me that the most dangerous time was when you didn't have the ball. Nevertheless the first forearm smash as I burst into the box came as something of a surprise. The other issue I faced was that I couldn't communicate with the rest of the team. My shouts of 'over here' and 'knock it long' fell on deaf ears and it wouldn't be until later that I learnt the phrase 'solo' for 'I'm free'. Star midfielder Francisco whistled through his teeth when he wanted the ball. As I could only whistle with my fingers in my mouth, that wasn't very practical.

I was disappointed to lose my first game and to not make more of an impression. Jock took me off with ten minutes to go but seemed pleased enough with my performance. My lack of a regular run in the first team at Rangers and the delay in my transfer meant I wasn't in tip-top condition however, and the gaffer wanted me to sharpen up. His solution was to introduce me to our translator Bob Chipres, who was something of a fitness fanatic. Bob was a forty-three-year-old, five feet six inches all-American action man who got up at the crack of dawn to pound the streets of Seville. I would spend a lot of time with him and his two young sons Stuart and Sean in the coming months and got to know them really well. He was an ex-marine who'd fought in Vietnam and had come to Spain to become a bullfighter. After surviving but not excelling for eight years, he began working on an educational programme with the University of Wisconsin, teaching Spaniards English and expats Spanish. He was actually a fan of Real Betis, our deadly rivals, but he was more than happy to help out with Jock and me when asked by the club.

The day after the Cadíz game Jock arranged a game of squash between Bob and me at the Antares Fitness Club near his apartment. He thought the ducking and weaving required on the court would be beneficial with my runs on the pitch. Bob was a dab hand at the game and Jock enjoyed watching him thrash me as he sat back with a beer on the balcony. His amusement was short-lived however, when after thirty minutes of punishment I landed heavily on the wooden floor. I heard a crack in my right foot and doubled up in pain. Jock summoned the club physio, who took off my shoe and sock as the top of my foot began to swell up. Between them they decided it would be a good idea to get some heat into the injury and plunged me into scalding hot bath. When it had no noticeable effect, I was whisked to the hospital where an X-ray revealed what we all feared – I'd broken my foot again.

This time it wasn't the one that I did in the Skol Cup semi-final at Hampden, so there was no suggestion I had an inherent weakness. But it was shattering news and I just couldn't believe my bad luck. The club had scrimped and saved to raise the £200,000 and had been rewarded by getting just eighty minutes out of me. Jock looked like a lottery winner who'd just lost his ticket.

The Spanish media went bonkers. Jock got both barrels. What the hell had I been doing playing squash in the first place? Were all the players going to be subject to this suicidal fitness regime? Who'd be the next one hospitalised and how long was I going to be out for? Six to eight weeks was the diagnosis from the quacks. They couldn't get a full plaster on initially as my foot was too swollen so they bandaged the top and put a plaster on the sole and up the back of my leg. I was given a single crutch and told to make my way back to the ground.

It was there that I met the president for the first time, and he wasn't very impressed. As I tried to make light of the injury he kept asking Bob 'why?' The poor bloke was totally bemused and eventually wandered off shaking his head. Bob took me out into the sunshine and showed me round the ground.

The Ramón Sánchez Pizjuán stadium had been built in 1957 and was the venue for the previous summer's European Cup Final between Steaua Bucharest and Barcelona. It had also played host to the World Cup semi-final between Germany and France, which became notorious for goalkeeper Harald Schumacher's assault on French defender Patrick Battiston. The Spanish national side have still not lost a game there, which is a proud boast in the city. To me, it was a fairly ugly-looking concrete bowl unfortunately, with none of the character of the grounds I was used to in Scotland. The hard-core supporters stood at the North end of the stadium and called themselves the Biris after a Gambian player called Alhaji Momodo Nije (nickname Biri-Biri), who played for the club in the 1970s. They paid 100 pesetas to rent small cushions to sit on, but as often as not launched them at us when we weren't playing well. Fortunately, they took to me straight away and admired my honest approach to the game and the fact I always gave 100 per cent. Like Jock they'd seen me playing out of my skin in the UEFA Cup and were very excited about my arrival. They were understandably disappointed when I got injured after my first game. For some reason, probably because they couldn't pronounce McMinn, they christened me Manolín, which is the shortened, affectionate version of Manuel. Years later, when I had my operation, they sent me their 100th anniversary shirt that had the names of their best players stitched on it. I was the only one to have his name written twice, just above a certain Diego Armando Maradona. It was one of my regrets during my short stay in Spain that I didn't play more games for those fans. They were a great bunch.

The flat I moved into, which was sourced by the club, was just 200 yards from the ground in the Nervión area of the city. It was a small, modern, two-bedroom affair with a tiny kitchen, a bathroom and a living area. It was fully furnished and more than adequate for me. Out of one bedroom window I could see my place of work and out of the other was a charming view of a large Corte Inglés supermarket. Fortunately Bob was always on hand to make sure I didn't make any ill-advised purchases there. On the one occasion he wasn't I managed to order enough Serrano ham to feed the five thousand.

Bob also helped introduce me to the other players, though the language barrier remained a problem throughout my stay in Spain. The lads were all Spanish other than two Uruguayans called Pablo Bengoechea and Carlos Amado Nadal. Bengoeachea was a midfield free kick specialist who was nicknamed 'The Professor' due to his educated displays. Nadal was a long haired centre forward, who was often kept out of the team by fellow frontmen Ramón and Cholo and the league's strict two foreigner ruling. The undoubted star of the show was midfielder Francisco López Alfaro, who could do no wrong in the eyes of the president or the fans. Francisco, as he was known, had been at the World Cup in Mexico with Spain and was rewarded on his return with an unprecedented ten-year contract to ward off the European big boys. He was a hugely talented player who sparked into life when he had the ball.

But he was lazy as hell off it and went missing for long periods every game.

I was determined not to go missing during my convalescence. My initial thought had been to go back to Glasgow to put my personal affairs in order. But Jock told me that my work permit only allowed me out of the country for thirty days a year. The team's next game was away at Atlético Madrid, so I decided I'd go and watch them. In those days in Spain injured players or even those who weren't picked for the squad never travelled with the team. The president was a tight bastard and wouldn't stump up for my flight, so Bob and I paid for a sleeper coach on the train out of our own money. Twelve hours later we emerged in Madrid to the amazement of my new teammates, who thought I was completely mad. Seville-based journalists, and later the fans, thought it was brilliant.

One of the reporters persuaded me to cover the game on radio. What followed was ninety minutes of the most bloody awful commentary ever to go out on the airwaves. Sitting up in the Gods, I did my best to describe the match knowing none of the players we were up against and very few of our own. As I spoke next to no Spanish, my fellow commentator had to translate what I'd said and then asked me questions in English. I could be describing a dramatic goal-mouth incident one minute and, by the time he'd finished, the ball could be out for a corner at the other end. Had it been a Hollywood movie it would have gone straight to video. On Betamax.

Seville ran out 2-0 winners in the end and it was a massive result for the team. Jock was delighted and you could see the relief on his face. The victory probably stopped him from getting the sack as the team had been on a bad run. He never complained about the pressure like some modern managers, as he'd probably had to put up with much worse when he was in the army. But his lovely wife Daphne helped pick him up on the rare occasions he was down. She was also very kind to me after I signed and looked after me like a son. I'll always be really grateful for the way she helped me in those first few weeks. Her husband might have broken my foot, but she and her home cooking put me on the road to recovery.

As far as Jock was concerned, that road took a detour towards his holiday apartment near Torremolinos. Had I been expecting a brisk stroll along the prom I was sorely mistaken. I got my plaster off in the first week in March and Jock got me doing gentle jogs up and down the beach. No dunes for a change, but plenty of sand. He then came up with the idea that salt water would aid the healing process. I think he must have seen a programme about racehorses that recovered more quickly from injuries that way. And so, like Ginger McCain and Red Rum at Southport, I was made to run into the freezing cold sea in a t-shirt and shorts as he barked orders out from under his hat and scarf. 'Get in there up to your waist, ya big poof,' was just some of the encouragement I was given. What the few brave souls mad enough to be out walking their dogs in the wintry conditions must have thought is anyone's guess. Had I been a horse they'd probably have phoned the police. It was so cold I couldn't feel my good foot let alone my bad one.

Jock also got me running with Bob every day when we got back to Seville. Rather than a gentle jog this was a ten-mile run each morning to build up stamina. Whether I'd been out on the beers or not the night before, he'd ring my doorbell at 6 a.m. sharp every morning. We'd then run round the narrow lanes of the old town as the city slowly came to life. It was murder at first, but I came to enjoy it after a while. I'd have a quick shower and a bite to eat then get a taxi to the training ground for the first session of the day. We trained in the morning and in the evening to avoid the worst of the Andalusian sun. Thanks to Bob's extra sessions I got fit again quickly and was very close to a first team return when disaster struck again. It was during an evening session, this time at the stadium. We had a drawbridge over the moat that divided the pitch and the stadium and I remember Bob scurrying over it and running up to Jock. After whispered discussions I was told to stop training and was informed that my dad had been involved in a bad car accident.

He'd been hit head-on by a German tourist towing a caravan just outside Dumfries. He was in intensive care with serious head injuries and had broken a number of ribs. I was distraught and told Jock I would get on the next plane home. He shook his head and said he'd spoken to the club. The president didn't want me to go home because he didn't think I'd come back. As far as they were concerned they'd spent an awful lot of money, I'd stupidly got myself injured and now I was running home to my family having played just one game.

Things were different then, but I couldn't believe their insensitivity. As far as I knew, my dad was at death's door and they thought I was going to do a moonlight flit. I went up the wall and threatened the beloved president with all sorts of things. Fortunately Jock calmed me down before I could do any damage to him or myself. 'Let's see how he is in the morning,' he said. Fortunately, his condition improved and I was able to get regular updates from my brother Mitchell. The club at least allowed me to make regular telephone calls to the hospital. After a week he got out of intensive care and eventually made a full recovery.

I still feel guilty that I never went back to see him. But it was difficult, as my employer wouldn't let me. After just two short months in Spain, I was feeling a hell of a long way away from home.

9

WOAH THERE, TONTO!

Jock Wallace never did things by half. Some people probably thought he was gruff and lacking in subtlety. His strong will and determination might have been mistaken for stubbornness or even arrogance. But he had an unswerving faith in his ability and the knowledge he'd acquired from life outside football as well as his years in the game. He didn't suffer fools gladly. Neither did he shirk difficult decisions, which is why it didn't surprise me when he dropped the club prima donna and gave his number six shirt to me. Unfortunately it came as a huge surprise to him, not to mention his thousands of adoring fans on the terraces.

I'd eased my way back into the first team after my broken foot and was playing quite well. But it was frustrating. We'd do ok for a game or two and then the wheels would come off and we'd lose games we shouldn't have. Jock needed to change it. Francisco was the blue-eyed boy as far as the supporters were concerned and could do no wrong. But big Jock hated the fact that he didn't track back and was hopeless when we didn't have the ball. He wanted everyone to play as a team whether we were attacking or defending. So he dropped him. The howls of derision that greeted the decision when it was announced over the tannoy could be heard in the changing rooms. As Jock made his way to the dugout he was pelted with cushions as the fans told him exactly what they thought of his team selection. He later admitted to me that it had probably been the wrong decision. But it highlighted the guy's inner strength and demonstrated that he was boss, whether the players liked it or not.

The reaction of the Seville fans also demonstrated the passion they had for the game and the team they supported. Most important of all were the biannual matches with local rivals Real Betis. Almost the first Spanish I picked up from meeting Seville fans was 'verde blanco caca', which translates as green and white shite. That was fair enough as far as I was concerned, given my previous employer in a city with a passionate derby of its own! The build up to the game was always intense and it would often be the sole topic of conversation for weeks on end. To make sure we didn't get too wound up, President Cuervas would take us away for a few days to a hotel down the coast. Jock had no objections as it gave him the opportunity to practise some routines away from any prying eyes. Souness had started to introduce something similar at Ibrox, but it was still fairly new to me.

Also new to me was Spain's most famous dish – paella. Before boarding the bus to take us away, I decided it was high time I tried it out. After much pointing at pictures on the menu, I selected the seafood version and wasn't disappointed. Full of enough saffron rice, prawns and mussels to sink a battleship, I then met up with the other players, feeling just a little more Spanish than before. Jock handed everyone an itinerary for our short stay, pointing out mealtimes, training sessions and when we'd be having our team meeting. The first couple of hours at the hotel had been designated as free time, which usually meant a walk with Jock given the language difficulties I had with the other players. But I was pleasantly surprised to be invited down to the beach by one of the Uruguayans, Nadal.

As well as the usual sun-seekers and swimmers, the resort had horses for hire. The nags were several notches up from donkeys at Blackpool and we decided to give it a whirl. It turned out that Nadal lived on a ranch back home in South America and was a skilled rider. I'd never so much as sat on the back of horse, but didn't think it could be that difficult as I handed over my money. As omens go, smashing my hatless head on the stable door as we reversed out wasn't a good one. But all seemed fine as I wobbled off down the beach in my vest and shorts.

Nadal immediately galloped off into the distance at great pace, returning from time to time with a great flourish. Had someone given him a mask and sword he could easily have passed for Zorro as he got his horse to rear up on its hindquarters. He even had it rolling in the sand as a crowd began to gather. I would have loved to have enjoyed the show, but was finding it difficult to concentrate. I'd come out without my sunglasses and was suffering in the bright sunshine. The motion of the horse was beginning to disagree with me too, so with great reluctance I left Nadal to his adoring public and made my excuses.

By the time I got back to the hotel I could hardly see and had a red rash on my face and arms. I'd also lost my paella behind a bus shelter and there were ominous rumbles at the other end too. The sanctuary of my room couldn't come quick enough and I spent the next two hours alternating between the bog and the bidet. When Jock phoned to ask why I'd missed the team meeting I told him I was in a bad way. He was having none of it and ordered me to grab a toilet roll and meet him in reception.

I did so with great reluctance and we headed out for a walk. There then followed the longest twenty minutes of my life as I continually interrupted Jock's thoughts on the forthcoming game to jump over the sea wall for one emergency evacuation after another. We finally got back to the hotel and Jock realised he'd have to send for a doctor. With him as interrogator, Bob as interpreter and me as occasional mime actor, the inquisition began. It wasn't long before the doc ascertained that I was allergic to horses, but the sickness and diarrhoea had her stumped. What had I been eating in the previous twenty-four hours, she asked? As she and Bob tried not to laugh and Jock tried not to hit me, I innocently informed them how some of the mussels in my paella had been a bugger to open.

After being given an injection, I was told to rest up and take plenty of fluids. The game was still forty-eight hours away and I was determined not to let my teammates down. After a fitful night's sleep I wasn't much better in the morning and had a terrible training session. Jock was under pressure from the president who wanted to know why his expensive import was in such a bad way again so soon after breaking his ankle. In fairness to Jock, he was keen that I didn't play despite the criticism he knew it would attract. But I insisted I was fit enough to take the field and did so in front of a packed house. I wish I hadn't.

Expectations were very high and we let our supporters down. I was woefully off the pace and chased shadows for much of the game. Whenever I went on a run my stomach gurgled and my bowels rumbled. All I could think of was a large bowl of mussels. Mid-way though the second half Jock put me out of my misery and hauled me off. We were 2-0 down and ended up losing 3-0 as Betis played us off the park. Jock and I were greeted with angry catcalls as we made our way back to the changing rooms. None of the fans knew I'd been ill and just thought I'd had a bad game. I shouldn't have played and Jock was annoyed having listened to me rather than himself. He left the field with a bowed head. The pressure was growing.

It didn't get any better in the coming weeks when Spanish football chiefs decided to experiment with the league, splitting it with ten games to go. The top four would play each other to decide who would win the title, whilst the bottom four would battle it out to avoid relegation. We were left with nothing to play for in the rump in the middle along with Betis, Atletíco Madrid, Real Sociedad, Valladolid, and Murcia. The good ship Seville quickly dropped anchor as its scurvy crew lost interest and all but one of their remaining games. With nothing to play for it was difficult to stay motivated and a shameful apathy set in.

Captain Jock did his best to rouse the troops with his pre-match team talks. We'd both been trying hard at our Spanish lessons and Jock was rather better at it than me. He'd start off quite coherently, pointing at the whiteboard in the changing rooms and discussing tactics. The players would nod and show interest as Bob whispered in English for my benefit. But their eyes would glaze over and brows would furrow as he descended into a foul-mouthed rant. Bob would then do his best to keep up, racking his brains to translate such choice phrases as 'get right intae these bastards' and 'dinnae take any fuckin' prisoners'.

Bob later admitted to me that he sometimes struggled to

understand Jock himself, particularly when they were called on to do interviews together on Spanish television. Just like Juande Ramos and Fabio Capello do now, Jock would give the TV crew the benefit of his wisdom in his native tongue. Bob would then do his best to decipher the Scottish accent, which got broader the more Jock got frustrated. As often as not the poor American would just have to make it up, trotting out some well-worn football clichés as the watching nation looked on oblivious. It was pure slapstick.

Despite the doom and gloom, such incidents helped to keep our spirits up. Fortunately they didn't need to be raised for our visit to Barcelona and their magnificent Nou Camp stadium. Jock and I had been looking forward to it for weeks. Both of us were eager to pit our wits against Terry Venables and Gary Lineker. We couldn't help but be impressed by the ground as we got off the bus from the airport. It towers over the city and presents as intimidating a sight for visiting teams as the club's formidable record. It certainly seemed to get to our Spanish players who were unusually quiet as we made our way to the changing rooms.

We did our warm-up on the pitch as the crowd began to filter in and I then made my way back to the changing rooms through the cavernous stadium. Jock was talking tactics with Bob and was all set to launch into one of his infamous team talks. The problem was the team hadn't followed me back. With ten minutes to go until kick-off I was dispatched to find them and began hunting high and low. I started to panic when various puzzled Barcelona officials said they hadn't seen them either and I wondered if they'd bottled it.

After what seemed like hours had passed, I finally stumbled through a door and found them all on their knees in full kit in front of a large cross. The Nou Camp was so big that it boasted its own chapel and they were keen to stock up on spiritual guidance. After much pleading, I eventually got them back to the dressing rooms where a worried Jock was stood shaking his head. Whether it was divine inspiration or not, the impromptu prayer meeting seemed to work and we ran out 2-1 winners in the end. The result added to the heat on Venables and he was sacked not long afterwards. The demands, particularly those made of the expensive imports at the top clubs like Barca, were as high as they are today. They didn't tolerate failure.

Jock's answer to the stresses and strains he was under was to take me out for a quiet beer. I'd moved to the old part of Seville by now, known as the Barrio de Santa Cruz. The area, which is famous for its tapas bars, lay to the east of the Guadalquivir River, near the city's famous cathedral and Alcázar. I'd get a taxi every morning from there to the training ground in the suburbs. At least once a week I'd be picked up by a Betis fan who'd frown at me in his rear-view mirror as I tried to describe my destination. Until the club provided me with a map, with an 'X' marking the spot, I'd often be dropped with a cheerful wave miles from where I wanted to be. Getting back was easier fortunately, as all I needed to do was pretend to be a tourist and ask for the cathedral.

My tiny two-bedroom flat was above one of the famous tapas bars. Jock would ring the bell and get the first round in as I made my way downstairs. Any passing British tourists would often be invited over to join us. Bemused couples from as far afield as Brighton and Buckie would then be pumped for news by two homesick Scotsmen. Long before closing, Jock would send me back to the flat to get my beauty sleep. He'd sometimes then carry on late into the night with anyone who cared to keep him company. I used to lie in bed with the windows open trying to get to sleep in the non-air-conditioned flat and would finally hear the shutters going down on the bars in the wee, small hours. As often as not I'd also catch snippets of a Scottish voice quietly singing 'Follow Follow' to itself. The words would echo down the narrow cobbled streets as I smiled to myself in the dark. You could take Jock out of Rangers, but you could never take Rangers out of Jock.

A couple of our favourite haunts lay on the other side of a notorious park called the Murillo Gardens. During the day it would be filled with families and I'd often take Bob's kids there for a kickabout after training. But after dark it became a hang-out for homosexuals, who were preyed on by local youths. Jock didn't scare easily and would walk straight through regardless of the danger. He believed they were less likely to attack couples so would take my hand and mince through as best he could. When we reached the other end he'd then drop it like a stone, hoping no one had seen us. A keen-eyed photographer could have sold the story of the 'Gay Football Manager and his Star Signing' for a fortune these days, but we always managed to get away with it.

We were less lucky on one occasion when we returned through the park to Jock's club car. We'd both had a few and were in no fit state to drive. But the police turned a blind eye to drink-driving so we'd decided to risk it. As we made our way down the street to where he'd parked his car, we discovered a number of windows had been smashed. The city had a large gypsy population who took the blame, rightly or wrongly, for the craze of stealing car stereos. Sure enough, ours had been nicked too and the seats were covered in glass. Jock insisted it was still fit to drive and would hear none of my requests to get a taxi. After carefully removing the jagged shards, we took our seats only for him to announce that all was not well. He couldn't put his finger on it, but something was definitely missing. As we both slowly began to sober up, we realised that they'd also pinched the steering wheel!

The dalliance with the dashboard was a prelude to my own brush with criminality. In September 1987, Ally McCoist, Ian Durrant and I were finally hauled up in court for our part in the East Kilbride punch-up. The incident had been the beginning of the end of my Ibrox career and the prospect of legal proceedings had been hanging over us like a black cloud. The top brass at Seville were genuinely worried about the prospect of me being convicted and there were endless discussions before I boarded the plane. They reluctantly agreed to lend me £1,000 to pay for my airfares and hotel accommodation, as there was no way I could afford it on my monthly allowance.

Thankfully money wasn't so tight at Rangers who recruited the finest legal brains in the country to fight our corner. It was just as well as I was extremely nervous. Having been inside some of Scotland's prisons during my brief spell playing for the warders of Dumfries Young Offenders Institution, I had no desire to return.

It was open season in the media. On our first day at Hamilton Sheriff Court, the press benches were full and many of the reporters had to be accommodated in the equally packed public gallery. The three of us avoided the scrum outside the court after being smuggled in through a back door. But they were all waiting for us inside when we stood up in the dock. We were deeply concerned about how events were going to be portrayed and were fearful for our careers and the reputation of the club. We were also worried what witnesses were going to say and how lurid or even far-fetched their evidence was going to be.

The gravity of the situation eased when the procurator fiscal began questioning us about the events of the ill-fated night. We told him in turn how we'd been drinking at the nightclub and had run into the alleged victim, who turned out to be a teenage tax officer called Craig Sampson. He then alleged that we'd threatened to give his dentist 'something to worry about'. Coisty had been boasting about the power of his punch, thinking he was Rocky Balboa. But the fiscal rained on his parade when he then revealed that the two teeth he'd knocked out of the nineteen-year-old's mouth had been false ones. 'Fucking hardman my arse,' whispered wee Durrant as we tried not to giggle.

The evidence against us never really stacked up over the course of the trial. The sheriff took as dim a view of Sampson as he did us. Our legal team also made much of the Celtic tattoos on his hands and the fact we'd been repeatedly goaded. News that I'd been daft enough to chase the guy into a police station raised a laugh in the public gallery and it was hardly my finest hour. But after three long days and much stress, Durrant and I were handed not proven verdicts and McCoist fined £150.

Neither of us really knew what the verdict meant and hung around uncomfortably in the dock until we were told we could leave. We did so quickly, fearing the sheriff might change his mind. We'd been stupid going out on a Thursday night and even more stupid getting involved in an altercation. McCoist and I at twenty-four were old enough to know better and the case taught us a thing or two about our responsibilities and how we conducted ourselves. Whilst it had been nice to get back to Scotland for a few days, albeit in the wrong circumstances, it also reminded me of one of the reasons why I'd left.

The return home would have been an ideal opportunity to put my personal affairs in order had they not been in such a mess. Within just two or three months of getting married I'd known things weren't right with Jackie and me. Rather than domestic bliss, I'd found marriage to be domestic drudgery. All I seemed to do was train, home, bed, train, home, bed every day. At least I had some good mates. As well as my circle of pals in Dumfries I had new friends in Glasgow as well. Her roots were still in Dumfries and it was there I preferred to send her when I went out with the lads. She must have got bored of being told that she couldn't come and hearing me get in on a Saturday at three or four in the morning. My dad's solution to the problem was to give Jackie some freedom of her own and for me to buy her a car. We went to a dealership in Ayr and came away with a Volkswagen Golf. She thought it was great and I thought it was a free lift to training every day. After a couple of weeks of being at my beck and call she quite rightly spat the dummy and stormed back to Dumfries. It was a good job as I'd already started seeing someone else.

June Newman worked as a barmaid in the Village pub in Shawlands. She was very pretty and had caught the eye of a number of the boys on our nights out. I got chatting to her one time after Jackie and I had had a blazing row and plucked up the courage to ask her out. She turned me down flat but eventually relented after weeks of persistence. I told her that my marriage was over and she accepted that things had gone beyond repair. So too did her lovely parents, Tom and Isabelle, who always made me very welcome.

Not long before I left Rangers I was in bed with June one

Sunday morning, sleeping off the excesses of the night before, when there was a knock at the door. I looked out of the window to see if I recognised any cars parked below. As I was doing so, a key turned in the door and my Dad began to enter the flat followed by Jackie. With surprising speed he cottoned on that I had someone else in there with me. Ushering Jackie out he gave me a withering look and made some excuse about taking the dog out.

My guilt increased after I'd got rid of June when they returned twenty minutes later, announcing that they'd come to sort out my finances. Despite the way I'd treated her, Jackie had confided in my Dad that I was drowning in debt. The finance on the car was the main thing. But I also had a stack of unpaid bills that I'd stored in a kitchen cupboard, hoping they'd go away. I confessed that I'd been stupid and broke down in tears. Dad was very calm about it, asked me how much I owed and said he would lend me the money. He wrote out a cheque and told me I'd give it back interest-free at £50 a week. I did so and never missed a payment.

If only my marriage had been so easy to sort out. Jackie's kindness was completely at odds with my selfish behaviour. It's difficult to explain now, but I probably wasn't mature enough to deal with the responsibilities back then. I don't know if she'd realised why Dad had performed a hasty U-turn in the flat – maybe I'm not giving her enough credit – but we both knew in our heart of hearts that it couldn't go on much longer the way it was. As we did from time to time, we resolved to give it another go and turned over a new leaf. I don't really know why we bothered. The car was involved in a smash soon afterwards and we had to get rid of it. To all intents and purposes our marriage was a write-off too.

10

SO IT'S GOODNIGHT FROM ME

The common complaint in football these days is that managers don't get long enough to prove themselves. Financial considerations in the top European leagues mean that they have to be successful quickly or they're out. Television revenues are so important to clubs with high wage bills that nervous chairmen have become trigger-happy. It has reached ridiculous levels now, but it wasn't much better during my career. I'd heard of teams getting off to bad starts and we were all familiar with the bookies' dreaded sack race. But the speed at which my old mucker Jock Wallace was despatched in August 1987 took all of us by surprise. We hadn't even played a game.

The writing had probably been on the wall the previous season when our campaign fizzled out with a series of lacklustre displays. But we'd followed it up with a relatively successful pre-season and Jock and I were raring to go. He'd taken us up to Pamplona in the Basque country for training, reasoning that the cooler climes would be ideal for some heavy-duty running. We'd also taken part in a tournament with some local lower league clubs that we'd won comfortably with some impressive displays. From there it was on to another tournament called the Carrera Trophy in Cádiz, where we beat the home side before losing to Brazil's Vasco de Gama, whose set-piece routines were too good for us. Jock was full of it and couldn't wait to get his teeth into the league programme.

The problem was the players. Jock had sown the seeds of discontent when he dropped Francisco from the team. They'd almost forgiven him when he decided to take one of the courses off them at their pre-match meals. The gaffer reckoned the vast quantities of grub they were putting away was the reason why they were sluggish on the pitch. It was meat or fish as far as he was concerned and not both. He also wanted a few of them to shift some weight and introduced extra running sessions reminiscent of the torture he'd put the Rangers players through at Gullane.

The Spanish players hated running. They could do it all day if they had a ball at their feet but they moaned like mad when the long distance stuff came out. The fact that half of them were heavy smokers might have had something to do with it. Discontent quickly began to smoulder behind the bike sheds and I caught snippets of conversation that were obviously directed at Jock. With just two days to go before the first game of the season all out rebellion engulfed the team.

The end came quickly. Jock was called into the president's office and told he was no longer needed. He phoned me that afternoon and urged me to hang in there. Bob did so too and delivered a similar speech to the one Walter Smith had given me after my bust-up with Souness. My immediate thought was that I'd soon be on my bike again as I didn't see a future for me at the club without my mentor. I was gutted he was gone. The guy wasn't just a great boss, he'd also become a pal and a confidant. His outlook on life was so like my Dad's that he had become a father figure to me. But now that had all been taken away. I was guilty that my displays as well as those of the other players had contributed to his downfall, in my case, for the second time. I felt out on a limb, distant from my colleagues, like unwanted baggage. Surely Jock's successor wouldn't want his cast-offs?

I didn't have long to find out. The new guy came in the day after Jock was sacked, suggesting the president's decision had not been made on impulse. He was former Athletic Bilbao centre forward Xabier Azkargorta, who had previously been in charge of Real Valladolid. He had a large black moustache and looked like a heavier version of the Spanish waiter Manuel from the TV comedy *Fawlty Towers*. After watching us train he introduced himself to the players in Spanish one by one. When it came to my turn he said in English that he wanted a word in his office. If I was expecting my P45, I was pleasantly surprised. He said he knew I'd been close to Jock and would be upset that he'd gone. But he wanted to reassure me that I was in his plans too and had a bright future at the club as long as I kept putting in the work. As introductions went, you couldn't ask for any more than that.

The new regime got off to a roller-coaster start. After losing to Betis in the opener, we beat Barcelona in the Nou Camp again and then won and lost in five successive weeks. True to his word, Azkargorta did include me in his plans, but only when we played at home. After long away trips by coach or on a plane I'd find myself as a substitute as he tried out a more defensive formation. It was deeply frustrating and no good for building up any kind of consistency, which, as a player, I always craved. I reached the bottom on an away trip to Zaragoza in the autumn. The teams probably fly direct now, but in our day we got a plane to Madrid before piling onto a coach for a four or five hour bus journey. We travelled all the way up the day before and a few of the lads broke curfew that evening and went out on the town. Many of them had girlfriends in the different cities we played in and Zaragoza had particularly rich pickings by all accounts. I'd learnt my lessons about wine, women and song at Ibrox and wasn't one of their number. But I was fed up the next day when the team sheet was handed round and I was warming the bench again. Some of the boys were still rotten after their late night and I feared we were going to get a doing.

Sure enough, within twenty minutes we were 5-0 down and dying on our arses. None of them looked like they'd ever played together before and at least one had been sick on the pitch. It was Sunday league shite. Azkargorta motioned at me to warm-up and I told him exactly where to stick it. If he thought I was going on to save that lot he could think again.

It was the single most unprofessional thing I ever did. The problem was I knew I'd take the flack, whatever the score was when I came on. The Spanish media had a horrible habit of questioning the performances of the foreign players first. I couldn't read their pearls of wisdom of course, but Bob translated the articles for me and we'd often both wonder if we'd been at the same game as them. It was a petulant thing to do and I should never have insulted the integrity of Azkargorta. But the one-man protest summed up just exactly how I felt.

For once the reporters didn't hear about my transgression. They had enough to report after the team ended up being stuffed 8-1. To his credit Azkargorta kept it to himself and showed no desire for a public dressing-down à la Souness. Jock found out, however, and was far from impressed. The big man was still in Spain having slipped away to his holiday home near

Fuengirola after sorting out his compensation. He still watched the highlights programme religiously on a Sunday night and got blow-by-blow accounts from Bob. He'd phone me up in the flat for a chat usually to offer friendly advice. If I needed a bollocking he'd hand one out too, as if his dismissal had never happened.

Following the Zaragoza disaster I told Jock I had to get out but he convinced me that the only way I would attract attention from other clubs was by playing consistently well in the first team. There was no point sulking with the stiffs in the reserves. The problem was, with Jock no longer there and Bob coming less and less due to his work commitments, away trips were becoming a prison for me. It was hours upon hours of travel in a foreign country with people I could barely talk to. And usually it was to sit on the bench.

Ironically it was another away trip, this time to Las Palmas, that promised light at the end of the tunnel. The opposition, who played on Gran Canaria, were a typical yo-yo side that bounced between the first and second divisions. But the trip held out the prospect of meeting a few British holidaymakers, which meant at least I'd have someone to communicate with. We flew in on the Saturday, played Las Palmas in the sweltering heat at 8 p.m. the following evening and emerged with a 2-1 victory. The boys were in fine fettle and went back to the hotel for a meal and a few glasses of wine. We had to catch a bus to the airport at 6.30 the next morning and were told to be in bed by midnight.

Nobody was in the mood to head off early. After a few beers in the hotel bar a few of us headed down the fire escape and snuck into a nearby nightclub. The Spanish players quickly latched on to another group of girlfriends and I was left on my own

113

again. Try as I might to strike up a conversation, there were very few English speakers about so I headed outside with a large bottle of beer. I strolled down to the beach and walked along the shore. It was a beautiful warm evening and there were plenty of folk still about. But I felt very lonely on my own and felt more homesick than I ever had before. I was also drunk and had no desire to hurry back for our early-morning flight. Instead, I took off my socks and shoes and settled down for a kip.

If you've never been woken up by the sea, I wouldn't recommend it. The first thing that crossed my mind as a wave splashed over my legs and sloshed up my back was that I'd had a terrible accident. The second thing was that I was in an awful lot more trouble than that. The morning sun was already high in the sky as I desperately tried to come to my senses. My shoes and one of my socks had been swept out to sea, so I made my way back to the hotel barefoot. The next problem was that I didn't have a clue what hotel we were staying in. After stumbling from one reception to another I eventually found it and crashed up the stairs at 6.25 a.m. My room mate Ricardo Serna was just putting the finishing touches to his tie and brushing his jet-black hair.

The salt had started to dry on my suit and was leaving large white patches. I was sweating profusely and stank of B.O. and beer. Had I been wearing a string vest I might well have invented the character Rab C. Nesbitt. Serna wasn't impressed. He shook his head, walked past me and said just one thing: 'Tonto'. Azkargorta thought I was mad too when I turned up in the foyer five minutes later. I'd managed to put on a pair of white training shoes but still looked a complete mess. He didn't even ask me if I'd been out and I can't remember if he fined me in the end. I think he was just glad to have me on the coach in one piece. The only thought in my head as we took off for the mainland a couple of hours later was that I had to get home. And I didn't mean to my flat in Seville.

One of the newspapers back home heard that I was homesick and flew a photographer out to take some pictures. I then did a 'come and get me' piece putting myself in the shop window for any clubs that were interested. Sitting in our Shawlands flat, Jackie spotted this and chose to do a piece of her own. June was pregnant with my baby. Rather than tell Jackie face-to-face I wrote her a letter from Heathrow Airport on one of my trips back to the UK. I told her that our marriage was finally over and that June was due in April.

With the help of three reporters, the *Daily Record* put me on the front cover under a banner headline screaming 'ADIOS!' Every gory detail was then revealed inside between our wedding photo and one of me looking sheepish next to a suit of armour that they'd dug out of the archives. Jackie, who struck a pose with the offending letter in an orange blouse, vowed to take me for 'every penny'.

Jackie didn't want me but fortunately there were others out there who did. Not long after my impromptu dip in the sea, Jock phoned to say he'd been contacted by a number of English clubs. Watford, Newcastle United and Derby County were all interested. There was also speculation in the Spanish papers that Bayern Munich were sniffing around. But I had no desire to go off and learn German after my failure with Spanish. Jock repeated his advice to keep playing well, convinced that something would come up.

Matters came to a head one evening when I got a ring on the buzzer in my flat. I answered and heard a Spanish voice say: 'Ted, teléfono!' I didn't have my own phone in the flat at the time and so was using the one in the bar downstairs. Just like I did back in Dumfries with the payphone in the street, I gave out my number so people could ask for me. The difficulty was nobody who picked up the phone spoke English and it was hit or miss whether someone understood or could be bothered to go and fetch me. This time it just happened to be Newcastle United manager Willie McFaul.

Willie had had people watch me and was keen that I signed. The board had put the money in place and had agreed a deal with Seville. All we had to do was thrash out personal terms. Jock, who was acting as my unofficial agent, returned to Seville the next day. We phoned Newcastle back from a hotel room he'd hired and examined the deal a bit closer. They offered me a three and a half year contract for £1,000 a week in wages and a signing-on fee of £25,000. It was £250 more than I was on with Seville. More importantly it was a ticket back to Britain and to one of the big clubs at that. I put the phone down on Willie after telling him I was very interested in signing. As I did so Jock told me there was someone else I should meet who was coming up from the coast in the morning. 'His name's Stuart Webb and he's a director of Derby County,' he said.

I knew next to nothing about Derby. My only memory was of seeing Archie Gemmill score against Nottingham Forest for them on a cabbage patch of a pitch in the FA Cup. Webb didn't look like he'd been lifting vegetables. He and his wife had been staying on a luxury yacht in Marbella harbour owned by Rams Chairman Robert Maxwell. I was impressed with his appearance but also that he'd come out to see me. Webb also offered me a three and a half year deal with £750 a week in wages and a £60,000 signing-on fee. The wages were less than Newcastle but the signing-on fee was much better so I was left in two minds. Webb suggested I got on the phone to Derby manager Arthur Cox.

As soon as I spoke to Arthur I knew I wanted to sign for him. He was like Jock Wallace with an English accent. There was no time for small talk.

'Hello Ted,' he growled. 'I've been chasing you for five years since you were at Queen of the South and I want to sign you. What seems to be the problem?'

I began to stumble over my words and heard myself say, 'Well, er, it's the car Mr Cox. I want a car.' Quite why I wanted a car still puzzles, particularly as I didn't know how to drive at the time. I think I presumed that all the big stars had their own cars so I needed one too. This had Arthur foxed but he asked to be handed over to Webb and obviously thrashed it out. Webb had not come all the way to Spain for a holiday and said he'd make sure I got a car.

I signed a piece of paper and shook Jock's hand when Webb left the room. There was now the small matter of telling Newcastle that I wasn't going there. Jock refused to phone them on my behalf claiming my name would be mud in football if I didn't do it myself. When I finally got through to Willie McFaul he was very disappointed. He was even more disappointed that I was going to Derby to join up with former Newcastle boss Arthur Cox. He promised to go back to the board for more money and said there would be a ticket for a Newcastle flight waiting for me at Heathrow when I arrived back from Spain. I thanked him for his efforts and felt bad about letting him down after provisionally saying yes. But I was delighted that I was finally going home and was very excited about joining Derby.

Before I could do so I had to play my last game for Seville.

The president had refused to let me go before the local derby against Betis. By now news of my departure had leaked into the papers and our opponents took great delight in boasting about sending me on my way. I wasn't in the greatest of shape as I'd picked up a nasty bang during a recent defeat against Real Mallorca. The fullback had sliced open my knee after catching me with his studs. Four young members of the medical staff had then stretchered me off. But in a moment of painful farce, they'd dropped me onto my feet again as I slipped off the stretcher when they took me up the steep-sided stand. Because it was on the crease in my skin, the knee kept opening up again whenever I ran. It was a heavily-bandaged target as far as my opponents were concerned.

Tensions were running high as we approached Betis' old Benito Villamarín stadium. The team bus had been stoned on our last visit there and police feared a repeat. But we passed through unscathed. The game was as passionate and full-blooded as ever. The first thing I had to do was pick myself off the grass after my opposite number went straight through the back of me, taking a large chunk out of my sock and calf with his boot. I emerged from the rest of the game unscathed and played quite well in a deserved 1-0 victory. Ramon got the goal in the second half and we celebrated in front of the small knot of Seville fans who been let into the ground. I then had to endure one of the country's trademark post-match inter-views, in which neither the person asking the questions nor the one answering them knew what the hell was going on. I wouldn't miss them one bit. However, there was a large part of me that was very sorry to be leaving Spain. I'd been terribly homesick and was ready to go home. But I'd learnt a lot as a player and a person and had loved living in Seville.

11

HOME RUN AT THE BASEBALL GROUND

I remember watching David Beckham sign for LA Galaxy in a $250-million deal and thinking football had moved on a long way since my day. Before he actually put pen to paper with the MLS side there was a live satellite link-up to Madrid, in which he announced he would be coaching at his own academies. The press, who had a field day revealing he was best mates with Hollywood A-listers like Tom Cruise, also announced that he would be making an awful lot of money. His move from Manchester United to Real Madrid had attracted almost as much attention a few years before. Madrid had televised his arrival in the Spanish capital, his triumphant arrival at their Bernabeu stadium and even his medical at an exclusive private clinic. I'm glad they didn't show my medical on the public wards at the Derbyshire Royal Infirmary because I wasn't wearing any pants.

I'd gone commando since taking the decision as a child that I could do without my brothers' hand-me-down underwear. By the time they reached me their vests and skid-stained Y-fronts were full of holes. The vests kept me warm but I didn't need the pants. It didn't occur to me as I was asked to take my trousers off and lie on the bed by an attractive nurse that other people might not be so keen. Derby's long-serving physio-therapist Gordon Guthrie, who had taken me to the DRI, was horrified that the club might have signed some sort of sexual deviant. Fortunately the nurse had seen it all before. After one of those little 'tuts' that women do so well, she spared Gordon's blushes by ripping off a piece of paper towel and covering the offending part of my anatomy. The rest of the medical passed without incident. I didn't look very clever with an ugly cut on my knee and a chunk out of the back of my calf from the Betis game. But the tests and X-rays revealed I had no problems internally. I was fit to sign.

I'd flown into Heathrow the previous day, Sunday 31 January 1988. The club had asked me to get on a flight and I didn't know if there would be anyone there to meet me, let alone any of the razzmatazz that marked Beckham's dramatic arrival. After clearing customs I noticed two elderly men in three-quarter-length football jackets scanning a photograph and shaking their heads as passengers filed past. I wasn't making it easy for them as I was wearing a thick jumper, leather jacket and shades like Dumfries' answer to the Fonz. One of them asked me if I was Ted McMinn and then relieved me of my bags when I answered yes. Without introducing themselves, they then escorted me to a car. I wasn't entirely sure whether they worked for Derby County or I was being kidnapped. They maintained a stubborn silence for most of the journey and it wasn't until we turned off the M1 at junction twenty-five that I definitely knew I was heading for the Baseball Ground rather than St James' Park.

My first meeting with Rams manager Arthur Cox and his assistant Roy McFarland the following morning was a little less dramatic. I'd liked the sound of Arthur on the phone and wasn't disappointed in the flesh. With his closely-cropped hair and his craggy features he looked like the hard-as-nails detective inspector in a thousand TV cop shows. I knew there wasn't going to be any bullshit; what you saw was what you got with the tough-talking West Midlander. I was aware of Roy Mac as the classy centre half who'd floated above the Baseball Ground mud in the Championship-winning teams of Clough and Mackay. He seemed a very decent bloke.

The old ground was little changed from those heady days and I could hardly wait to step out in front of its tightly packed stands. It was much more like some of the old Scottish grounds I'd played at rather than the soulless concrete bowls of Spain. Roy introduced me to my new pals, none of whom I recognised. But I was hardly a household name myself, certainly not like England internationals Peter Shilton and Mark Wright, who'd both signed from Southampton earlier that season. Private and often aloof, Shilts would always remain something of an enigma. He kept himself to himself, possibly because he was much older than the other lads. But I struck up an immediate rapport with Wrighty. Despite being an international, he wasn't big-headed and was fiercely loyal to his friends and family. His sense of humour and easy-going nature suited me down to the ground.

Wrighty was to score on my debut when we took on Portsmouth. The long coach journey down to Fratton Park was a great opportunity to get to know the boys and I was quickly welcomed into the card school. We'd play a bit of brag and occasionally hearts, but the real game of choice was always shoot pontoon. Nigel Callaghan and Rob Hindmarch enjoyed a game, as did Wrighty and Shilts. We'd start off playing for fifty pences and the odd pound and as the pot grew bigger the tension would mount. As we approached our destination there was often up to £50 at stake for the winner. That was plenty big enough for us and there were never any of these crazy amounts gambled by the current crop of England internationals. It's no wonder some of them can't concentrate on the game in hand if they're losing tens of thousands of pounds at cards. Ironically, it was also our England man Shilts who always wanted to play for big money. As we approached the service station near his Leicester home where we'd drop him off if we'd been playing down south, he'd always challenge the banker for big bucks. He'd lose just as many times, if not more, than he won. I was saddened when I later heard he had gambling problems and had lost a lot of money. But, unfortunately, I can't say I was too surprised.

It had been quite a gamble for me personally joining the Rams, despite my desperation to leave Seville. After successive promotions in 1986 and 1987 had taken us from the Third division to the First, the team was struggling to hold its own. The gulf in class was beginning to show. From 12 December onwards we suffered six straight defeats. We were fourth from the bottom with only Watford, Oxford and Charlton below us in the table when I joined. Alan Ball's Portsmouth were only three places above us but they beat us quite comprehensively on my debut despite the closeness of the scoreline. Vince Hilaire tapped in their opener after Terry Connor had bundled into Shilts. Wrighty's majestic header cancelled that out, but a glancing one from former Derby apprentice Mickey Quinn restored their advantage. The pitch was heavy after being cut up by an FA Cup tie and I had to receive treatment twice after being scythed down by Lee Sandford and Barry Horne. But there was a great spirit in the team and it didn't appear to be burdened by any big egos. Despite that I realised it was going to be hard work to stay in the top flight. We had some big games coming up. None more so than my home debut on the Wednesday night against Manchester United, who were joint second in the table with Nottingham Forest. Derby hadn't beaten the Red Devils at the Baseball Ground since a Charlie George double helped them to a 2-1 win thirteen years previously.

The weather for the crunch clash was appalling. It was freezing cold and the sleat swirled around the old ground's floodlights in an arctic wind. But the place was rocking. I remember emerging from the narrow players' tunnel and being struck by the amount of noise generated by the crowd, who were huddled together for warmth. We'd often had double the 20,016 attendance for a big match at Ibrox. But the massed ranks of Rams fans sheltering under the 'Welcome to the Baseball Ground' sign on the Popside terracing created a cracking atmosphere.

Sadly it was the visiting supporters exposed to the elements at the Osmaston end who had more to sing about. Wrighty was immense at the back alongside Hindmarch, who was playing his first league game since August. Mickey Lewis and Geraint 'George' Williams battled away in midfield, with Cally on the left, me on the right and thirty-two-year-old John Gregory in a makeshift centre forward role. We matched them for grit and endeavour but lacked the extra skill and fell behind to a Norman Whiteside sitter on seventy-one minutes. They wrapped it up with two minutes to go when Viv Anderson played Gordon Strachan in and he side-footed past Shilts. Or so they thought.

I was determined we weren't going to surrender so easily. With just seconds left on the clock and the crowd beginning to filter away, I picked up the ball in front of the dugouts and charged off down the right wing. Fellow Scot Arthur Albiston had not long come on for Mike Duxbury at left back, but I caught him flat-footed and beat him on the inside. I didn't really know what else to do next, so just lashed it goalward with my left foot as it sat up on a divot. As soon as the ball left my boot I knew it was in and so did goalkeeper Chris Turner. A huge roar of joy and renewed optimism greeted the goal. But despite sprinting to retrieve the ball, there was barely enough time to restart the game before the referee called proceedings to a halt.

I was delighted to have scored the best goal of my career, yet gutted to have finished on the losing side. I hadn't had the best of games and wanted to let Arthur know there was better to come. I had to dash off after the match to catch a flight to Seville, but I knocked on his door and assured him he hadn't seen anything yet. With a gesture I would come to recognise, he winked and tapped me on the shoulder before moving past me into the corridor. He was a man of few words and didn't believe in lavishing praise on anyone, no matter how well they'd played. But he knew who to put his arm round and who to give a bollocking to.

There were one or two bollockings to dish out that season as it happened. The United defeat was our eighth one in a row in the league. It equalled an unwanted record set 100 years previously in the club's first ever league season and matched across two seasons in 1965. Fortunately, my goal gave us the fillip we needed and we embarked on an unbeaten run of seven games. We hardly set the heather on fire against Oxford United, but the *Derby Evening Telegraph*'s Gerald Mortimer described the point we got in a drab draw as a 'drink of water to a man dying in the desert'.

We followed it with a 1-0 win against West Ham United.

Nigel Callaghan's diving header got us out of jail after my penalty struck goalkeeper Tom McAllister's right-hand post before rolling behind him and out for a goal kick past the left-hand one. We then kept our third consecutive clean sheet in another bore draw at White Hart Lane before Cally earned us another point at home to Charlton, having been appointed penalty taker. Liverpool, who would equal Leeds United's record of twenty-nine games without defeat during the next game, then showed why the back pass rule would shortly be outlawed. But our largest crowd since 1980 were rewarded for barracking their boring play when Mickey Forsyth crashed home the equaliser with five minutes to go.

The team was a long way from being the worst in the league. We just lacked a decent centre forward. Robert Maxwell, who had taken over from his son Ian as chairman at the start of the season, was reluctant to put his hand in his pocket unfortunately. He loved nothing better than stirring it up in the media, however, and wasn't averse to making things up. As a result we didn't know what to make of the story in his own newspaper the *Daily Mirror*, that he'd invited Dutch legend Johan Cruyff to become Derby's director of football. Arthur Cox did and hit out angrily at the rumours in an outburst similar to the one that would cost Oxford's Mark Lawrenson his job the following season.

Luckily he survived and got his wish for more strike power when Republic of Ireland captain Frank Stapleton arrived from Holland and not Cruyff. Stapleton had played just a handful of games for Ajax's second team after recovering from a serious back operation. But his signing had an immediate effect when we recorded our best win of the season in a 3-0 demolition of Coventry City at the Baseball Ground. Mickey Forsyth got his second goal of the week, before Phil Gee and 'George' Williams completed the rout.

Stapleton had not spent his time on the sidelines idly sitting about. Instead he'd built up a mini clothing empire selling sports gear that he brought into training in several large suitcases. The eyes of the apprentices lit up as Dublin's answer to Santa Claus paraded his wares at knock-down prices. It wasn't until a few weeks later when the tracksuits had faded in the wash and the crocodiles had fallen off the polo shirts that we realised that all that glittered was not gold.

Sadly the Coventry game turned out to be my last one of the season. I'd been playing with a niggling groin problem that I'd first picked up in Spain. It felt fine when I ran in straight lines, but if I tried to jink from one side to the other I'd get sharp stabbing pains deep in my pelvis. Fullback Mel Sage also had a groin injury so we were packed off to a Harley Street clinic with physio Gordon Guthrie. It turned out both of us had sports hernias, or 'Gilmore's groin' as the syndrome was named, after the London surgeon who first spotted it.

We checked into the Princess Grace Hospital the day after our consultation and were operated on. After three days they got us up and took us for a walk in nearby Regent's Park. The problem was that we weren't allowed to walk fully upright as they feared we'd burst our stitches. We must have presented quite a sight as we shuffled past Madame Tussauds with our nurses, doubled in two and staring at the ground. My nurse was to have worse to come when she gave me a suppository to aid my first bowel movements the following day. She asked me if I'd taken them before and I said I had. Wondering why she'd left a single glove with the large white tablets, I put them both in my mouth and swallowed them down with a swig of

Lucozade. She returned an hour later to find nothing had happened. Another hour after that she enquired why, before impatiently snapping on the glove and remedying the problem with a little more haste than was strictly necessary. It's a mistake, let me tell you, that you only make once.

Derby made a better fist of it in my absence and managed to survive automatic relegation by eight points. But we were only a single point off fourth bottom Chelsea, who became the first top flight club for ninety years to lose their status via a play-off when they surrendered to Second Division Middlesbrough. Liverpool won the title comfortably from Manchester United after new signings John Barnes and John Aldridge defied the doubters who said they wouldn't challenge for honours after selling Ian Rush. We certainly wouldn't have survived without Shilts and Wrighty, who were ever present at the back. They were helped by Rob Hindmarch, who returned for the United game in February and stayed until the end of the season, with Paul Blades reverting to right back.

Our real problems were up front however, where a severe striker shortage meant we only hit three or more goals in one of our forty league games. Phil Gee battled away all season but, along with John Gregory, could only muster six efforts, the lowest ever by a Rams player. It was obvious we needed a decent forward. With the greatest respect in the world, that wasn't an aging Frank Stapleton and his suitcase full of sartorial surprises.

I used the remaining weeks of the season to get fit. But medical matters of another kind were also keeping me busy when the spring brought the birth of my first child. June delivered the little bundle of joy we called Dayna in Glasgow's Rottenrow Maternity Hospital on Friday 8 April 1988. Things were hardly ideal with her living up in Glasgow whilst I found my feet in Derby, but the injury gave me a chance to sort things out. It was a very emotional time with the birth, my move back from Spain and my efforts to establish myself at a new club. The messy, two-year divorce with Jackie had eventually gone through and I left her with my Glasgow flat that had cost me every penny of my signing-on fee with Rangers.

June and I moved into rented accommodation in the Derbyshire village of Swarkestone soon after and settled down nicely. Wrighty had found the house, which just happened to be near his own on a quiet country lane near a pub called the Crewe and Harpur Arms. June was happy looking after Dayna and I could be the doting Dad whilst I trained to get fit again, escaping to the boozer with Wrighty for the odd Sunday session when we felt the need. For the first time ever I felt settled and the people around me felt like a real family. Dad had done his best bringing us up, but this seemed to be what it was all about.

Our happiness had been temporarily threatened by the reappearance of my mum for the first time in over twenty years. I never actually saw her myself, but news of her presence in Derby followed a knock on the dressing room door. She'd tried something similar just after I'd signed for Rangers, when she wrote a letter and sent it to the club. But this time she'd turned up in person. Arthur, who hated being interrupted when we were in our bubble, was in the middle of a team talk. He threw open the door and angrily confronted a member of staff who was shifting nervously on the balls of her feet. She blurted out that my mum was at the front desk and was looking for a couple of complimentary tickets. The woman wondered if I'd like to meet up with her afterwards. As the other players all looked on, I said the first thing that came into my head: 'I don't have a mum, tell her to fuck off!'

That was good enough for Arthur, whose only comment was 'you heard the man' before he slammed the door. He'd checked out my background as any decent manager would and knew that Dad had brought me up on his own. He knew it had been tough but he wasn't going to let someone mess with my emotions now. This had been only my second opportunity to find out why she'd abandoned us in over two decades. Yet just like at Rangers I felt I hadn't needed her in my life up until then, so why did I need her now? The fact she was looking for comps said it all as far as I was concerned. It might seem harsh to anyone who hasn't been through what my dad, my brothers and I had but, having been abandoned by her and completely ignored for so many years, that's exactly how I felt about her and I certainly didn't feel like forgiving and forgetting after what she'd put us all through.

12

WHITE HART PAIN

The importance of a good pre-season should never be underestimated. For all we hated them at Rangers, Jock Wallace's annual trips to the seaside got the fitness into our legs that served us well throughout the season. Souness and Seville just weren't the same. Arthur Cox's equivalent of Gullane was Allestree Park Golf Course. The tree-lined park with its eighteen hole course and stately home is on the A6 just three miles north of Derby city centre. I managed to stay out of the sand in the bunkers, but got plenty of practice on the hills when I went back a week early with the youth team and the apprentices. By the time the first team jetted back from their holidays I was flying and felt fitter than I'd ever done before. In the second week we switched to nearby Moorways Athletics Stadium to work on our sprinting and again I was miles ahead of the others. I couldn't wait to get back on the pitch.

Yazz and the Plastic Population enjoyed a five week spell at the top of the charts that summer with their hit single 'The Only Way Is Up'. The song's optimism reflected the mood in the camp. We'd done little more than survive last time out, but all of us felt we could prosper this term. Joining us on our quest was Trevor Hebberd, who arrived from Oxford United for

£275,000 with Mickey Lewis going the other way in part exchange. John Gregory left to take up a position as player-manager at Portsmouth but was replaced by Nick Pickering from Coventry City and free-transfer-gamble John Chiedozie. When Andy Garner left for Blackpool in August, Paul Blades was the sole survivor from pre-Cox days at the Baseball Ground. Most significant of all however, was the capture of centre forward Paul Goddard for £425,000 from Newcastle United. All of us desperately hoped Goddard, or 'Sarge' as he would forever be known, would be the final piece in the jigsaw that would allow us to climb up the league.

Sarge was a big one for the fashion of rolling up the waistband of your shorts, exposing your thighs and much else besides. It certainly did enough to put off the Middlesbrough defenders when he capped an impressive debut with the only goal of the game in our opener at the Baseball Ground. I had to watch his bulging muscles and the match from the stands after Arthur preferred Gary Micklewhite on the wing. I also missed our 1-0 defeat at Division One newcomers Millwall seven days later. But I was brought back in against Newcastle United, the team I'd very nearly signed for, when Chiedozie's knee injury provided an opening. I eagerly grabbed the opportunity, helping set up both goals in a 2-0 win, as we sent the Geordies and their revolting yellow and green change strip packing. I thoroughly enjoyed the standing ovation I got when I was replaced with three minutes to go and the result teed us up nicely for my first local derby against Nottingham Forest.

Mark Wright did his best to wind me up ahead of the game as we made our way down the A52 on the team coach. Forest had a great side at the time and had reached the semi-finals of the FA Cup the previous season, before finishing third in the league. My opposite number – England international Stuart Pearce – was the one I had most to worry about, according to Wrighty. He told me I'd better watch my back as Psycho had been bragging at a recent England game that he was going to take me out. Still, I wasn't fearful when I took to the pitch at what seemed a pretty dilapidated stadium for a club with its recent successes.

We began brightly encouraged by the Rams fans massed at the Bridgeford end, but then had to contain Forest for much of the first half. Referee John Key made a meal of the game ordering Arthur and Roy Mac back to their dugouts before booking Wrighty and Nigel Callaghan for tackles on Gary Crosby and Stuart Pearce. I then brushed aside Neil Webb on the touchline before being clattered by Pearce. After Gordie came on to treat me, Pearce was quite rightly booked. So was I for a foul on Webb inexplicably, much to the joy of the home support. They had much more to celebrate a few minutes later when Colin Foster pounced on Wrighty's error at a corner to avenge the own goal he'd notched the previous year. But we were far from beaten, and just seconds after the restart 'George' Williams passed out to Mel Sage, who set me free to centre for Hebberd. The former Oxford man controlled the ball and smashed it past Steve Sutton for the equaliser, and I took great pleasure in celebrating in front of the Main Stand.

Wrighty and I carried on the celebrations at a country pub in his native Oxfordshire. Despite being a worldly-wise England international, he was a shy, country boy at heart and loved nothing better than escaping back to nature. His idea of fun was getting tanked up at an old village pub before pouring himself out of bed at dawn to shoot whatever he could point his gun at. And so at stupid o'clock the following day, I was dragged out into the semi-darkness and presented with a twelve-bore shotgun. I didn't know one end of a gun from the other and was more than a little wary as I trudged off over the fields in my borrowed boots and Barbour.

It wasn't long before Wrighty and his dad had dispatched a couple of pheasants and a rabbit that were gleefully collected for the pot by the family Labrador. I was told the next one was mine. As we approached a hedge a bird broke cover and I put the gun to my shoulder. But unlike the accomplished marksman at my side, I hadn't anticipated the kick from the gun. Much to their amusement, I was flung backwards into a muddy puddle. Several further attempts yielded similarly unsuccessful results and I resigned myself to gathering my grub at Tesco's like everyone else. My bruised shoulder was eyed sympathetically at training the following day by a number of teammates, many of whom thought my first encounter with Stuart Pearce had taken its toll.

Little did we know that our equaliser against Forest was to be our last – at the right end at least – for four league matches. After losing 1-0 away at QPR, we were toothless in a 0-0 draw against Southampton before entertaining Norwich City at the Baseball Ground. We were 1-0 down to a Mark Wright own goal that would eventually put the Canaries top of the league that evening, when all hell broke lose. Norwich's Trevor Putney tripped me up and I tried to hold onto the ball with my legs. As I lay on the floor he began trying to stamp it away to the annoyance of the Derby players. Wrighty was particularly incensed and charged forty yards to wrestle Putney over the advertising hoardings. Arthur then grabbed the big defender and gave him an almighty bollocking, hoping it might spare him. But referee Alan Seville had little choice but to send them both off. Despite laying siege to the Norwich goal we couldn't force an equaliser. The defeat was followed by another 0-0 draw at home to Charlton. We were into our seventh week of the season and only two players had managed to score – Trevor Hebberd and Paul Goddard.

Despite new arrivals in the summer we were still woefully short of firepower. Some of the papers were linking us with former Sheffield Wednesday striker Lee Chapman, who would eventually sign for Forest. But Chairman Robert Maxwell pulled it out of the bag in the last week of October when we signed Dean Saunders from Oxford United. Cynics suggested he was moving the transfer money from one pocket to the other. But the club's decision to break the million-pound barrier for the first time certainly gave the players a lift. Deano also excited Derby supporters with his speed, flair and sheer love of the game. But it was his eel-like ability to turn defences that tied Wimbledon in knots on his debut, when we hit as many goals as we had in the previous eight games. Saunders got two of them, one of which I tried to claim, with Mel Sage and Gary Micklewhite also negating Vinnie Jones' brave header in a 4-1 win.

The performance was followed by a 5-0 hammering by West Ham in the League Cup in which we were bloody awful from start to finish. And things didn't look good for our second visit to the capital in four days, when we lined up against Tottenham on the Saturday. Spurs confirmed our worst fears after just six minutes when Paul Stewart grabbed his first goal for the club since signing from Manchester City. Chris Waddle was threatening to run riot. But against the run of play I managed to equalise past the hapless Bobby Mimms from an acute angle.

Terry Venables' side, which was rock bottom of the table at

the time, then went to pieces. In the sixty-second minute I found a gap between Mitchell Thomas and Gary Mabbutt and buried Wrighty's through ball from another tight angle. Deano then wrapped it up eight minutes later when he ran on to a Paul Goddard header and we recorded our first away victory since March. We were cock-a-hoop in the changing rooms afterwards and things got better with a knock on the door. Tottenham's sponsors Holsten had given me the home team's man of the match award and handed over a crate of lager. I was then asked to go up to the hospitality area where I was presented with three bottles of spirits and an engraved silver plate from two other appreciative sponsors. I've still got the plate somewhere in the loft, but the booze didn't last much beyond Watford Gap services.

The Spurs victory set us up for a great November in which we drew against Manchester United at home and then beat Aston Villa and Arsenal by 2-1 scorelines. We should have buried United but twice let them back into the match. Chairman Robert Maxwell had called for bigger crowds at our games and the 24,080 in attendance were not disappointed with what they saw. I was in my element taking on Mike Duxbury and was paid the ultimate compliment by Alex Ferguson when he switched him with Clayton Blackmore in an effort to limit the damage. I should have scored on a couple of occasions but was denied by Scottish international Jim Leighton, who was having one of his better days. Dean Saunders showed me the way as he did when we took on Villa the following weekend. His superb header was his sixth in five appearances and gave us our first top flight victory at Villa Park in over fifty years. But even that was overshadowed by Phil Gee's spectacular effort against Arsenal. His left-foot thunderbolt secured the points and silenced the doubters who'd groaned when it was announced that he'd be replacing the injured Paul Goddard.

I did rather better against Coventry City who we took on after a disappointing home defeat at the hands of Luton. Deano put us ahead against the Sky Blues, before Cally missed a penalty. I then scored when I beat Greg Downs for the umpteenth time that afternoon and smashed it past Steve Ogrizovic. My only other league goal that season came on a bitterly cold and windy day at Middlesbrough in March. With just seventeen minutes on the clock I took a corner with my left foot on the right-hand side in front of the travelling Derby fans. Aiming to put it in at the near post, I hit it flat and hard and repeated my trick all those years ago against Dumbarton by beating Stephen Pears. My jig of joy was a little more muted this time, but it gave the supporters something to remember on their long trip home.

Terrific performances on the road were to become a feature of the campaign and we relished getting on the team bus. We could have done even better than we did had we picked up more points at home. Defeats at the Baseball Ground against QPR, Norwich, Luton, Liverpool, Millwall, West Ham and, most painfully of all, Forest, stunted our progress. But in a topsy-turvy season we earned draws at Sheffield Wednesday and West Ham, beat Coventry 2-0, Aston Villa 2-1 and Newcastle, QPR and Middlesbrough all by a single goal. A lot of teams froze when they approached Old Trafford. But we didn't fear anyone that season and got off the bus the following April full of confidence. Gary Micklewhite's goal after just three minutes put us in charge. When Paul Goddard's header doubled our lead fifteen minutes into the second half the locals streamed for the exits. As we were to find out at full-time, they were lucky to be able to do so.

We'd obviously been aware of the FA Cup semi-final taking place on the same day. But our pre-match preparations meant all our focus was on our own big game across the Pennines. It was a great result to beat them on their own ground and we were laughing and joking when we got back into the dressing room. Arthur looked unusually serious as he closed the door and told us to sit down. He then said he'd heard there'd been people crushed to death in Sheffield. Details were still sketchy and we all presumed that the football hooliganism that had claimed lives at Heysel had returned to haunt us. It wasn't until we got back on the bus and turned on the radio that the full extent of the horror at Hillsborough began to emerge. We should have been celebrating a great day for Derby and its supporters. But it was a particularly bleak one for fans of the game across the world and we drove back to the Midlands lost in our own gloomy thoughts.

Despite the tragedy the league still had to be completed. We followed up the Old Trafford wins by beating Sheffield Wednesday and Aston Villa but were hammered 3-0 at Luton and Charlton, who were both scrapping to stay up. We then put in a great display in our eighth and last away win of the season when we took on title challengers Arsenal. I missed the game with a slight groin strain but was delighted for Deano, who capped a fantastic season with a wonderful goal. Derby finished fifth in the end, their best league placing since Dave Mackay's last full season in charge in the mid 70s. Only three years after climbing out of the Third Division the team was one of the top teams in the country. We would have been back in Europe had it not been for the ban on English clubs. But in a season when ninety-six fans lost their lives in another football tragedy we were realistic in our disappointment.

The 1988/90 campaign was an ideal time to kick on. With a couple of decent signings in the closed season I'm convinced we could have mounted a more serious challenge in the league. As it was, the only man to put pen to paper was Arthur Cox, who signed a five-year contract. David Penney added to the Maxwell/Maxwell transactions when he joined Oxford for £150,000, but nobody else came in. We'd got our fingers burnt in the transfer market in January when one of Maxwell's audacious publicity stunts blew up in his face. The club were said to be signing Czech internationals Lubos Kubic and Ivo Knoflicek, who had defected to the West whilst on tour with Slavia Prague. Everyone was excited by the arrival of the Czechs, who looked like the real McCoy in training. But after parading them in front of the crowd before the FA Cup tie against Southampton, we were embarrassed to find out that FIFA would not sanction a move without a transfer fee. Maxwell flatly refused. He wouldn't spend any more money in the summer either, which meant the only change to the team was the replacement of our blue shorts with traditional black ones.

We began the new season with low-key draws against Charlton and Wimbledon before Manchester United came calling. With people's minds still on the Hillsborough disaster, the game was delayed by twenty-five minutes to avoid unnecessary crushing. But it was worth the wait after a penalty by Saunders and a goal from Goddard combined with some world-class saves from Shilton to deliver our first victory. Saunders was in great form again in our 6-2 aggregate win over Cambridge in the League Cup. He helped himself to a hat-trick and I notched the last in our 5-0 win at the Baseball Ground as we overturned a first leg defeat at their place. My close range effort was my first on home soil since my debut twenty months ago.

The future's bright, the future's orange – my brothers Martyn (5), Mitchell (8) and a 4-year-old me (left) pose for a school picture in garish jumpers knitted by our granny Peggy.

Father Christmas – my Dad William Wallace McMinn and I enjoying the festivities on the sofa at Mitchell's house in Dumfries.

The only green kit I ever wore – me and my fellow Dumfries High School Former Pupils being presented with our new strip in the grounds of the school.

Rubbing shoulders with a legend – the closest I ever came to the late, great Davie Cooper during the first leg of Queen of the South's League Cup tie at Ibrox in August 1983.

Nutmeg anybody? – beating Celtic's hapless full-back Derek Whyte for the umpteenth time in the first televised Old Firm game at Ibrox in August 1986.

Fan-dabby-dosy – pressing the flesh with the Gers supporters in the Copland Road End after finding the net against Clydebank.

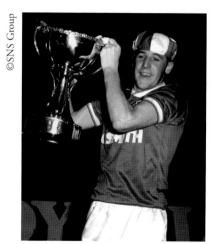

Kidding the kidder – winding up Celtic's Peter Grant, the man who loved to wind up Rangers supporters.

My cup runneth over – celebrating winning the Skol Cup at Hampden in October 1986 in the obligatory daft hat.

The Three Amigos – Ally McCoist, Terry Butcher and I show what it means to beat Celtic.

Singing the Blues – the post-match karaoke kicks in.

Passing the torch – showing off the Skol Cup to the next generation of Rangers supporters.

He ain't heavy – celebrating Ian Durrant's winner in our 1-0 victory.

Rather you than me pal – leaving England goalkeeper Chris Woods to his knee-high fifty-fifty with Graeme Souness on the training ground.

Above: Drowning our sorrows – in the bar with my mentor Jock Wallace after a Seville defeat.

Left: Hasta la Vista – playing up to the tabloids on the steps of June's mum's house in Steppes the day before swapping Glasgow for Seville.

The odd man out – on the edge of a team photo before a pre-season tournament in Pamplona just days before Jock was sacked.

Gunning for goal – about to pull the trigger for my spectacular strike against Manchester United on my home debut for Derby.

Up, up and away – flying high in front of C Stand after my second goal in our League Cup win over West Bromwich Albion.

You'll never beat Des Walker – trying to protect my dodgy knee in the heat of battle at the City Ground.

You've definitely got ginger hair – sharing a joke with Tommy Johnson on the Bowling Green at Raynesway.

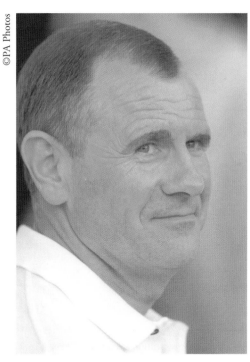

Eyes right – Arthur Cox kept me on the straight and narrow at Derby and pulled no punches when my time was up.

Dark days – donning the black armband for my career at Birmingham City as goalkeeper Kevin Miller and I watch another goal go in.

Fingering the culprit – reacting angrily to Stockport's Michael Wallace after he hacked me down then spat in my face in Burnley's play-off final win at Wembley.

Hands-on approach – taking my first steps in management with Mark Wright in the dug-out at Southport's Haig Avenue ground.

On yer bike – setting off from Ibrox on my sponsored cycle ride, six months after my operation.

Every father's dream – watching my son Kevin play in the blue of Rangers during my testimonial game was a proud day for both his grandad and me.

The kids are alright – Dayna, Kevin and me on holiday in Tenerife.

Rock of ages – my beloved wife Marian, who's stuck with me through thick and thin.

I saved some of my best performances of the campaign for the League Cup competition as I had done in Scotland. After late goals from Goddard and Saunders saw us past Sheffield Wednesday, we were paired with West Brom in the last sixteen. Arthur promised he'd buy me a pair of Adidas World Cup football boots if I scored against the Baggies. I'd been wearing Diadora that season after Wrighty's agent Kev Mason had secured me a boot deal. Wrighty got paid to wear Lotto boots as he was an England international. I had to make do with two pairs of boots, some training shoes and two luminous green shell suits that would have been better on Harry Enfield's Scousers. That was it. There was no suggestion they'd pay me to wear them and I couldn't phone up to get replacements. The boots were made from beautiful Italian leather but they hadn't been designed for the Baseball Ground mud. Fortunately they held out long enough for me to score not just one, but two against West Brom. Both were right foot curlers from in front of the C Stand Paddock as I gave fullback Daryl Burgess a torrid time.

Boot manufacturers might not have been too interested in my performances, but the media and other managers were taking note. Gerald Mortimer in the *Derby Evening Telegraph* speculated in his match report that an international call-up couldn't be far away. The *Sunday Mail* back home also had a double page interview with former Scotland boss Tommy Docherty in which he was fulsome in his praise. He suggested I should be chosen to spearhead Scotland's attacking options at that summer's World Cup. It was flattering in the extreme.

Andy Roxburgh took note and came to watch me on several occasions that autumn. Knowing he and other scouts were in the Directors' Box gave me an extra lift during the games. I was in the form of my life and desperate to play for my country. I really believed that after years of graft I could finally cut it at the top level. Just as importantly, maturity had brought self-confidence and I no longer doubted my ability. I was twenty-seven years old and on top of the world.

Arthur wouldn't let me wear my new boots against Tottenham. After presenting me with them at training he told me to give them to an apprentice to break in. My existing ones might have had a hole in, but he didn't want me getting blisters. He didn't like making changes either and was reluctant to introduce new things into the set-up. We always had the same routine for away trips, stayed at the same hotels with the same players rooming together and even had to sit next to each other on the bus. The only thing that was different was our choice of music. Nigel Callaghan, who was a keen amateur DJ, would spend hours putting together his own tapes for us with the latest chart tunes. We'd travel the country playing cards and reading the paper with our very own version of Top of the Pops going on in the background. It used to drive Arthur mad.

The away trip to Tottenham was no exception. We travelled down south the night before to stay at the Swallow Hotel just off the M25. We then went to the ground the following morning in confident mood, having won there the previous year. I'd also bagged the two goals and was chirpier than ever on the bus and in the changing rooms. I just had the feeling it was going to be my day. We were given our notes on the opposition and I was expecting to play against Mitchell Thomas again. The notes were a series of observations on the strengths and weaknesses of the players compiled by Jimmy Sirrel, who was scouting for us after retiring from management at Notts County.

The only problem for Jimmy and I was that I wasn't being marked by Thomas. He'd switched wings and had been replaced by Pat Van Den Hauwe.

The Wales international was on me from the first whistle. He never let me settle and was constantly snapping at my heels. He was the type of player who'd rake his studs down the back of your calf or stand on your toes at a corner. We fell behind to an early goal from Paul Stewart, who'd also hit the opener the previous season. It was a struggle and we looked like we'd be lucky to go in just the one goal behind at half time. With five minutes to go to the interval we had a throw in on the halfway line. I went to flick it on in the air and felt a nudge in my back from my marker. I was knocked off balance but thought I'd recovered to spin inside. As I landed on my left leg, my foot slipped down the banking at the side of the pitch. My studs had caught in turf as the rest of my leg and body continued to turn.

The main thing I remember initially was not the pain but the noise. There was a sound like a drinks can being crushed and my leg went completely limp. As I lay in a crumpled heap I turned in desperation to the dugouts. The first face I saw as the searing pain shot up my leg was Tottenham manager Terry Venables. I screamed in agony and he shouted across: 'Get up you diving bastard!' I was then joined by Gordon Guthrie and heard Arthur shout: 'Tell him to run it off.' I got to my feet and keeled over as soon as I put my weight on it. Gordie realised I was in a bad way and called for a stretcher. Unlike in Majorca they managed not to drop me and I was rushed to the treatment room. Tottenham was much more advanced than Derby and had a lot of medical equipment including an X-ray machine. But every time they moved my leg I was in agony and my whole knee was beginning to swell up. They managed to get some images and a lot of ugly faces were pulled when they saw the results. I was then bandaged in cotton wool and told to wait.

Word got to Arthur that it was a bad one. It was decided that my best bet would be to get a lift back to the Derbyshire Royal Infirmary with *Telegraph* reporter Gerald Mortimer. Gerald was summoned but it turned out he'd parked his car at the end of the tube line in a bid to beat the traffic. As I lay in terrible pain on the treatment table they discussed taking me on the tube. I couldn't believe what I was hearing and was relieved that the idea was soon abandoned. Realising I'd have to go on the bus, they wheeled me through to the Derby changing room. The atmosphere was subdued like it had been at Old Trafford and none of the players wanted to look me in the eye. Nobody knew the extent of the injury, but they realised I was in trouble. In a gesture I didn't fully appreciate at the time, all of the Spurs players including Paul Gascoigne and Gary Lineker came in to wish me well after the game. The only exception was Van Den Hauwe.

I was given a pair of crutches, limped out to the bus and was helped up the steps by Wrighty. I then lay with my leg up across one of the seats as the players filed silently by. For some reason I was starving hungry. I hadn't eaten since breakfast and had thrown that up as part of my pre-match routine. After away trips we usually got a round of ham or cheese sandwiches as well as a banana or an apple, washed down with a can of Carling Black Label from the players' bar at the Baseball Ground. There was no water let alone isotonic drinks, vitamin shakes or bowls of pasta. Given the likelihood that I would need an operation when I got back to Derby, I was told I couldn't have anything. I made the long trip back with a throbbing leg and a rumbling stomach.

Roy MacFarland and Gordie gave me a lift to the DRI, where the club had phoned ahead and summoned leading surgeon Alex Cargill. I was wheeled into a consultation room to find him in his civvies already examining my X-rays. He didn't say anything for a long time and then had a whispered conversation with Gordie. He then approached the bed. 'I'm not going to mess you about Ted,' he said. 'It doesn't look good. But I'm not going to know exactly how bad it is until I get in there. I'll operate first thing in the morning.' Roy and Gordie shook my hand and went home as I was left on the ward overnight with my thoughts. I phoned my dad in Scotland, who'd heard about the injury on the radio, and hoped he'd say something positive. But I didn't get the reassurances that I wanted.

Had my ambition to play for my country gone up in smoke? Had the fledgling dream of playing in Italy been shot down before it could fly? Or had my whole career just been ended? As I lay there waiting for the morning I cried until I could cry no more. The nurses checked on me regularly but there was nothing they could do. Sat on the chair at the side of my bed was my kitbag full of my stuff. Staring at me through the open zip were Arthur's wretched World Cup boots.

13

THE LONG AND WINDING ROAD

I was violently sick when I woke up from the operation after discovering that general anaesthetics didn't agree with me. I then looked down at my leg and discovered that it was encased in plaster from hip to ankle. There were four tubes coming out of my knee connected to two bottles on either side. They were full of blood and other fluids that looked like they were being pumped in and out. The agony of the previous day was gone but there was a dull pain, like the worst possible type of toothache. I didn't know what I'd done or what they'd tried to fix, but all became clear with the arrival of Mr Cargill. The last time I'd seen him had been after the long trip down to theatre that morning. He'd put me at ease with some reassuring words before marking my knee with a pen where he intended to make the incisions. I'd then prayed for the best as the fog came down.

Mr Cargill said he wouldn't know if the operation had been a success for months to come. But he was confident I'd make a full recovery in time. He'd opened my leg to discover that I'd severed both my cruciate and medial ligaments and had torn most of my cartilage. He'd had to insert a pin in the knee to hold it all together. It was, he said, the worst injury he'd

144

ever seen and was going to take a long, long time to heal. As he was explaining the recovery process, June and the kids walked in after getting off a train from Glasgow. My son Kevin had been born that summer and I was delighted to see their friendly faces. I'd need a lot of support in the months that followed. The club said they'd help out too. Arthur was on the phone as soon as I awoke and said they'd do everything they could to get me fit again. He'd also spoken to Andy Roxburgh, who'd promised to give me until April to prove my fitness for the World Cup. It was 26 November and the clock was ticking.

A more pressing engagement was my forthcoming wedding to June. Having vowed to never marry again after Jackie, I'd reluctantly agreed to make an honest woman of her. It seemed like the best thing to do for the kids. We'd set the date for the weekend before Christmas at Derby Register Office. The first dance might have to be put on the back burner, but it was full steam ahead as far as she was concerned. With my ability to help with preparations limited to telephone calls I could make from the sofa, boredom soon set in at home. I had to ditch plans for a stag night and could only look on as June dashed around making last minute arrangements. The spell was broken by the club's Christmas party, which had been pencilled in for the night before the wedding. Wives and girlfriends were invited too and excesses were kept to a minimum. But it was great to see the lads again after over a fortnight away from the club.

Despite downing a good few pints of lager I woke the next morning feeling surprisingly clear headed. But my leg wasn't too clever and felt like it was going to burst inside the cast. The toes of my left foot had gone black and blue. I phoned Gordon Guthrie at home and he advised me to report to the DRI at once. Despite it being a Saturday, Mr Cargill rushed

145

straight in to check me out. He didn't like the look of it one bit and began to saw off the plaster there and then. My thigh had shrunk with the lack of exercise and it dawned on me that it really would be a long road back. Yet much more noticeable was the huge bruise spreading down my shin and calf. The discovery provoked some consternation on the ward and a nurse was quickly instructed to give me an injection. I had a blood clot and was whacked full of Warfarin. Breathing a sigh of relief I made to get up off the bed, joking that I had an important appointment at 2 p.m. that afternoon. The ward sister wasn't impressed and pushed me back. Had the blood clot travelled up my leg and reached my heart I might have died, she said. I would be staying in hospital for a week. The wedding was off.

June was understandably gutted. She'd spent a lot of time organising the ceremony and the reception at an Italian restaurant called La Villa. Her parents and friends had travelled all the way down from Scotland. She even suggested we get the registrar to come to the hospital so that I could tie the knot in bed. But we quickly discovered that the marriage licence rules of the day didn't allow it. Selfishly, my main concern was my own health and the outside possibility that I could still make the World Cup in Italy. I felt sorry for June whose big day had been spoiled. But the pressing priority was getting fit and continuing my career. I should perhaps have realised that the whole thing was a terrible omen.

When I got out of hospital they refused to put the full cast back on my leg, fearing it may encourage another clot. Instead I had a brace fitted that contained a calliper to hold my knee in place. From being set in the straight position it was adjusted by a couple of degrees every week to slowly get movement back into my knee. Only five weeks after my operation, Arthur decided I'd be better off going for some intensive treatment at Lilleshall. There wasn't very much I could do at our Raynesway training ground and I was beginning to get depressed watching the lads in action. The former stately home between Telford and Newport in Shropshire was the home of the Football Association's Youth Academy and Britain's olympic gymnasts. It was also where sportsmen and women went to recover from serious injuries.

Lilleshall was a cross between a boarding school and a gym, with the emphasis being on hard work. You checked in on the Monday morning and would train from nine until five every day, escaping at midday on a Friday. The accommodation was basic to say the least. You were allocated a small room with a single bed, a dressing table and a wardrobe. You shared the shower and bathroom with the person in the room next to you and none of the bedrooms had televisions. The only entertainment was a poky little bar on the ground floor, which had a small television in the corner. It was poor man's Butlins without the redcoats.

I got the calliper off my leg in March 1990 and was allowed to start doing resistance work on my leg. The idea was to gradually increase the weights you pushed against on the various machines without bursting the tender muscles you were trying to rebuild. I spent hours moving small weights tiny amounts. It was both painful and mind-numbingly dull. But the goal was making that plane to Italy with Scotland and I never stopped working towards it. At the end of each day we were divided into two teams to play sit-down volleyball. The losing team on a Friday would have to cycle two miles down to the gates and back as punishment whilst the winners went home early. At the end of March I was allowed to start hopping on my bad leg and then to do some gentle jogging. After months of dark depression, it felt like there was a light at the end of the tunnel.

The dark days were also lightened by the camaraderie of my fellow professionals. Every week there'd be a new arrival from one of the professional clubs on either side of the border as new players picked up injuries. We were also joined at various times by jockeys, rugby players and tennis stars. Among the big names to drop in during my time were Liverpool's Alan Hansen, Southampton's Mickey Adams and my old pal Ian Durrant, following the horror injury he suffered at the hands of Aberdeen's Neil Simpson. Durranty and I held court in the bar and set about teaching everyone drinking games. One of those who liked a pint or two was legendary hardman Mark Dennis.

Mark, who was given the nickname Pyscho long before Stuart Pearce, was a bit of a volatile character and people wore kid gloves around him. But he was keen to come on night outs with us. These consisted of a trip to the only pub in Newport that had a pool table. On one occasion a couple of Birmingham City supporters were in and were heard to say that Mark's decision to leave the club had been the worst one he ever made. It was a red rag to a bull, and he quickly got into a scuffle. We were then barred from the pub by the landlord, which denied us the only source of entertainment for miles around.

When I wasn't getting chucked out of pubs, I'd travel back to Derby to watch the lads in action. Midweek games were particularly good news as it meant I could escape early. I remember watching the first League Cup quarter-final replay against West Ham. My abiding memory was of Derby's Steve Cross going down under a crude challenge from George Parris. I knew as soon as I saw it that Crossy had done his ligaments and would join fellow crocks Gary Micklewhite and me at Lilleshall. We were also visited by promising youth team players Justin Phillips and Kris Sleeuwenhoek and staff used to joke that we could put out a Derby County volleyball team of our own.

Eight first team players were out by the time of the second West Ham replay, including the suspended Mark Wright and Rob Hindmarch, and we went down 2-1. Victory by the same scoreline at Manchester United thanks to goals from Wrighty, who was then harshly sent off, and Nick Pickering, took us up to seventh in the league. But we sank back into the bottom half in March with successive defeats to Sheffield Wednesday, Southampton and Aston Villa.

April came round quickly as did my deadline for making the Scotland team. After months of work at Lilleshall, I paid a visit with Gordon Guthrie to Mr Cargill's surgery on Vernon Street in Derby. I was a nervous wreck when I went in but he put me at ease by telling me I was miles ahead of where he'd expected me to be. The strength in my knee was terrific and it looked like I'd make a full recovery. He then paused and took a deep breath. 'You're doing brilliantly, Ted,' he said, 'but I'm afraid there's just no chance you're going to be ready any time soon. You're not going to the World Cup.' He also said that he didn't think I'd play again until the following calendar year but I'd stopped listening by then. As Gordie put his arm round my shoulder I buried my head in my hands and began to sob. I'd known in my heart of hearts that there was no way I'd be fit. I hadn't even kicked a ball, for God's sake. But to actually be told by the surgeon was like being hit by a freight train.

I could barely watch Scotland take to the field against Costa Rica in Genoa that June, such was my disappointment. Had it not been for a freak injury it could have been me. I'd jumped for thousands of headers in my career and landed safely. When I needed to most I couldn't. But I wasn't quite so bitter ninety minutes later when they trudged off after losing 1-0 to the Central American minnows. Maybe I wasn't so unlucky after all. The boys beat Sweden 2-1 in the next game thanks to goals from Stuart McCall and Mo Johnston, setting up a make or break game in Turin against Brazil. But a single goal from Muller ended the dream before it had begun.

I was back at Lilleshall throughout May and June, emerging for pre-season at Allestree and Moorways in July. The knee was getting stronger but my fitness and pace had suffered. When I reached for another gear on a sprint it was no longer there. When the balls came out I was like a kid in a sweetshop, racing around all over the place and shooting from the halfway line. Arthur was concerned that I would burn myself out and told me to calm down. We started working on set piece routines and I crossed a number of free kicks from wide positions quite comfortably. We then finished the day with some five-a-side matches.

With next goal the winner, I tore down the left side of the pitch and feigned to cross the ball with my left and dragged it back onto my right. My marker, centre half Justin Phillips, didn't read it and clattered into my left knee. I heard a loud click, screamed in pain and collapsed to the ground. Justin stood over me with a look of horror on his face and begged me to get up. But there was no way I could. Something had gone. As I was helped from the field Arthur launched into big Justin, who was mortified about what he'd done. It wasn't his fault, but Arthur feared I was in serious trouble again. Surprisingly, Mr Cargill decided not to operate. He suspected that the cartilage may have gone again but wanted to wait for the swelling to go down. When it did I was straight back to my cell at Lilleshall for more fitness routines.

There was no way I'd make the opening game of the season. In my absence, the lads got off to a pretty dreadful start. They didn't win until 10 October when they squeezed past Carlisle 1-0 in a League Cup replay. Their first victory in the league wasn't until a fortnight after that, when they saw off Southampton. They'd picked up just three points out of a possible twenty seven in their opening nine fixtures. I made the squad for the game against Aston Villa on 15 September and trained at Raynesway the day before. The last thing we did on a Friday was a five-a-side game on what we called the bowling green next to the car park. I felt great until my knee locked up again as I went to pass the ball. I was taken to the DRI and Mr Cargill carried out keyhole surgery to tidy up the cartilage at two o'clock that afternoon. And wouldn't you know, it was then back to leafy Lilleshall.

November brought renewed hope for the team and a 2-1 victory over Luton Town. A penalty from Dean Saunders, who'd already missed two spot kicks that season, and a fierce right-foot drive from Callaghan did the damage. They then held Manchester United to a no score draw before heading up to Leeds United. Elland Road was never the happiest of hunting grounds and the 3-0 reversal didn't come as much of a surprise. But it was a warm-up for the main event, which was the visit of Nottingham Forest seven days later.

I watched the game with the Rams fans in A Stand, feeling for the first time just what the tension of a local derby was like for them. Things didn't get off to a good start when Mel Sage and Steve Cross were ruled out with injury before the game and Geraint Williams had to limp off with a knee injury on his 100th consecutive senior appearance. It got even worse when Steve Chettle thumped a post and then hit a deflected shot past Shilts from the resulting corner. But then Gary Micklewhite slid in Craig Ramage at the Normanton End and his measured clip over Steve Crossley gave us our first league goal at the Baseball Ground against Forest since 1979.

Wrighty grazed the crossbar with a header early in the second half, before Deano showed him the way by beating the supposedly unbeatable Des Walker to a Micklewhite centre and nodding past Crossley for the winner. The jubilant Derby fans around me spilt out onto Shaftesbury Crescent at full time as I made my way down to the dressing room. I bumped into Brian Clough on the way and wondered how he felt. He grabbed my hand and praised our performance and then wished me all the best with my recovery. The game, he said, was missing me. It's amazing how a few words of kindness from a remarkable man can lift your spirits. Not that they needed much lifting that night.

Despite the euphoria that surrounded the victory, a winter of discontent set in at the Baseball Ground. Robert Maxwell had put the club up for sale for £8 million a week into the season but wasn't being inundated with offers. Despite the departure of Paul Blades to Norwich City for £700,000 and Rob Hindmarch to Wolves for £300,000, no new faces came in. Things came to a head in the New Year when the fixture against Tottenham Hotspur on 20 January saw unrest in the stands. The game was the first to be televised live from the Baseball Ground for three years. Rams fans made the most of the cameras to vent their frustration at Maxwell. An offer for the club from local millionaire Lionel Pickering was rejected. He lost patience waiting for an answer, went public with the news and was promptly told by our absentee chairman he was no longer welcome at the ground.

The Derby supporters gave me a far better reception when I finally made my comeback against Sheffield United on 26 January. Despite the fact that we were stuck in the bottom three, around 5,000 fans made their way up the M1 for the relegation dogfight. The roar from behind the goal as I jogged out for the warm-up brought a lump to my throat. It meant the world to me just to be able to put on a white shirt again and take to the field. The cards and letters of support they'd sent during the long fourteen months had been wonderful. But for any footballer with a career-threatening injury to hear a crowd singing their name again is something special. I'd come through a reserve team game against Aston Villa in the midweek and was pleased to have suffered no reaction. But deep down I was worried about how the knee would hold up to the strain. Gordon Guthrie insisted that I wore a large white elasticated bandage as protection and I went out onto the pitch looking like a skateboarder. It was as good as a bullseye target for the United players.

Unsurprisingly, Vinnie Jones was the first to notice it. Like a James Bond baddie he told me he was going to get me and unlike the famous special agent there would be no wriggling out of it. He waited until ten minutes to go before poleaxing me in the centre circle. The ref blew his whistle for a free kick and a scuffle broke out as the Derby players rushed to my rescue. Mark Wright was in the thick of it as he had been with Trevor Putney. Dave Bassett loudly accused me of diving. But as I lay in the mud receiving treatment I was secretly delighted. Jones had nearly broken my ankle yet he'd also done me a favour. He hadn't actually tested the knee, but in clobbering me he'd removed any doubt I had about my ability to take a tackle. It was kill or cure coming back from an injury and I'd just found the antidote. We lost 1-0 but I was back.

We also lost in our next fixture at Villa Park despite goals from Mick Harford and Mel Sage and it was clear that I wasn't going to turn things around single-handedly. Yet the disappointment of losing was tempered by Arthur's decision to hand me an extension to my contract after the match. He was taking a gamble as I'd only played two first-team games since returning to fitness. But the year's extension and his kind words in the media gave my confidence a massive boost. I tried to do the same in an interview with Alex Cameron in the *Daily Record* who rang me up for a comment on Ian Durrant. The little midfielder had experienced setback after setback and was beginning to wonder if he'd ever play again. I was living proof that he could.

The joy of being back playing football again was in stark contrast to the dire form of the team. The statistics made grim reading. From the turn of the year we won just once in nineteen attempts. We hit rock bottom on March 23rd when Liverpool visited the Baseball Ground and thrashed us 7-1. We were well in contention in the first half and Dean Saunders even equalised Jan Molby's penalty. But they ran riot in the second half, inflicting only the third ever seven-goal defeat in the club's history. We managed to score six ourselves in the penultimate home game of the season when we brushed aside a hapless Southampton team with the help of a Paul Williams hat-trick. But it was too little too late. The death knell had been sounded at Maine Road three weeks earlier, when we lost 2-1 to ten-man Manchester City. They played without a goalkeeper for sixty-seven minutes and Deano missed his fourth penalty of the campaign. He and my old pal Wrighty would be sold to Liverpool for large transfer fees at the end of the season in a bid to shore up the club's leaky finances. It was a sad way to bow out for both of them.

I missed the Man City game as my knee had swollen up and Arthur had told me to take it easy. There had been nobody taking it easy a couple of weeks before when we went to the City ground looking for our first win on the banks of the Trent since 1971. Maxwell had shot his mouth off in the lead up to the game, claiming he couldn't wait to rub Brian Clough's nose in it. They were fired up as a result. Our case wasn't helped when we lost Wrighty to a calf strain early in the second half. The gap caused by his absence allowed Roy Keane in to head home Ian Woan's cross for the only goal of the game. I had my usual running battle with Stuart Pearce and was battered and bruised when I was taken off with seven minutes to go. I was booed off the pitch by the home support who gave me all sorts of abuse as I approached the main stand. You develop a thick skin being a footballer, but listening to several thousand rednecks calling you a wanker isn't pleasant.

I wasn't expecting to be helped on my way by Nigel Clough, however, who shouted 'piss off' as I walked past him. I stopped and asked him to repeat it but he turned away and laughed. He was less amused when I called him a 'Daddy's boy' before finally being dragged off the pitch by Gordie. I was wound up as I made my way to the bench and the Forest fan who spat on me as I took my seat didn't alter my mood. I told Wrighty I was going to knock Cloughie's head off at full time. 'Bollocks you will,' he replied, totally unimpressed. 'The problem with you Ted is that you're all mouth and no trousers!' But I convinced him I was serious and we then plotted an ambush in the tunnel, like two bank robbers planning a heist. The only fly in the ointment as far as I could see was Pearce, who I didn't fancy having to tackle as well. Thankfully Wrighty pledged to deal with him.

We nursed our wrath by twice complaining to Nottingham Police about the behaviour of the Forest fans in the last ten minutes of the game. They wouldn't stop baiting us and constantly banged on the clear Perspex roof of the dugout. On both occasions we were told by the coppers to sit down unless we wanted to be arrested. When the referee blew for full time we moved quickly up the tunnel and took up our positions. As the jubilant Forest players came off the pitch I launched myself at Clough and pinned him by the throat up against the wall. I drew my fist back to lamp him but was hauled off by an angry Archie Gemmill. After much pushing and shoving, tensions were eventually diffused and we were thrown into our respective changing rooms. I drew some satisfaction from letting Clough know that I meant business. But I began to realise I'd made a fool of myself. The presence of several senior police officers was worrying too.

The inevitable knock on the door came when I was in the bath. Arthur, who'd missed the fracas, was not impressed and ordered me into the corridor wearing just a bath towel. A sourfaced police inspector said he intended to cite me for breach of the peace before asking me to escort him to the referee's room. Many refs would have been in their element at this point. The one that day also claimed to have seen nothing and did his best to calm the copper down.

It seemed obvious to me that Notts Police hadn't lifted anyone that night and were spoiling for a bit of action. It would have been a great tale for the lads down at the station if he could tell them he'd pulled a Derby player. It looked like he'd get his wish until Brian Clough stuck his head round the door to see what all the fuss was about. He told the 'young man' not to worry and pledged to sort out the misunderstanding with a gentlemanly handshake.

Still dressed in a dripping towel, I was marched into the Forest changing rooms where the players were downing bottles of beer. A naked Stuart Pearce with all his tattoos on show was standing on one of the lockers leading Ian Woan, Steve Hodge and Des Walker in an anti-Derby song – just like we would have done had the boot been on the other foot. They were jubilant after beating the old enemy. Notable by his absence was Nigel Clough who, like me, had retreated to take a shower. But he was ordered out by his old man and we stood opposite one another clutching our towels. Head bowed like a pupil in front of a headmaster, Nigel then explained what had happened and complained about what I'd called him. Much to my amusement Clough senior immediately took my side. As the Forest players began to snigger, he told his son: 'Well you are a daddy's boy and I think you should apologise to Mr McMinn. He deserves some respect after coming all the way from Derby to play a game of football.' Nigel went bright red, mumbled an apology and shook my hand. His legendary father then ushered me back to the away dressing room, wishing me a pleasant trip back down the A52. What a man!

The disappointing defeat and the handbags that followed didn't stop us going out for a drink after the game. As soon as we got back to Derby we dumped our stuff and headed out to drown our sorrows. During my time at the club we always went out for a pint as a team, win, lose or draw. Health and fitness professionals these days will no doubt baulk at the suggestion that it was good for us, but it ensured that morale was always high. We were generally well behaved when it came to match preparations and there were few if any curfew-breaking incidents like there had been at Ibrox. Yet we very rarely troubled the cocoa manufacturers on Wednesdays and Saturdays. During the week we usually ended up in a city centre nightclub called the Pink Coconut, which attracted revellers from all over the Midlands. At the weekends we'd end up further afield, usually at Paradise, a big barn of a place next to an out-of-town roller-skating rink.

A lot of us went out after the Forest game, which probably didn't look too clever in retrospect. But there were plenty of others who'd had a bad day at the office so we didn't feel guilty. After a couple of drinks nearby we breezed into the Pink Coconut, where I was asked for a picture by a couple of girls with a camera. As I turned to pose with them, I was smacked in the face with a glass ashtray and fell to my knees. Blood began trickling down my cheek from a large gash above my right eye as I tried to recover my senses. I had no idea who'd hit me and by the time I got to my feet the offender had been dragged away. The embarrassed club owners ushered me into a back room and packed my swollen eye with ice. The police also turned up and took me to the Derbyshire Royal Infirmary.

By the time I'd had six stitches inserted in the wound without an anaesthetic, half of Derby had heard what had happened. Some, including a teammate, even knew why it had happened. I emerged groggily from a consultation room into the chaos of casualty to find him chatting to the two officers who'd brought me to the hospital. Before I could make a statement, he dragged me into an empty room. It turned out that he knew the culprit and, perhaps more importantly, also knew his wife. He'd been having an affair with her and the husband had found out.

Because I was a pal of his, and considerably less intimidating, I'd taken the brunt of his revenge. The problem he faced, if I decided to press charges, was that the resultant publicity around a court case would alert his wife, who was blissfully unaware of the impropriety. After first getting him to promise that he'd sort the whole sorry mess out, I went out to tell two disappointed coppers that I'd prefer to go home and forget all about it. Talk about taking one for the team!

14

PLAYING THEM OFF

Why it took me a year to marry June after my injury put paid to our original plans puzzled people, her not least of all. We were supposed to have tied the knot in December 1989, only for the White Hart Lane pitch to raise an objection. Afterwards I'd been fully focused on regaining my fitness and saving my career. There was also the travel to and from Lilleshall, which was time-consuming and tiring. But they seemed to be pretty lame excuses to those looking in on our world. The thing they didn't appreciate was the fact that I didn't really want to. It seemed a good idea for Dayna and Kevin's sake, as it was still the done thing in society. But not unlike my first attempt with Jackie a few years previously, I can't say that I was raring to go.

I wouldn't have been either, had I known what June would say to me on our wedding night. It was December 1990 and we'd done the deed at Derby Register Office with a few friends and family present. Having seen my last lot of wedding pictures end up in the *Daily Record*, I persuaded my new bride to dodge out of a side door and avoid the local newspaper photographers. We then enjoyed the reception at the Italian restaurant that we'd had to cancel last time, before heading back to our house in Mickleover. In time-honoured fashion and despite my dodgy knee, I picked her up to carry her across the threshold. As I did so, she fixed me with an icy stare and said: 'If you ever shit on me, I'll take you to the cleaners.' It came as something of a surprise and didn't get either the wedding night or the marriage off to the best of starts.

Fortunately, the 1991/92 season in the First Division began with a little more promise. The main benefit from the transfer of Dean Saunders and Mark Wright was the club's ability to buy out Robert Maxwell's shares. Deano's fee of £2,900,000 was a record between two British clubs. The new administration reinvested some of it when they splashed out on Aston Villa's twenty-three-year-old centre half Andy Comyn for £200,000. Middlesbrough defender Simon Coleman then signed for £300,000. Both fitted in well at the back as we gained a 1-1 draw at promotion favourites Sunderland on the opening day thanks to Mick Harford's diving header.

Comyn had a shot cleared off the line at Roker Park but went one better against Middlesbrough in the next game, when his tap-in and a volley from Harford handed us only our second home win of 1991. Things were looking up on the road too, when a 2-0 victory at the Valley on 1 September delivered our first away win in nine months. I was really enjoying my football again and relished charging up and down the wing as the Pop Side roared their approval. The injury had probably robbed me of a yard of pace but I felt I was playing as well as I had at any time in my career. What I lacked in acceleration I now made up for in experience and guile. Sadly my crosses weren't being met, however, and the goals began to dry up. Following the win against Charlton we drew two and lost two, scoring just once in the process.

161

Arthur's answer to our difficulties was to hand sixteen-year-old Mark Stallard his debut on a trip to Oxford's Manor Ground. Unfortunately he looked like a little boy lost as we went down 2-0 on Peter Shilton's forty-second birthday. We needed someone to score goals, but with little money to spend, it would be difficult. The answer came in the form of two loan signings. First up was Ian Ormondroyd, who arrived on a three-month deal from Aston Villa. But the one that captured the imagination of the Baseball Ground crowd was Bobby Davison, who signed for a month almost four years after leaving for Leeds United.

Bobby was a natural goalscorer and a wide man's dream. He scored his 99th goal for the club on his home debut against Brighton and grabbed his hundredth in a 2-2 draw at Newcastle. He netted five times in total as we rattled in fifteen goals in six games. I even got in on the act myself when I beat Alan Knight of Portsmouth from a tight angle to record my first goal for twenty-three months in front of our biggest crowd of the season to date. My last strike had been against West Brom in the League Cup after which Arthur had bought me my World Cup boots. I might as well have won the World Cup given the way I celebrated.

We won at Millwall following that, but it would be my last contribution for three weeks after I tweaked a thigh muscle in training and lost my ever-present status. Whilst I was recuperating, local businessman Lionel Pickering bought the majority shareholding in the club. He'd made his money founding a free newspaper called the *Derby Trader* and was determined to improve the team. He had plenty to be pleased about with his investment during the month of November. After slipping to successive 1-0 defeats to Port Vale and Tranmere, we won four out of our next five games and began to climb up the table.

But then we stumbled again through December and January, failing to win in five attempts. The last of those was a defeat to Sunderland, our sixth at home that season. The loan signings in September had lifted the team and Arthur knew he had to pull another rabbit out of the hat if we were to continue our upward trajectory. This time he had money to spend and he did so by buying the man the Roker Park faithful had once called Marco Goalo.

Marco Gabbiadini arrived for a million pounds between our FA Cup replay win over Burnley and our away fixture at Portsmouth. He'd had a nightmare four months at Crystal Palace after leaving the North East and didn't have to think too hard about joining us, despite dropping down a division. Just like me he scored on his debut and we were hopeful he'd provide the missing piece of the jigsaw. Paul Simpson also scored on his debut when he signed from Oxford United a month later. He netted his second for us on 7 March in a 1-1 draw at Plymouth, who had been boosted prior to kick-off by the unveiling of new player-manager Peter Shilton. Shilts had wanted to try his hand at management for some time and was grateful when Arthur didn't stand in his way. I was less enthusiastic, however, when he sent Argyle out to kick me off the park. They eventually succeeded when I hobbled off with fifteen minutes to go after being rattled by Tony Spearing.

I missed the next game at home through injury and watched from the Main Stand as we ripped apart bottom of the table Port Vale 3-1. Paul Kitson did everything but score after recently signing from Leicester City for £1.3 million. I watched with a mixture of admiration and anxiety as all professionals do when they fear new arrivals might keep them out of the team. There was a real buzz around the Baseball Ground as the Pop Side chanted the name of Lionel Pickering. His millions were making it possible for Arthur to manage.

The pair dipped into the transfer market again to capture the signature of Tommy Johnson from Notts County. He too arrived for £1.3 million and helped the team score three against Tranmere. But the Prenton Park side, inspired by loan signing Pat Nevin, managed to hit four. Tommy was a really likeable lad with an infectious Geordie personality. Unlike Gabbiadini and Kitson, who thought rather more of themselves, he fitted into the dressing room immediately. He was just a young lad and a bit rough around the edges, but he had bags of talent. As much as I liked him, that also made him a threat.

A combination of my injury and the new arrivals meant I missed two games in March and was on the bench for another two. I took revenge on Shilts and his physical approach by finding the net in the home fixture against Plymouth, when I came on for the injured Paul Williams. A couple of weeks later Arthur handed me the captain's armband after Geraint Williams got injured. It was a great honour to be made skipper and I was surprised he hadn't asked Mickey Forsyth, who was the longest serving player at the club. It was the first time I'd ever captained a team in my career, but I made the most of it and presided over a comfortable 3-0 victory, our ninth away win of the campaign. But in tackling Ian Banks from behind during the second half I earned a caution and twisted my ankle in the process. Simon Coleman took over the captaincy after I limped off and didn't fair much better, getting sent off in the closing minutes for two bookable offences. The team went on to gather six more points without me in trips to the coast to play Grimsby and Brighton. But they dropped two at home again against Oxford, despite Paul Simpson scoring against his old club.

PLAYING THEM OFF

I returned for our penultimate home game of the season against Newcastle United wearing the unfamiliar number five shirt. Arthur had asked me to play in the middle. The game soon took on an unfamiliar look too, as referee Brain Coddington sent off the opposition's Kevin Brock, Kevin Scott and Liam O'Brien. Things quickly turned into a farce with eleven against eight and we moved up to third place after a thumping 4-1 win. We held on to the position after 2-1 wins in our last two games against Bristol City and Swindon Town. With thirteen minutes to go in the Swindon game we were going up as runners-up. But ten-man Middlesbrough recovered to beat Wolves at Molineux and clinch the second promotion place behind Ipswich Town. We traipsed round the pitch at the end thanking the fans for their support throughout the season and couldn't help but feel deflated. I was a little chirpier than some of the other players knowing I'd won the place money on a £100 each way bet at 16/1 that a few pals and I had had with our local bookie! And besides, we were heading for the play-offs and a day out at Wembley if we could just beat Blackburn Rovers.

A fanzine appeared around the Baseball Ground at around the time of our charge to the play-offs called 'Hey Big Spender'. It poked fun at the people who claimed Mr Pickering had tried to buy success in his short time in charge. If there was one club spending more than us that season it was Blackburn Rovers, where Kenny Dalglish was getting rid of Jack Walker's money like it was going out of fashion. Rovers had scraped into the play-offs in sixth place after winning their final game at Home Park and consigning Shilts and Plymouth to the third tier of English football. They had limped over the line after a dreadful finish to the season, having lead the league by fifteen points at one stage. But they had beaten us quite convincingly home and away, and we were more than a little wary as we made our way to Ewood Park in the hot summer sunshine.

A lot of the Derby fans had yet to take their places in the ground when Marco Gabbiadini opened the scoring with a diving header after just three minutes. Some ten minutes later Paul Simpson put Tommy Johnson through and he slid the ball past Bobby Mimms for the second. But the dream start turned into a nightmare as we switched off, imagining ourselves to already be under Wembley's famous twin towers. We lost shape and discipline and Blackburn poured forward. They were level at halftime as Paul Williams and I, deputising for his name-sake Geraint, failed to support our defence. David Speedie added to our woes in the second half by scoring two more and my ineffectual display was brought to an end when I was with-drawn to make way for Craig Ramage. Having been on 'easy street' after the first fifteen minutes, we'd left ourselves with a mountain to climb in the second leg.

Arthur strapped on the crampons for his team talk and persuaded us that we could scale the summit. We were also roared on by our magnificent supporters who were crammed into the Baseball Ground. They had something to cheer after just twenty-three minutes when Andy Comyn headed Tommy Johnson's cross past Mimms. There could have been more before half-time, but Jossie Williams, Simon Coleman, Paul Simpson and Paul Kitson all contrived to miss good chances. If we could just get another goal and keep a clean sheet we would be edging through on away goals. The half-time tea was drunk amid talk of keeping it steady and holding our nerve and we charged out believing that we could do it.

Disaster struck just four minutes into the second half when

Kevin Moran's weak back header beat Steve Sutton to hand them an undeserved equaliser. From being one goal away from Wembley we now had to score twice to stay in the match. Arthur quickly reorganised midfield and threw me out onto the right to get more crosses into the box. The change paid dividends almost immediately when the ball broke my way inside the box and I smashed in a goal to put us 2-1 up on the night. Try as we might we couldn't get the extra goal we needed. Jossie missed another good chance with a volley and Mickey Forsyth clipped the bar with a bullet header. It just wasn't to be.

At the final whistle, a couple of Derby fans took out their frustration on David Speedie, whose combative style had wound them up over the two matches. I'd had a bit of a ding-dong with him in the first half too when he'd picked up the ball at a free kick to waste time and then thrown it back in my face. I thought Speedie was a nasty little shit on the pitch and he wasn't widely liked by other players or fans. But you'd have had him in your team if you had the chance because he was a great wee player. He had the last laugh over us as well in securing his team a place in the final at Wembley. As Gerald Mortimer in the *Derby Evening Telegraph* said in the opening paragraph of his gloomy match report the following day, we'd won the battle but Blackburn had won the war.

We were gutted after losing and sat in the changing rooms feeling we'd wasted the whole season. But on reflection it had been no disgrace. Within three years Blackburn would be Premier League champions as Walker's fortune took them to the very top. Following the disappointment of relegation and the disruption behind the scenes caused by the protracted sale of the club, we'd expected it to be a very hard season. Yet we'd plugged away and only just missed out on automatic promotion by two points. Big-money transfers had arrived in the New Year and provided good news for the long-suffering supporters. Despite their presence I'd made thirty-five starts in the league in my first full season back. Not only that, the fans had made me their player of the season. I was both surprised and chuffed to bits with the announcement, which reinforced what a great relationship I had with them. I was a few months short of my thirtieth birthday and felt in good shape. The award was a real pat on the back for all the hard work I'd put in through the long dark days when I wondered if I'd ever kick a ball again. But it was also a show of thanks to Mr Cargill, Gordon Guthrie and all the staff at Lilleshall, who between them had spent thousands of hours putting both my leg and my life back together.

Had my home life been as contented as my football one I'd have been a happy man. But I wasn't receiving any awards for being a good husband. Within six months of marrying June, the doubts I'd had at the altar had been confirmed. We fought like cat and dog over the most trivial of things and I spent less and less time at home. On one of my many nights out I met a pretty blonde called Heidi Cole. She was a very attractive girl who was nine years younger than me and I was flattered by the attention she paid me. At around the same time June began alternating between our house in Mickelover and her parents' place in Glasgow. Dayna was growing up fast and wasn't far off starting school and her mum was struggling to cope with bringing up a young family with an absentee husband. I lived out of a suitcase, flying up to see them in Scotland or welcoming them back to Derby if June was down. It wasn't easy but I hoped they wouldn't be old enough to be affected by all the toing and froing. Unbeknown to June, I also began seeing Heidi in Derby. I didn't view it as a long-term commitment and neither of us fully trusted one another. But it suited us both to meet up from time to time for a drink and a bit of company.

Unfortunately the two worlds collided when my philandering finally caught up with me. It was at a reserve-team game of all places. I wasn't playing in the match at Stapenhill near Burton, but I'd gone along with Heidi to watch with the intention of taking her to the pub afterwards. None of the players batted an eyelid when we walked into the ground and to our position behind the goal. But it hadn't occurred me that the wives and girlfriends might have something to say about it. One of them must have phoned June, as the next thing I knew she was striding along the touchline towards us. She was carrying Dayna in her arms and was bright red with anger. I suggested to Heidi, who had until now thought my marriage was over, that she might want to slip away to the pub early. In the short time before June arrived I couldn't come up with any excuses and steeled myself for a slap in the face. But she took me aback by thrusting Dayna into my arms and charging off after Heidi.

It occurred to me that if I went the other way, Dayna and I could leave them both to it. But when I glanced in the direction of the wives and girlfriends on the touchline, I was greeted with some icy stares. Nobody was now watching the game, preferring the public execution that was about to take place instead. I headed to the car park and found June and Heidi running in and out of the cars in a Benny Hill style chase. June was screaming at her rival and threatening all sorts of revenge if she ever laid hands on her. A crowd of spectators built up before I managed to use my wing wizardry to get between them. I then persuaded June to come back to Derby with me, gallantly abandoning Heidi fifteen miles from home. She gave me the earful I was expecting on the way back as I mumbled in time-honoured fashion, 'it's not what you think'. But it was exactly what she thought and I'd been caught red-handed. The cat with the cream had just had it tipped over his head.

I felt like shit that night for messing June around when she was at home looking after my kids. I also felt guilty for lying to Heidi and leaving her to fend for herself. But the thing I felt most of all was stupid. How daft was I taking Heidi to a match with all the other wives and girlfriends? The Brain of Britain title was certainly safe for another year! Arthur got to hear of the incident at training, as it was the source of much amusement among the lads. Afterwards he offered me some words of advice as a friend rather than a manager. He had an old-fashioned view of his job and believed he had a duty to keep the players on the straight and narrow as well us guide us on the pitch. He also had an old-fashioned view of marriage but spared me a lecture on morals. Instead, the wise old owl suggested that family would always be more important. Not only that, he said the grass was very rarely greener on the other side. I nodded in agreement and vowed to see the error of my ways. But sadly, it would take me several more years of heartache to realise that he was right.

15

PUNCH-UPS AND PIZZAS

I've been lucky enough to fall out with very few players and managers during my career. I don't know if it's because I've always enjoyed a bit of banter that I've generally been well-liked in dressing rooms. I've never been shy in coming forward either and I hope I can laugh at myself as well as others. Graeme Souness and I obviously didn't part on the best of terms and I think he treated me harshly towards the end of my Rangers career. But by getting involved in the court case and breaking curfew I didn't leave the guy with an awful lot of choice. Managers just can't have players carrying on like that and expect to maintain team discipline and morale. The exception that proved the rule in my good relations was Marco Gabbiadini.

I'd never really seen eye to eye with Marco from the day he walked through the door at Raynesway. Fellow new boy Paul Kitson, who arrived from Leicester City soon afterwards, was supposed to be the temperamental one. Yet Gabby managed to match him strop for strop. I don't know if it was the big transfer fee, his reputation at Sunderland or his failure at Crystal Palace, but I always felt he had a point to prove. In doing so he often rubbed the opposition and quite a few of his colleagues up the wrong way. I have to say that I always thought he was a great player and I respected his ability on the park. I just didn't feel the need to be best pals with the guy. You can't get on with everyone after all. In fact, it suited both of us just to stay out of each other's way for the most part. Until he crossed the line one day.

We'd done our pre-season and were honing one or two drills on the bowling green ahead of the 1992/93 season. The club had a fixture in the Bass Vase competition that night against local non-league outfit Gresley Rovers. We played in the tournament every year and used the fixtures to blood some of the apprentices and reserves pushing for a place in the first team. I wasn't expecting to be picked and had made plans to go out with Heidi. But I was surprised to hear my name was the first to be read out and even more surprised that I was the only senior player in a team full of kids and stiffs. Arthur looked me in the eye, perhaps expecting a reaction, and told me he wanted me to captain the team and get a result. There were some frowns on the faces of the other players as they went back to the routine they were practising. But as I turned to go for a shower and ready myself for the evening's entertainment, Gabbiadini said in a loud voice: 'Can you collect the bibs and the balls for the first team before you go, Ted.'

He was joking and as an old hand at mickey-taking I should have laughed it off and walked away. But he'd unwittingly poured salt into an open wound. From the moment I'd sat with my leg in pieces on the team bus leaving White Hart Lane, I'd worried if I'd ever play again. I'd woken up on a hospital ward with blood pumping out of my knee then spent fourteen long, hard months at Lilleshall. I'd wondered on a daily basis if I'd kicked my last ball. In a freak accident my own teammate had done me again and then Vinnie Jones had cut me in half in the Bramall Lane mud. But I'd battled back and been told by the club's supporters that I'd been the best player last season. And here was this million-pound gobshite with a face like a smacked arse telling me to collect the bibs and balls.

The red mist came down and I went at him like a whirling dervish, swinging for all I was worth. Months of pent-up frustration oozed out through my fists and feet. Who the fuck did he think he was? Before I could do much damage to him, or him to me, we were dragged apart. Now I wish the incident had been recorded because from where I was standing not all of the punches landing on Marco were mine. When I emerged from the scrum I noticed Arthur was standing nearby with steam coming out of his ears. I'd never seen him so angry. A punch-up with a player was one thing, disobeying his instructions and undermining his authority was quite another. 'Get in the fucking shower, Ted and then fuck off back to the Baseball Ground,' was all he'd say.

By the time he finally joined me across town his reaction was both carrot and stick. The stick came out first as he told me he was very disappointed with my lack of professionalism. He'd expected me to set an example to the others and was surprised I'd reacted to a bit of banter. As there'd been a few fans watching and word would no doubt get round, he had no choice other than to fine me two weeks wages. But in the same breath he offered me another one-year extension to my contract. It seemed like a fantastic conclusion to a training-ground punch-up, until he told me that my new role was to bring the younger lads on. I wouldn't be starting in the first team and would only be called on as a substitute as and when required. Instead, I'd captain the second team and be responsible for nurturing the club's emerging talent. It was less than three months since I'd won the Player of the Year award and here I was being cast aside. As I put pen to paper on the contract I felt like I'd found a penny and lost a pound.

On reflection, the writing had been on the wall for months. The new signings who'd come in during the spring had increased competition for places. Tommy Johnson was playing well in my position and justifying the money that had been spent on him. I'd only really hung on to a shirt in the first team at the back end of the season because Geraint Williams had picked up an injury and Arthur had shoved me in the middle. Pre-season training had also been unusually hard on my bad knee. It was never something you looked forward to, but the fortnight of pounding the fairways at Allestree and haring round the track at Moorways had kept Gordon Guthrie busy with the ice pack each day.

Lionel had also given Arthur more money to spend in the summer and he'd brought in a number of quality players. Luton were persuaded to sell Wales international Mark Pembridge for £1.25 million and Darren Wassall joined us from Forest for £600,000. After Geraint joined newly promoted Ipswich Town, Arthur signed Martin Kuhl from Portsmouth for £650,000 and Dutchman Richard Goulooze from Heerenveen. But his most adventurous dip into the transfer market would come with the capture of Craig Short, who made the short journey from Notts County for a club record fee of £2.65 million.

Despite my personal disappointment at the prospect of playing a bit-part role, there was an air of optimism about the club as we embarked on another attempt to get into the top flight. It quickly dissipated as we lost our opening three fixtures and failed to win any of our next five in the league and League

Cup. I sat on the bench for our opening fixture against newly-promoted Peterborough listening to the home fans singing 'what a waste of money' at us. Ken Charley, who'd won them the play-off final the previous year, grabbed the only goal of the game.

There was more of the same when we lost at home to eventual champions Newcastle before I was restored to the starting line-up against Leicester City. Gabbiadini was dropped and I moved into the wing position vacated by Tommy Johnson, who was told to play down the middle. We looked much better in an entertaining game, but lost 3-2 thanks to two goals from my old colleague Phil Gee, who put us to the sword and would have had a hat-trick had a post not intervened. We picked up our first point of the season in a dire game against Watford next up. Jason Kavanagh became the first Derby player to be sent off for a professional foul under the new directives, but it was just about the only point of interest in the whole game.

There wasn't a lot of enthusiasm for the Anglo-Italian Cup either, but that was next up with a midweek game against Notts County. The competition, which pitted English First Division teams against those from Italy's Serie B, was designed to improve relations between the two countries after the Heysel Stadium tragedy. But to reach the international stages and actually play an Italian side you had to win your domestic group first. Notts County didn't put up much of a fight as we took the game seriously, hoping a victory would kick-start our lacklustre season. We won 4-2 thanks to goals from Paul Williams, Mark Pembridge, Paul Simpson and Marco, who came on for me after I received a nasty cut across my knee. I missed the next game against Barnsley at the end of September but another

175

goal from Pembo and a fine strike from Richard Goulooze ensured the Italian Job was on.

First up was Pisa who boasted Denmark's Euro '92 winner Henrik Larsen and a nineteen-year-old called Christian Vieri, who would later move from Lazio to Inter Milan for a world record £32 million. Neither proved a tower of strength as we scored two early goals through Tommy Johnson and Mickey Forsyth. I had a good game and the Italians didn't know what to do when I ran at them and crossed the ball for Tommy, who had switched to the middle to replace the injured Paul Kitson. They resorted to kicking me in the second half and an Argentinian called Jose Antonio Chamot, who would play in three World Cups for his country, was given his marching orders after scything me down from behind on the hour mark. They didn't put up much of a fight after that and Pembo finished things off with a great volley that sailed into the top corner of the net. A crowd of just over 8,000, higher than anywhere else that night, watched us in the club's first competitive game against European opposition for sixteen years.

Our game against Cosenza had a similar feel about it a fortnight later. We won comfortably as they tried to kick us off the park. I started in place of the injured Paul Simpson and had an easy game on the wing. But that was more than could be said for poor Darren Wassell, who had to be taken off at half-time with a huge stud hole in his knee. By then we were 3-0 up and cruising thanks to headers from Andy Comyn and Paul Kitson and a neat finish from Gabby. The only threat from them, other than a series of scandalous tackles, was striker Marco Negri, who would go on to have a short but spectacular career with my old club Rangers. As soon as he lost interest, the small band of Derby supporters who'd made their way to the San Vito Stadium in Calabria were guaranteed to go home happy.

We then had two games in the competition in the space of eight days during December and emerged with mixed fortunes. First up was Cremonese at the Baseball Ground. They were by far the best team we faced and scored three times within the first eighteen minutes. Yugoslav striker Matjaz Florjancic got two of them and forced Darren Wassell to concede an own goal. The Italians then gave us a lesson in defending, until Paul Kitson got in for a consolation.

Reggiana were top of Serie B when we arrived in thick fog in the town of Reggio Emilia, near Milan on 7 December. But the side that emerged contained only three members of their first team and we cruised to a 3-0 win with goals from Kitson, Pembridge and Gabbiadini. We'd topped the English section after Pisa held West Ham to a draw at Upton Park in the night's other important game. Next stop was Brentford in a two-leg semi-final.

I missed the first leg due to injury but watched from the stands as we edged a seven-goal thriller. Mark Patterson, who had nearly been sold to Preston, scored two invaluable goals as the home side launched a determined fightback after finding themselves 3-0 down in the first half hour. The away goals proved a godsend as we lost 2-1 at home in the return leg. Gabbiadini put us in front on the night towards the end of the first half. But Gary Blissett grabbed two goals in four minutes to ensure a nervy finish for the crowd of 14,494 who'd turned out to support us. They eventually got their trip to Wembley when we hung on, even if it hadn't been achieved in quite the way we'd hoped.

Despite playing in the majority of games in the competition

Arthur left me out of the squad to face Cremonese at Wembley. I can't say I was distraught not to be included, but it was disappointing to miss out on a Wembley Cup Final, whatever the competition. The Rams fans that travelled down to London to make up the vast majority of the 37,000-strong crowd were also left disappointed as the team went down 3-1 again. Cremonese, who were heading for promotion to Serie A, played us off the park. They were far better than us in every position other than goalkeeper. Had it not been for Martin Taylor, who saved a penalty and pulled off a string of great saves, the margin would have been far greater.

Missing the final typified how miserably the season was turning out for me. After being named in the eleven for the nil-nil draw at Watford, I didn't start another first-team game until we entertained West Ham on 10 January. I wished I hadn't after Julian Dicks booted lumps out of me before he was finally sent off for the eighth time in his career. Derby fans had to watch us lose our eighth home game of the campaign and quite rightly booed us off at half-time and at the end. Arthur didn't then pick me again until our home game against Leicester at the end of February. We managed to win 2-0 with temporary captain Mickey Forsyth immense in the middle of the back four. But I was forced off again with a knock and was replaced by Richard Goulooze.

Part of me quite enjoyed playing in the reserves, as unambitious as it sounds. The first team were under an awful lot of pressure due to the fact Arthur had spent the best part of £10 million trying to get us promoted. There was far less tension away from the media spotlight and I was still picking up the same wages. But at thirty years old, when I should have been in my prime, I was beginning to wonder if trotting out for the stiffs was how it was going to be for the rest of my career. Arthur definitely wanted me around and said so on numerous occasions when he could see the doubts creeping in. I was good for bringing on the youngsters and he liked me geeing the lads up with a bit of chat and the odd practical joke. He probably reckoned he'd had the best out of me as a player and that I was never going to be the same again after four operations on my knee. But there came a point during the season when I sat in the dressing room pulling on the number twelve shirt and thought: I don't want this anymore. I want to be wearing one to eleven. And most of all, I'm fed up putting the red nose on and playing the court jester.

Some players in my position would have slackened off in training and moped about with their bottom lip out. The ones these days would have been straight onto their agents to sort out a lucrative transfer for them. I didn't have an agent and didn't want one so I just tried harder. Arthur had told me that I wasn't part of his plans at the start of the season. He wasn't going to throw Tommy in the reserves and give me a run. But he was also good enough to tell me that one or two scouts had been watching the reserve games and I began to contemplate life away from my beloved Baseball Ground. When the other lads were getting showered and pulling on their golfing slacks, I'd stay behind after training and cross another hundred balls. As Jock Wallace had told me at Seville, the only way to get a move was to earn one. The extra sessions put a strain on my knee and Gordon Guthrie began to worry that I was over-doing it. But as painful as training was on my leg, it was better than the alternative of going home.

June, who'd moved out permanently by now, had started divorce proceedings. True to her promise on our wedding night, she began taking me to the cleaners. I arrived home from training one day to find she'd stripped the house of practically everything that wasn't screwed down. The only things she'd left were the television and the sofa in the lounge. I watched a rerun of the student sitcom *The Young Ones* that night with a takeaway pizza and a warm can of beer, envious of their luxury lifestyle. A few days later a letter landed on the carpet where the doormat had once been. It was a maintenance payments demand from the Child Support Agency.

Things weren't much better with Heidi. We'd been seeing each other on and off for months now but the initial excitement of having an affair soon subsided and was replaced by the usual domestic drudgery. After June moved out we saw more of each other but the regularity of our meetings belied a lack of permanence in our relationship. Then she announced she was pregnant.

Our little baby girl, Jordan, was born on 4 July, 1993 or Independence Day as it is known in the United States. Her mother certainly had to be independent as I wasn't present at Derby's City General Hospital. I had no desire to be recognised on a maternity ward with someone who wasn't my wife. It only needed someone to do the maths and pick up the phone to a newspaper and my private life would have been feasted on again. I got a taste of rejection myself a few weeks later when Arthur called me in after training and announced that he was going to listen to offers for me. Nobody had made a bid but he could see that I was going to find it hard to play in the reserves again. Filled with misplaced optimism, I'd put in a good shift in pre-season and had been hoping that I could fight my way back into the team. But Arthur was as good as telling me I was finished at Derby.

I spent several weeks in limbo waiting for the phone to ring before Birmingham City expressed an interest. I was again hauled off the training pitch and told to get myself to St Andrews for a lunchtime meeting. I drove as quickly as I could and was stopped for speeding on the A38. Luckily, the traffic officers were less officious than their colleagues in Nottingham and let me off when I explained why I was in a hurry. I parked up outside the ground and wasn't particularly impressed with my surroundings. The Baseball Ground was hardly a thing of beauty, but at least it looked like it had seen better days at some point. St Andrews looked like the Luftwaffe had recently paid a visit.

Assistant Manager Trevor Morgan greeted me at the door and took me upstairs to the boardroom to meet Manager Terry Cooper and Chief Executive Karen Brady. She told me that the club had agreed a £200,000 fee with Derby and all I needed to do was sign on the dotted line. The sticking point was that they could only offer me £1,000 a week, which was a £300 a week pay cut on my existing wages. What they could give me, however, was regular first-team football and a signing-on fee that would ease the financial difficulties brought on by the CSA. Brady was charming and very persuasive and told me I was just the sort of player they wanted. They were an hour's drive down the road from Derby and in the same division. It sounded like the best of a bad job to me.

16

SINGING THE BLUES

It's important to get off to a good start when you join a new club. Scoring on your debut or having a good game can ease the weight of expectation and endear you to your new supporters. I had all of this in mind when I made my debut with Birmingham in a pre-season tournament in Italy. Sadly it went out of the window within five minutes when I managed to get myself sent off. Terry Cooper had made me captain, figuring that my experience in Spain would help us against continental opposition. It was a three-team affair against a couple of villages, with each of us down to play forty-five minutes against the other two. A couple of minutes into the first match I had an altercation with their fullback. As I got up to move away he spat in my face and I grabbed him round the throat. The referee took a dim view of both of us and sent us packing. As I was walking off down the tunnel their physio came and had a pop and I found myself fighting him and the player. George Parris then ran off the pitch to my aid as the poly-tunnel wall bounced to and fro. It wasn't a great start.

Things didn't get an awful lot better when we went down 1-0 at the Valley in our opening fixture of the season. My knee then swelled up in the 2-2 draw with Wolves and I missed the next half-dozen games. But the team got a fillip when Danny Wallace joined from Manchester United in October. Despite being just five feet five inches tall he headed the winner on his debut against Watford and we moved up to eighth in the table, and started to believe that a play-off place was a realistic ambition. That belief was reinforced when fellow new boy Carl Shutt, who'd arrived from Leeds, grabbed the second in a 2-1 home win over Bolton Wanderers.

Not long after the Bolton game we went down to Tiverton in Devon for a testimonial. It was a bitterly cold day and none of us felt like leaving the warmth of the team bus. Terry had left the trip to Morgie to organise and the first thing he did was order fourteen double brandies from the bar. Totally unprepared, we quickly went one down to a team who sensed they could capture a league scalp. The tackles were flying in all over the place and just before half-time I was caught by one of their defenders, who gashed my calf with a stud. Terry hadn't bothered to send our physio so the role had been given to BRMB radio presenter and lifelong Bluenose Tom Ross. Tom, who'd also been named as a substitute as a laugh, was a smashing bloke and was liked by all the lads in the team. But you could write what he knew about medical matters on the back of a fag packet. As he jogged on with the magic sponge to treat my cut I feared the worst and wasn't disappointed when he began rubbing some Vic into it. I can safely say I've never run so quickly in my life!

As the autumn and winter progressed the team picked up a series of injuries that sidelined a number of our better quality players. Fortunately they all got proper medical attention. Despite Shutty scoring the winner in a scrappy 1-0 win over Millwall, we lost five out of six games between the middle of

October and the end of November. A section of the crowd turned on Terry particularly after our 3-0 thumpings at the hands of Nottingham Forest and Tranmere Rovers. We arrived for training two days after the Tranmere game to be told by Trevor Morgan that Terry had quit. He'd threatened to do so at around the same time the previous season. But this time he meant it.

I felt sorry for Terry. He'd spent a fair bit of the new chairman's money trying to haul the club away from the foot of the table. But he was unlucky with injuries and just didn't have enough talent at his disposal to get the results the club and fans demanded. Morgie took charge of our second game in a month against Nottingham Forest when we travelled to the City Ground on 4 December. I was expecting a bit of stick as an ex-Derby player and was not disappointed. A good proportion of the crowd spent the ninety minutes calling me a wanker. Despite giving five years of service and leaving voluntarily, I was also a 'Derby reject'. Just to rub it in, we lost 1-0. My young son Kevin was at the game and I spent much of the drive back to Derby explaining to him what it was all about. It wasn't the nicest thing to have to do and reinforced my dislike of the city, the club and its supporters. To this day I do my utmost to drive round the place if I have to be somewhere east of Derby and I will never have a Nottingham postcode.

A great deal of uncertainty can creep into a club if a new manager is not appointed soon after the previous one leaves. Karen Brady and the board were no doubt working hard behind the scenes. But as players we turned up every day for training not knowing what was going on. Like the fans we resorted to reading the papers to find out who was being linked to the club and who might fancy it. Given our lowly position, there were precious few of the latter, but the general consensus was that Steve Coppell would be the man to take over. Whether the ex-Manchester United player was ever approached or simply knocked them back, he never arrived at St Andrews. Instead we got another former United man in the shape of Barry Fry. Coppell had played over 300 games for the Old Trafford side, including three FA Cup Finals, and represented England in the 1982 World Cup. Fry, playing in the generation before, hadn't even made the first team.

Despite his lack of success as a player and his relatively modest track record at Southend and Barnet, Barry's appointment was welcomed by the players. His bubbly character and endless jokes about his old chairman Stan Flashman brightened up training and brought much needed laughter back to a dressing room that had become accustomed to sombre silence. Doubts began to creep in over his suitability, however, when he named his team ahead of his first game against Crystal Palace. We'd travelled down overnight and stayed in a hotel, with the intention of letting Barry get to know the players. He proved he'd yet to do so by putting young defender Graham Potter at fullback. Graham, who was injured at the time, wasn't at Selhurst Park and hadn't even come down to London. Barry laughed it off but then surprised us again by asking who would like to be captain. As he went round the team finding out who'd done it before, it got to the stage where players were claiming they'd skippered their primary school side in a bid to exert their credentials. This, we would later discover, was just the start of the madness.

I've yet to meet a player who likes playing over Christmas. It's very difficult to abstain and concentrate on the football when everyone around you is enjoying themselves. But it's one of the few drawbacks of being a professional and most people just get on with it. We had Stoke City on Boxing Day 1993 and trained hard on Christmas Eve. We were expecting to be given Christmas Day off or, at the worst, be told to come in for a light session in the morning. But Barry had other ideas. He told us to enjoy ourselves, have our Christmas dinner and a few drinks and relax, before adding: 'I'll see you all for training at 7 p.m.' There was no way I could have a turkey and all the trimmings let alone a few drinks with the drive over from Derby. When we arrived at a deserted St Andrews, however, it turned out a few of the lads had taken him at his word. Carl Shutt, who'd come down from Leeds was half-cut and a lot of the lads were puffing and blowing just putting on their boots.

After getting changed, the floodlights flickered into life and we began a gentle jog round the pitch. We then did ten minutes of stretching and a couple of shuttle runs before Barry announced that he'd had enough and that he'd booked us all into the Arden Hotel near Birmingham Airport. After a sleepless night listening to the planes taking holidaymakers away for Christmas, we took the bus to Stoke for an early kick-off. Despite Paul Peschisolido getting his eighth goal of the season we went down 2-1. Why we'd had an evening training session and had to stay in a hotel for a fixture in the Midlands still puzzles me. But if Christmas was crazy, New Year's Eve would be worse.

After a convincing win over West Brom in front of our biggest crowd of the season, we were all set to see in Hogmanay at a hotel ahead of our visit to Southend. With Barry visiting his old club, we expected him to be keen to get a result and treat the trip professionally. But at the invitation of owner David Sullivan we went to a party at his mansion, Birch Hall, on the edge of Epping Forest near Theydon Bois in Essex. The whole first-team squad were asked to the bash at the fourteen-bedroom pile, which boasted its own cinema, bowling alley and two swimming pools. We drove there on the team bus and after making our way up the long gravel drive were greeted by a group of skimpily dressed dolly birds from Sullivan's *Daily Sport* newspaper.

They plied us with beer and wine all night as we enjoyed a huge meal at a twenty-four-place dinner table. There was a little stage at the end of table and halfway through the meal Motown band the Four Tops came on and began belting out their hits. It was a great party and everyone got stuck in, but there were more than a few of us concerned that the amount of food and drink we were putting away might affect our performance. Barry was oblivious and was in his element among the busty blondes, with a glass of champagne in one hand and a fat cigar in the other. The bus eventually arrived at around 3 a.m. to take us back to the hotel with all of us off our heads.

The changing rooms the next morning stank of booze as we tried to clear our heads and shape up for the match. Several of the lads were sick in the toilets before they could put on their shirts and we trooped out into the bitter January air looking like death warmed up. Southend seemed to have had an early night and buzzed around us like a super-fit youth side. The only player to emerge with any credit from our side was Pesch, who netted our consolation goal in a 3-1 defeat.

I felt very sorry for the Blues fans who'd curtailed their celebrations the night before to drive down to Essex and watch us. We let them down and should never have overindulged the night before. But you had to question the wisdom of the chairman and manager who had gladly let us do so. Sadly the hangovers hadn't cleared two days later when we took on Kidderminster Harriers in the Cup and became the victims of a giant-killing.

Their manager Graham Allner was a big Blues fan and didn't know where to put himself after the 2-1 win. He wanted to celebrate his team's victory but was upset by the shambles his favourite team had become.

I remember getting into the changing rooms after being booed off and feeling properly embarrassed. I don't wish to take anything away from Kidderminster as they were magnificent that day. But there is no way they should have beaten us, particularly in front of our own fans. For once in his life Barry was lost for words. He sat there in silence contemplating the enormity of our defeat, thinking no doubt how he was going to explain this one to the press. The club had lost to Altrincham at the same stage in the competition seven years previously, when John Bond had been in charge. But this felt like we'd hit rock bottom. We had massively and unforgivably under-achieved and it was easily one of the lowest points in my football career. The pain was eased by the fact that our conquerors also went on to humble Division One side Preston North End in the next round, before losing narrowly to Premier League West Ham United.

Things didn't get much better after the Kidderminster game when we lost in successive away trips to Notts County and Watford. I was on the bench against County as we were edged out 2-1 but was taken off after being named in the starting eleven when we got thumped 5-2 at Vicarage Road. Gary Cooper and Steve Claridge both got sent off as we finished with nine men. None of us were looking forward to the first game back at St Andrews against Mick Buxton's Sunderland. We anticipated that an increasingly disgruntled crowd would vent frustrations if we didn't make a good start. And we weren't disappointed. After the usual bluster from Barry in his pre-match team talk we made our way out of the changing rooms to face the music. I took a deep breath at the top of the tunnel and began to walk out into the weak winter sunshine, only to be hit in the face by a meat pie.

For those who've never been smacked in the chops by football's favourite savoury snack, it's a pretty sobering experience. It took me a few seconds to realise just what had happened. Once I'd cleared the puff pastry and sticky brown mess from my eyes, I decided I'd better chase after my assailant. As soon as I hurdled the barrier and landed among several hundred bemused Blues fans, I knew it was a bad idea. But with bits of meat hanging off my face I didn't feel I had much choice. I grabbed the nearest steward and began accusing a bloke in a bobble hat of pitching his pie at me. He was pouring Bovril out of a Thermos flask and had clearly been nowhere near the tunnel. But caught between anger and embarrassment I just wanted someone to be apprehended. Fortunately the referee spared my blushes by blowing several short blasts on his whistle to attract my attention. He was waiting to start the game and couldn't do so with me in the crowd. I clambered out of the stand rather sheepishly as my teammates choked back the laughter. Things weren't looking good for my Blues career.

I wasn't hit by anything else that day as we played out a drab nil-nil draw. But all of us were given pelters for our performance. The reception I got throughout my time at St Andrews surprised me after the great relationship I'd had with the crowd at Derby. I guess I got off to a good start with the Rams and scoring on my home debut against Manchester United must have helped. But I found them a likeable lot and enjoyed the banter I had with the Pop Side when the ball went out of play. In contrast, Blues supporters were aptly named and never seemed to be happy with their lot. Living in the shadow of their larger, more successful neighbours Aston Villa must have put a strain on them. In fairness, they didn't have an awful lot to be happy about in the six months I was there, and they'd eventually watch their side be relegated that season. Speaking to fans now, they tell me it was just about the worst it ever got at St Andrews. They also didn't see the best of me as a player given the problems I was having off the pitch, my dislike of the management set-up and the long hours of travel that took their toll. But if I had to choose one place for a cheerful night out, it probably wouldn't be Birmingham.

After spending most of December getting to know the squad, Barry spent all of January chopping and changing it. He would eventually use forty-six players that season, beating Coventry City's record of forty-three that had stood since 1920. He loved to wheel and deal and keep players on their toes, but there often seemed to be little rhyme or reason to his selections. Players used to dread knocks on the dressing-room door in the last hour before the game. A note would sometimes be passed or a message conveyed from one of the directors telling him to field a certain player because a scout had turned up to watch them. You'd be preparing yourself to start and suddenly be demoted to the bench after being told to hand your shirt to another player. It happened to me before our away game at Notts County on 11 January, when I'd been set to play and was then told I wasn't. I took off my shirt and handed it to Barry. In full view of the other players I told him I'd had enough.

It was no prima-donna tantrum and I'd never been one of those players who thought they had a God-given right to play. I'd spent most of the previous season in the Derby reserves after all. I just thought it was ridiculous how he carved the team up if he thought he could free up a few quid by selling a player to bring someone else in. I was one of the senior members of the squad with a proven track record. If I wasn't playing well or had been ill-disciplined then fair enough. But it was as if Del Boy from *Only Fools and Horses* was in charge of the team.

Being dropped coincided with Barry's hunt for an alternative training venue. We didn't have our own training ground but were usually put through our paces at the civil service training ground over at Shirley. It was a pain for me to get to on my commute from Derby and I used to hate sitting in the rush-hour traffic in the morning. It wasn't the best of grounds either, being directly on the flight path at Birmingham International Airport and continually covered in bird turds from the flocks of Canada geese that used it as a giant green toilet. But we didn't know whether to laugh or cry when he put down some bibs for goalposts in a local park near St Andrews and told us to play a game of five-a-side. The locals looked more than a little bemused as they exercised their bull terriers and Rottweilers, while we ran about like schoolkids. We were professional footballers playing in front of thousands of spectators every week and here we were booting a ball about at the side of a swing park. I suppose the dog shit made a change from bird shit.

On another occasion Barry had us slogging up and down the Malvern Hills for a week. It was the middle of the season and we were supposed to be at the peak of our physical fitness. Yet here we were doing pre-season training all over again without a ball in sight. Jock Wallace would have been proud of him, sending us up one muddy field after another as the rain poured down. If the running was his idea of the stick, his carrot was to take us to a health spa called Champneys Springs in Ashby de la Zouch, Leicestershire, the following week. Again there was no ball work in sight, just massages, pedicures, seaweed scrubs and jacuzzis. We spent most of our time lounging about in the pool and chatting up the staff in their white pyjama outfits. We didn't work out a single set-piece routine and didn't talk tactics for a whole week. But by the end there wasn't a single team in the division who had fresher looking skin or cleaner pores!

The problem with the spa, apart from the lack of proper football training, was the boredom. There was no bar at the place and not a drop of alcohol permitted on site. Barry was never one for curfews and was quite happy for us to go out locally for a few drinks as long as everybody was sensible. We went to a couple of pubs in Ashby on a few occasions but found the local nightlife a little tame. As a few of the lads liked a flutter, we decided that the only thing to do would be to go for a day at a local racecourse. If nothing else, it would get us away from the boredom of the spa.

We decided that our best bet would be to head for Nottingham and we did so in two cars. I took my battered Vauxhall Carlton, whilst Steve Claridge piled a few more into his sporty new Vauxhall Calibra. We left the M1 at junction twenty-four and were approaching the power station at Radcliffe-on-Soar when we hit heavy traffic. After sitting in it for twenty minutes I decided to turn round and head for a short cut I knew. Steve and his car were in front of me in the queue so I flashed my lights to alert him and spun round to the right. As I did so I noticed a car coming from my left and pulled onto the grass verge to avoid it. He missed me but in locking on his brakes slewed over to his right and ploughed straight into the front of Steve's Calibra with a loud bang. I jumped out of the car, held my hands up and apologised immediately. It had all been my fault as I just hadn't looked when I swung out into the oncoming traffic. The old guy in the car was quite shaken-up by the accident so I did my best to calm him down. I felt very sorry for him and guilty that I'd ruined his day. But as the others piled into my car I couldn't help but have a giggle at Steve's expense as we left him on the side of the road waiting for the tow truck. He backed a faller in the first that day.

When Barry's training methods didn't get any better and his team selections got more and more bizarre, I let him know in the politest way I could that I thought my future lay elsewhere. He didn't try to dissuade me, thinking I was either finished and had nothing to offer or that he could get some cash for me. The club circulated my name and let it be known that I was available. The following week the phone went at home. It was Jim Jefferies who wanted to know if I'd consider coming back to Scotland to play for Hearts. I wasn't averse to the idea at all despite the fact I would have to relocate, as I would be closer to my kids. I was also keen to play in the SPL again and finish my career in my native Scotland. The problem was he could only offer me £325 a week in wages, which was a dramatic drop from what I was on. Six months previously I'd been on £1300 a week at Derby and here I was swithering about a £1,000 a week pay cut. In the end I reluctantly told them that I couldn't take up the offer for personal reasons. I'd known life outside the Old Firm wasn't always a bed of roses but here was a stark example of the financial reality for clubs hoping to compete against Scotland's big two.

Salvation arrived the following week in the shape of Burnley boss Jimmy Mullen. I'd been impressed with Jimmy when his Burnley team came to play Derby a year or two previously. He was an honest pro who'd won promotions at Sheffield Wednesday, Rotherham and Cardiff City, before signing up for the school of hard knocks that was management. I spotted him in the Directors' Box at St Andrews one night when I was playing for the reserves. He'd been down to take a look at another player having heard good reports, but he was sufficiently impressed to give me and not the other bloke a call the following day. He said he couldn't promise the earth, but suggested that if I was looking for a change of scenery I could do worse than dropping down a division and coming up to Turf Moor to help in their promotion bid. I wasn't bothered at all about leaving the First Division, but his offer of a month's loan deal gave me the security of finding out what it was really like before I committed to the club.

True to their word, Burnley didn't offer the world. But their £600 a week was almost twice what Hearts could put on the table. If the loan signing turned into a permanent transfer they could also give me a £36,000 signing-on fee, spread over the two-year deal. The money would help plug some of the holes in my leaky financial affairs. I was spending a fortune on petrol every week getting to and from Derby and the Child Support Agency payments were also beginning to bite. Birmingham had been an unhappy interlude in my career and I'd achieved very little. But a new challenge had presented itself at Burnley and I was all set to give it a go at what was almost certain to be my last hurrah in professional football. As I travelled up the M6 to Lancashire, I felt like a man who'd just been released from prison.

17

ONE LAST DROP OF CLARET

The only time I'd played at Turf Moor before I signed for Burnley was in an FA Cup tie in January 1992. I had a stinking cold and had travelled up from Derby expecting to be on the bench. Arthur Cox had other ideas and told me I was starting. He ordered physio Gordon Guthrie to go into the first-aid kit and retrieve the half bottle of whisky he kept in there for 'medicinal purposes'. After a couple of gulps, I ran out onto the pitch and gave their fullback Ian Measham a torrid time for ninety minutes. We twice took the lead but were pegged back in an entertaining draw. At the end, Burnley boss Jimmy Mullins paid me the ultimate compliment when he told me to give him a ring if I was ever short of a club.

The Clarets were top of the old Fourth Division at the time and looked like a team who were going places. I was also very impressed with their support who'd packed the place out, particularly down the Longside terrace, and really got behind the team. I don't know what they'd been drinking when we played the second replay, but the thousands who travelled down from Lancashire sang their hearts out all night despite losing 2-0. They were still there long after the final whistle and I remember Jimmy having to go out and ask them to go home. After putting up with the miserable lot at St Andrews, I was looking forward to the backing of a proper set of fans and working with a manager who knew the game.

My first match on 5 March was away at Fulham and I very nearly missed the kick-off after getting lost following the team bus in my car. I eventually dumped it in a school playground and ran to the ground, following the match-day crowd. We fell behind to an early goal, before David Eyres equalised and Adrian Randall put us in front at halftime. But we conceded two in the second period and went home with nothing. I spoke my mind in the changing rooms afterwards and told skipper John Pender and fellow centre half Steve Davies a few home truths. I thought I'd probably gone too far but Jimmy told me afterwards that he liked the fact I was passionate and wouldn't stand for any sloppiness. It seemed to do the trick as we drew our next two games before thumping promotion rivals Bristol Rovers 3-1. I scored on my home debut against Stockport with a left-foot shot as I had for Derby and also grabbed the third in the dying seconds of the Bristol match.

The wheels then came off at Hartlepool when John Pender and Adrian Heath were sent off and we crashed 4-1. Pender made amends by scoring the first in a 3-1 win over Hull City, but we then lost by a solitary goal at Wrexham on Easter Monday. The defeat didn't stop me making my loan signing a permanent deal in the first week in April. Birmingham and Burnley had agreed a fee and I was only too pleased that I was moving on. Clarets fans appeared to be pleased as well, after singing 'sign him up, sign him up' at our last two games. We looked like we were in serious danger of blowing the play-offs but didn't lose another game in April. The highlight of our four wins in six matches was Tony Philliskirk's twenty-two minute hat-trick in our 5-0 demolition of Barnet. Despite conceding four ourselves in the last game of the season at already relegated Exeter City we finished sixth, three points ahead of Bradford City. The scoreline in Devon wasn't the only embarrassing thing that day. A group of Burnley supporters had made the long trip south wearing kilts and 'See You Jimmy' wigs in my honour. They made a great fuss when I came out for the warm-up and even joined the Scottish marching band, which was providing the pre-match entertainment. It was a far cry from the pie chuckers at Birmingham.

Our opponents in the two-legged play-off semi-final were also from Devon – Peter Shilton's Plymouth Argyle. The south coast side had finished a full twelve points ahead of us in the league and had missed out on automatic promotion by just three points. But we didn't fear them when we lined up at Turf Moor on Sunday 15 May. I was up against my old Derby teammate Mark Patterson, who'd lodged with me for nine months before heading to the coast. He wasn't the best fullback in the world and I reckoned I'd have the better of him over the two legs. What I hadn't reckoned on were the instructions from Shilts to nobble me at every opportunity. Sure enough, just five minutes in, I crossed a ball into the box and as everyone followed its flight, he slid in and caught my right ankle. He apologised straight away but admitted that Shilts had told him to do it. Soon afterwards my sock began to fill up with blood and my ankle began to swell. But I was determined he wasn't going to kick me out of the game and gave as good as I got. We huffed and puffed and created a number of chances but couldn't quite get the breakthrough and the 18,000 strong crowd went home without seeing a goal.

The Plymouth players thought they had one foot in the final

and were cock-a-hoop when they got off the field. We could hear singing coming from their dressing room and judging by the long faces in ours, it looked like many of our lot thought it was all over too. They'd already beaten us 3-2 at their place that season and we travelled down to the south coast concerned we'd blown our chance. Our away form was pretty ropey too, having won just four times in the league on our travels that season. But on the morning of the game I picked up a copy of the local rag in our hotel and discovered their chairman had put out an appeal to bus companies in Cornwall and Devon asking if they had any spare coaches for Wembley. I showed Jimmy and he pinned it on the dressing room wall that night and told all the players to read it. When we got out into the tunnel, their keeper Alan Nicholls was pretending to smoke a cigar and was boasting how easy it was going to be to beat us. It was all the team talk we needed and we went out and battered them 3-1. Despite falling behind, two goals from John Francis and one from Warren Joyce ensured that it was Lancashire coach companies and tobacconists who would be busy later that month.

Plymouth fans invaded the pitch at the final whistle and I realised for the first time how David Speedie must have felt when he was accosted by Derby supporters. A couple of the boys got a clip round the ear and were sent on their way by their beaten hosts. It took the police several minutes to clear the pitch and we wondered if it was safe to go back out. But when we did so, most of the travelling Burnley contingent was still in the ground. They'd had a very long journey down and would have another long one back. But the trip after that would be to the Twin Towers of Wembley for the first time in six years. On that occasion they'd seen their beloved team go down 2-0 to Wolves. Hopefully, this time, we could make amends.

ONE LAST DROP OF CLARET

Before we could do so the Chairman Frank Teasdale announced that he'd booked us in for another night at the Moat House hotel and that the bar was free. Never one to turn down an invite, I jumped in with both feet and celebrated in style. A couple of the Plymouth players came in and there was a bit of friction in the air. John Deary told a few of them to fuck off and it looked like it might kick off. But in fairness to Alan Nicholls, he came over and wished us all the best at Wembley. Steve Davies, Tony Philiskirk and I were the last men standing after a marathon session and we were still propping up the bar when other residents began coming down for their breakfast. We staggered out of the hotel having never made it to bed and crashed out on the coach taking us home. We'd won nothing yet, but we'd proved a few doubters wrong and were now just ninety minutes away from promotion.

I'd been to the national stadium with Derby and sat on the bench with a dodgy hamstring as they were out-classed in the Anglo-Italian Cup. It was a Mickey Mouse competition but I would still like to have played in the final. Here I was just over a year later with an opportunity to make amends. And this time there was considerably more at stake. The stadium had clearly seen better days and was in need of refurbishment (or demolition as it soon proved), but there was a real buzz on the team coach as we made our way in from our hotel near Waltham Abbey. Catching a glimpse of the Twin Towers for the first time made the hairs on the back of your neck stand up. Everywhere we looked there were thousands of Burnley fans who cheered as we drove past. Like Plymouth, Stockport had finished twelve points ahead of us in the league. Yet there was great confidence in the cavernous changing rooms as we pulled on the claret and blue for the final time that season.

If Mark Patterson had tried to out-muscle me in the semi-final, Stockport did their level best to do it to the whole Burnley team. They seemed more intent on crippling us than beating us and quickly removed any vestige of sympathy that the neutrals in the 44,806 strong crowd might have had for them. It didn't stop them taking the lead in the second minute, however, when Gary Parkinson had a free kick awarded against him and Chris Beaumont met David Frain's cross to head past Marlon Beresford. I'd hardly touched the ball and it was a hammer blow to go behind so soon. But the early goal helped to settle the nerves and we soon got into a rhythm. A few minutes after their goal, Peter Ward clattered into me on the wing. Our own John Francis then followed him into the book for a fifty-fifty challenge on their keeper. But the real damage was done to John's right knee and he limped off some minutes later to be replaced by Andy Farrell.

Before Andy could come on I was hacked to the ground again, this time by Michael Wallace. As I lay on the turf holding my leg he accused me of diving, trampled all over me and then spat in my upturned face. I got up to knock his lights out, but was dragged off him by players from both sides. Referee David Elleray had seen everything and immediately sent Wallace off, before booking me for retaliation. The Stockport players accused me of getting him sent off, but he got what was coming to him. It was only the second time in my career anyone had ever spat on me, and ironically, it had occurred in the same season as the first. If anyone can think of a more disgusting and degrading way to treat a fellow professional I'd like to hear it. David Eyres didn't fair much better when he was hacked down by Mike Flynn ten minutes later. But after lengthy treatment he came back on and replied in the perfect way by grabbing our equaliser.

Adrian Heath set the move up with a pass outside their area. Eyresy then beat two defenders and another on the edge of the box before bending a fantastic left-foot shot past their keeper. It was his twenty-ninth goal of the season.

Eyresy was having a great game and always looked dangerous up front as we pressed forward for the winner. Warren Joyce and Farrell when he came on were dominant in midfield and Davis and Pender were solid at the back after their early scare. Despite being booed by the Stockport fans every time I touched the ball I was also having a good game and had the measure of their defenders. We went in at halftime on the front foot after Elleray was forced to play seven extra minutes of stoppage time. Stockport's aggressive approach continued after the interval when Chris Beaumont elbowed Les Thompson off the ball and then trampled all over him. Elleray and a lot of the players missed the incident as they were following the play. But his keen-eyed assistant brought it to his attention and he was left with little choice other than to order Beaumont to join Wallace in the dressing room. Shortly afterwards, Gary Parkinson grabbed our winner with a deflected shot that looped over Keeley and into the net.

Things should have got easier after that but Stockport refused to lie down. We could have killed them off but Eyresy hit the bar when it was easier to score. Elleray played another seven minutes of stoppage time before finally blowing the whistle. The scenes at the end were fantastic as we all punched the air in delight and danced around on the pitch. We'd thoroughly deserved our victory and I was delighted for our fans, who'd given us fantastic support all season. I was also delighted for Stockport and everyone associated with the club who got exactly what they deserved: nothing. The few supporters that they managed to bring down to Wembley gave me dog's abuse as I made my way up the thirty-nine steps to collect my medal. But it was a great feeling knowing that we'd be playing in a higher division than them the following season. It was also great to know that a whip-round in the hotel that had produced £1,600 before the game had turned into £5,600 after we backed ourselves with a bookie, who'd offered us odds of 7/2 against a Burnley victory.

The winnings provided a welcome boost to my finances, which were in an increasingly parlous state. I went up to pre-season training seriously wondering if I could afford to put enough petrol in the car every week to continue playing for the Clarets. The thing I was relying on was the next instalment of my signing-on fee, which was due that summer. But I got a rude awakening when the Burnley secretary told me that he'd received a letter from the CSA demanding that it be handed over to June in lieu of the money I was supposed to owe her. After paying her and my mortgage off every month, I had £200 a week to live on and a significant chunk of that was going on transport to and from Burnley. June also managed to get some of my bank accounts frozen. On a number of occasions I'd go to the hole in the wall and be told to contact my bank. It became embarrassing using them and I began to stop doing so at busy times for fear I'd be spotted as it swallowed my card. I also wrote several cheques at around that time knowing full well that they'd bounce. It was a horrible position to be in.

My gloomy personal predicament was in stark contrast to the confidence surging through the club. Season tickets sales had boomed throughout the summer months as we prepared for our first season back in the second tier of English football for eleven years. Jimmy Mullin broke the club's transfer record fee, which had stood for sixteen years, when he signed England U21 international Chris Vinnicombe from my old club Rangers for £200,000. And it went again just a few days later when he spent £250,000 on attacking midfielder Liam Robinson from Bristol City. Despite the signings, we kicked off the 1994-95 season with a series of underwhelming displays. The only game we managed to win in our first seven league and cup outings was against York City in the League Cup.

Middlesbrough, Oldham and Barnsley all beat us and we scrambled 1-1 draws at Turf Moor against Stoke and Bristol City. Our first league triumph came at Luton when Robinson scored the only goal of the game. We won again in the south east, this time 3-2, after coming from behind at Millwall. The game was more memorable for referee Mike Bailey's decision to show me a second yellow card and then a red for an innocuous challenge. The problem was he'd never shown me the first yellow card. After consulting with Jimmy Mullen I pointed this out to him. He went as red as his card and told me I could carry on before running off. Who says referees never get it wrong? We certainly did in our next two games when we went down 1-0 to Wolves and their Black Country rivals West Brom at the end of September. We didn't win our next three games either, securing successive draws against Tranmere, Bolton and Sunderland. The derby against Bolton would be my last for the first team until New Year's Eve, after I aggravated my old knee injury in a tempestuous game.

When I returned, the team was hovering on the edge of the relegation zone and there was a great deal of tension around Turf Moor. That was lifted when we thumped a sorry Southend side 5-1 and everyone thought we'd turned the corner. The game witnessed the debuts of Craig Armstrong and Andy

Saville, who were drafted in on loan from Nottingham Forest and Birmingham City respectively. Despite Saville opening the scoring against Southend, neither player was able to do much as we then embarked on a run of eight straight defeats, equalling an unwanted club record that had stood for exactly a century. I started just one of the games and was then out for the whole of March. A combination of my knee flaring up every time I trained, hamstring troubles and problems off the pitch kept me out until 4 April when I came on as a substitute in our 2-0 home win over Charlton.

There was tragic news during that period when my old pal Davie Cooper died. His death came completely out of the blue for everyone in the Rangers family. He suffered a brain haemorrhage at Broadwood stadium whilst filming a training video for kids with Charlie Nicholas on March 22nd. He died the next day in hospital aged just thirty-nine after never recovering. As I drove up for his funeral at Hillhouse Parish Church in Hamilton four days later I couldn't help but feel that the game had been shorn of a legend. I'd also lost a good friend who I'd been on holiday to Florida with the previous year. He was fit as a fiddle and still went out for a run in the mornings despite the large quantities of beer we put away the previous nights. We also recreated our heady tennis days at Ibrox with a volleyball net on the beach. Coops, needless to say, beat me hands down. The great and the good of Scottish football were at the service. A huge crowd had gathered outside and the red, white and blue floral tributes covered the pavements, as they did the gates outside Ibrox. In his eulogy, Walter Smith said God had given Coops a talent and would not have been disappointed with how he used it. It was a sad, sad loss.

During my injury absence I was glad to miss Burnley's 4-0

hammering at the Baseball Ground. But I was delighted to start against my old team Derby when they came to Turf Moor on 15 April. It was nice to catch up with a few old friends in the changing room and I got a fabulous reception from the travelling Rams fans. I played well in the game, which we ended up winning 3-1, before being substituted in the second half. The result put pressure on manager Roy McFarland and contributed to him getting the sack at the end of the season following Derby's failure to make the play-offs. Another man under pressure was Jimmy Mullen, who was a relieved man after we secured the three points. But his relief was to be short-lived. Our defeat at Port Vale, for which I was injured again, all but sealed our fate. That was reserved for the home game against Portsmouth, when a half empty Turf Moor saw us bow out 2-1. It was the second time I'd been relegated and as I trooped off the pitch I felt every bit as sick as the first time.

If relegation was disappointing for both the fans and the players, a real tragedy occurred to me on 31 May when my dad died. I was down in London at the time seeing a girl called Sue Hanson, who I'd met at an away game. My brother Mitchell called my mobile and left a message telling me to phone him. I said to myself that I would do so in the morning, but then got another call at around 10 p.m., when he told me Dad was in hospital after a heart attack. I got straight into the car and drove through the night to Dumfries, arriving at around 4.30 a.m. Instead of going straight to the hospital I decided I'd be better getting my head down for an hour or two, so I let myself into Dad's house with the spare key. At 6 a.m. my older brother Martyn woke me up with tears in his eyes. Dad had had another heart attack and died that morning. He was sixty years old.

I felt guilty for not going to see him in hospital. I'd taken a split-second decision, not knowing his condition. People said I should go to the chapel of rest to say goodbye. But I'd seen him alive and well only a week before during a visit to Scotland and that was the image I wanted to keep of him. Ironically, I'd also had contact of sorts with my mother in recent weeks after a chance conversation in Burnley. A referee in a reserve game had approached me at halftime and said he knew her. She was working as a nurse at a hospital in the north west of England and wondered if I wanted to meet up. It was the first time she'd tried to contact me since my debut season at Derby and the answer was still the same. I told the ref that the woman must have made a mistake, as my mum was dead. She may as well have been as far as I was concerned, after abandoning us. Dad had struggled to bring the four of us up all on his own and had worked his fingers to the bone to make sure we were fed and clothed. Now he was gone too.

Football was a welcome distraction after a summer off spent soul-searching. But having started just seventeen league games during the 1994-95 season, I wondered how I'd fare in the following one. The answer quickly became apparent when Jimmy told me that he was going to use me sparingly during a chat at pre-season training. He said he was going to lighten the load on my dodgy knee by making sure I didn't have to train all week like the other players. He had a point. After driving for two hours to training, it would be stiff as a board when I got out at the other end. He suggested I just came in on a Monday and a Friday and I wasn't about to complain. Jimmy also intended to drop me for away games, which I presumed meant I could see more of my kids Dayna and Kevin. But in echoing Arthur Cox before him, he said he still wanted me to come on the team bus to keep the boys amused. I did it for a few weeks when we had trips down south. But I rapidly tired of hanging around in service stations for the team bus, like a circus entertainer waiting for his turn in the Big Top. All I needed was some oversized shoes and an exploding car. It wasn't what I wanted.

What I did want to sort out was my tangled personal life. Things came to a head when June and I had a final showdown in the Family Court at Derby Magistrates at the end of March. She was already getting £168 off me a week through the CSA but was applying to the court for more. The money came off my £600 a week salary before I was taxed and left me with just over £200 a week for my rent in Shardlow where I was staying with Heidi, food and petrol to and from Burnley. I was losing money every week. We'd also sold the family home for £68,000 four years after buying it in the boom for £70,000 and spending £15,000 doing it up. Things got off to a bad start when her smug-faced solicitor revealed to the court that I hadn't declared a non-contribution PFA pension, which had accumulated £23,000. She then asked the court if she could examine my dad's will to see if he had left me any money. June later admitted that she hadn't been responsible for the move, but I felt sick in the pit of my stomach when I heard the request.

The upshot of the two-day proceedings, which cost me £12,000 in solicitor's fees, was that I had to pay an extra £20 a week to June. A date was set in May for another hearing at Chesterfield Magistrates Court, when it would be decided what assets of mine she could get her claws into. My solicitor Peter Hare and I adjourned to a small room outside the court and I told him there wasn't a cat in hell's chance that I'd be at Chesterfield.

'That would look very bad, Ted,' he said in grave tones. 'In fact the judge would probably find against you straight away. It would be far better to be there to put up a fight.'

'I've no fight left,' I replied. 'And besides, I'm going to Australia.'

I'd begun hatching the plan a couple of weeks earlier. As my life was falling apart on the pitch, Burnley's was going nowhere fast on it. Jimmy Mullen had left the club following growing discontent among the faithful and four successive defeats in January. Clive Middlemass had taken over as caretaker, before Adrian Heath returned to Turf Moor. I got on well with Adrian and had a frank conversation with him a couple of days after he got his feet under the table. I'd played very few games during that season, most of which we'd lost. But the defeats no longer hurt. I was the first one in the shower, the first in his car and, due to the distance I had to drive, always the last one home. The hours behind the wheel were doing nothing to help my dodgy knee, which was only allowing me to play from time to time anyway. Heath told me to think about it but I'd made up my mind that I wanted out of my contract and away from English football. Secretary Mark Blackbourne said he had a couple of contacts in Australia, including former Everton player Mick Lyons who was managing in Canberra.

A couple of nights later the phone began to ring and I took a number of late-night calls from clubs across Australia. The most promising was from a Geordie called Paul Simmons, who managed a team called Joondalup City near Perth. He said they could pay me A$275 a week and would sort out a car and work for me if I fancied joining them. I had no idea what the exchange rate was, but signed up there and then. Paul said he'd pay for the flight after I had to tell him I didn't have any money and I went into a travel firm the following day to make some enquiries. The lad behind the desk must have thought I'd robbed a bank when I told him that a flight that night would be fine. There was one leaving from Heathrow to Perth at 10 p.m. and I booked it there and then.

The next job was to free up some money. The only saleable asset I had was my old Vauxhall Carlton. I took it to a local garage with my mate John Timmins where it was checked over by a sceptical mechanic, worried why two dodgy-looking blokes were keen on a quick sale. I'd taken the clock off the car in an attempt to save some mileage on the long drive to Burnley every day. John hastily reconnected it whilst I distracted the garage owner and he eventually agreed to buy it for £1200. It was worth more but I was in no position to argue. The snag was he didn't have the money on him and said he'd get it to me in the next few days. That was no good to me so I had to leave it to John to sell the car and send the money out to Australia later.

Before leaving Derby I went to the Baseball Ground to say goodbye to some old friends. The first person I saw was one of the club's secretaries, Marian Taylor. I'd known Marian for nearly ten years having met her on the first day I signed for Derby. We'd become very good friends over the years and she was upset that I was leaving. She'd always been a great help and had always sorted out my contracts and bills, when my own inadequacy had found me wanting. I couldn't help but feel that I might have been in a much better position if I'd married a woman like her rather than the three I had. She certainly made sure I was in a better position financially. Whilst I was saying my goodbyes to other people, she nipped out to the bank and returned with an envelope containing £500. She stressed that it was a loan, but smiled sympathetically when she said she didn't care when I gave it back. I felt terrible taking the money, but I didn't really have any other option. I'd arrived at the Baseball Ground full of optimism, looking forward to the future. I left it eight years later like a thief in the night.

John also gave me a couple of hundred quid when he drove me down to Heathrow in the pouring rain that evening, my mood every bit as black as the weather. I shook his hand and checked in all my worldly goods at the Quantas desk. They consisted of two holdalls containing a toilet bag, some spare clothes and several old pairs of football boots. Unlike most people boarding the busy flight, I had no intention of ever setting foot in Britain again if I could help it. I knew full well that that probably meant I'd never see my kids again. But I don't remember that being a particularly difficult decision to take. It was desperately sad, but there was nothing other than them keeping me in Britain. They'd be much better off with their mother after the court case had left me on my knees. What use to Dayna and Kevin was a washed up footballer with little money and fewer prospects? Apart from the other side of the world, I had no idea where my life was going.

18

THE TIN MAN MAKES IT TO OZ

Paul Simmons is the only bloke who's ever said I looked like a footballer. Throughout my career people poked fun at my hunched shoulders, skinny arms and unorthodox running style. I was proud of being called The Tin Man but it's hardly the most complimentary of nicknames. Paul said he recognised me when I staggered through customs at Perth Airport on April 3rd 1996, because I was 'every inch the sportsman'. He could have said anything in all honesty as it was 4 a.m. and I was knackered, having not been to bed for the best part of two days. He was bright as a button and his enthusiastic greeting went some way to easing my apprehension. I had no idea who I was meeting, where I was going or where I'd be staying. All I had was a scrap of paper with a telephone number on. I'd rung it between flights in Singapore and spoken to a bloke with a strong Geordie accent. Here he was, all six feet five inches of him, welcoming me to the Promised Land where my new life awaited.

That life was almost ended on a couple of occasions as we thundered up the Mitchell Freeway in the dark. Every couple of miles a kangaroo would hop out into the headlights prompting Paul to swerve or stamp on his brakes. I hadn't seen too many of them running around in Burnley, but the novelty quickly wore off. Paul, or Geordie as he preferred to be known, was more interested in selling Joondalup to me. It had a population of around 6,000 people and had been set up in the 1980s as neighbouring Perth spread its wings. The place was unusual in that it had the highest proportion of British-born residents in the whole of Australia. It was these people who'd set up and now played for the town's football club in West Coast Division One. I'd happily have had a more thorough history lesson had I not been so tired. But Geordie insisted he took me to the ground before I hit the hay.

From what I could make out in the headlights of his car, the Joondalup Arena was an oval with grassed banks and a solitary main stand. Summoning what enthusiasm I had, I asked him about attendances and was quietly impressed when he said they got around 'five' for the big games. I'd been used to playing in front of between ten and twenty thousand at Turf Moor and didn't think half that would be too bad. But when he said they averaged around 150 I quickly realised he meant hundred. It wasn't so much one man and his dog as one man and his kangaroo.

Geordie had emigrated to Australia in the early 1970s on a £10 boat ticket when the country was still welcoming immigrants with open arms. He'd been a policeman in Britain and had used his skills to set up a security firm on the other side of the world. His passion was Joondalup FC who he played centre forward for and managed. He was forty-five years old and looked it when the ball was at his feet. But he was dynamite in the air, using his height to score more than his fair share of headers. His enthusiasm was fantastic too and he was always first to lead the team in the club song after a victory. Apart from scoring headers, his forte was attracting sponsorship from local businesses. He used the money it brought in to pay the better players' wages. We'd agreed on the phone before I came out that my wage would be A$275. The pound was strong against the local currency but it was clear I was going to have to get a job to support myself. That was all very well, but I hadn't done anything other than kick a football for twenty years and didn't have a qualification to my name.

Geordie told me not to worry about money and invited me to stay at his house until I settled in. He lived with his wife Maureen and their two kids Greg and Danielle in a beautiful bungalow on Joondalup Golf Course. It had four or five bedrooms, a big snooker room and a swimming pool at the back that looked out onto the fairway. I'd arrived in Perth with the £800 in my pocket that John and Marian had given me and needed to start earning some money. Matters weren't helped when I managed to burn a hole in it buying my new team-mates a few beers on our first night out. We'd gone into Perth to see the sights and were getting on like a house on fire. But when midnight struck they rapidly cleared off leaving me drunk and on my own in the big city.

I managed to hail a taxi and asked him to take me to Joondalup Golf Course. As the driver pointed out, the town had two courses and the only thing I knew was that I lived on the fourteenth hole. He dropped me off outside the clubhouse of one and I staggered off as kangaroos skipped past me in the darkness. There were all sorts of weird noises coming from the rough and I began to fear for poisonous spiders and snakes. I'd been walking for about an hour when the ground suddenly gave way and I tumbled down a huge hole. After somersaulting to the bottom I came to rest in soft, wet sand and realised I was in a bunker. The face of it appeared steeper than Ben Nevis and it took me several goes to get out. When I finally did so I was covered in sand and mud and looked like I'd been washed up on a beach.

By chance I realised I was near Geordie's back fence and managed to clamber over. I got through the door after two or three attempts and walked up the white carpet to the kitchen. After fixing myself a late-night snack I then tried an airing cupboard, a bathroom and several other people's bedrooms before finding my own, where I crashed out face down on the bed. It felt like I'd just closed my eyes when a woman's voice screamed: 'Oh my God what a fucking mess!' I opened an eye and found Geordie at the foot of my bed. His house-proud wife had got up to discover a trail of sand and kangaroo shite in her home and was understandably pissed off. It was time to find some alternative accommodation.

I managed to do so, avoiding the bunkers, on another part of the golf course. It was a beautiful new apartment and expensive. But my teammates and people connected with the club were hugely generous in helping me out. Within a fortnight of moving in I had all the furniture, crockery and bed linen that I needed. The rent wasn't cheap but I'd also landed a job working for another exiled Brit called Barry Greenwood. Barry ran a company that installed air conditioning at hotels and big industrial units. Despite my work experience running to a couple of years in a sawmill, he was happy to take me on. When I turned up for my first day on site I was denied access because I wasn't a member of a union. They seemed unimpressed when I told them I was in the PFA and sent me away with a flea in my ear. Barry asked me what union I wanted to be in and quickly fixed me up with an ID card for the Association of Plumbers. I was then let back onto the site by the same bloke who'd stopped me in the first place. This is all above board then, I thought.

I was now a member of a union but I had no idea where Phillip was when Barry asked me to get his screwdriver. Barry was 100 feet up at the top of a raised platform at the time, drilling holes to attach the air-conditioning pipes to the ceiling. I had a quick rummage around in our toolbox before setting off to look for his mystery colleague. The first bloke I stopped was called John and didn't know who he was and the second guy just shook his head. I carried on in a similar vein for five minutes before Barry shouted down from the platform to ask me what I was doing. He didn't know whether to laugh or cry when I told him that I couldn't lay my hands on his mate or his screwdriver. But he quickly gave me a crash course in tools, showing me the difference between a Phillips screwdriver and a normal one and leaving me in doubt that anyone could own a Stanley knife.

If working for a living was proving tough, the football most certainly wasn't. Our first game was on the Saturday after I arrived, against a Perth team called Queen's Park. The name had a familiar ring to it from my days playing in Scotland, but the standard left a little to be desired. I've always thought that real-life football is very difficult to replicate in films. No matter how skilful the actors involved, the action always looks wooden. I can only think that the worst directors model their scenes on Queen's Park players, who threw themselves around like they were in Roy of the Rovers. I was passed the ball in the first minute and, without doing anything fancy, set off in a straight line. Numerous defenders lunged about comically as I proceeded towards the goal. I got to the byeline, crossed the ball and watched as it was headed home. A couple of spectators in the sixty or seventy-strong crowd were heard to shout 'that's why we bought him'. It dawned on me that I might just have travelled to the other side of the earth to play pub football.

We ended up winning the first game 4-2 and I never really broke sweat. I didn't in any of the games as we went through the season as the standard didn't improve. We were playing in the First Division, which was one below the Premier League. That in turn was one below the Australian National League. But we could never have progressed even if we had been good enough, as Western Australia was only allowed one representative and that was Perth Glory. The games came thick and fast and we kept winning them. We'd train on Tuesdays and Thursdays, using the streetlights as floodlights, and play our games on a Saturday. We beat all of the teams in our area including Armadale, Sorrento, Freemantle and Rockingham.

Rockingham were trained by a Scottish manager, who clearly had it in for me from the moment we arrived at their ground. I heard him call me a big-time Charlie and noticed he'd put a huge aboriginal guy to man mark me. I knew I was in a game when he kicked me three or four times in the first ten minutes. Geordie, who wasn't the most politically correct, had told me that the best way to wind Aborigines up for some reason was to say that they had 'blow job breath'. I tried this during the first half and he went mad, chasing me over the fence and into the car park. We then spent a minute or two dodging between cars as I apologised and he put me straight on the various child abuse scandals that had afflicted his people.

I was more sensitive with my sledging after that, but still got my fair share of whacks from the opposition. Most of them tried to man mark me and I got little or no protection from the referees, many of whom were used to the rough and tumble of Aussie Rules. I was booked for retaliation during one of the last games of the season after my frustration got the better of me. We were drawing 0-0 and needed to win to confirm our place at the top of the league. With five minutes to go I collected the ball on the left, cut inside and thumped one with my left foot from outside the area. Remarkably it sailed into the net and I ran off to celebrate, hurdling the barrier and jumping into the crowd. As I went to retake my place on the pitch I saw the referee reach for his cards to send me off.

I was desperate to win the player of the season award, which was voted for by the refs and linesmen. If you got sent off at all during the campaign you were disqualified. After much pleading he took sympathy on me and decided to book our captain John Peacock instead. If only life had been as easy as that back in Britain! John, who was a centre half with a nose like Steve Bruce, was one of the better players in the team. We also had a Scottish lad called Joe Sweeney who'd played amateur football back home. Together we held the rest of them together and with Geordie grabbing header after header we won the league at a canter.

The league ended in September and with it went my additional income. I was under the impression that I'd be paid throughout the year, but it turned out the club could only afford my salary when we were playing and they themselves were earning revenue. I didn't complain too much as the people had been very welcoming since I'd arrived in the country and couldn't do enough for me. The lack of funds showed itself in other ways, however, which did nothing to disabuse me of the idea that the club wasn't much more than a glorified pub team.

Geordie had promised me a car when I'd spoken to him initially in the UK, but after a couple of weeks nothing had materialised. When I made some polite enquiries it turned out that they were waiting to get it back from a former player called Ritchie Watson. I'd been promised a pretty smart piece of kit which would help me get to and from the matches and training and was surprised when a royal blue mark one Escort dating back to 1970 turned up. The leather upholstery had seen better days and it appeared not to have any windows in the back. The one in the front on the driver's side dropped down into the door cavity when you touched the handle, the windscreen wipers were temperamental and the petrol gauge didn't work. Out of sheer embarrassment I used to park it about a mile from the ground when I went for training and made sure I never gave any of the other players a lift. The dodgy gauge did for me one evening when it ran out of petrol and I had to trudge back from training in the rain. David Beckham and his fleet of luxury cars it was not.

My lack of wages meant I had to live on the A$600 a week salary that I got from the air conditioning firm. Help was at hand, however, when Barry got a contract to do some work in the Aborigine township of Pannawonica. The settlement, which was an iron ore mining town, was a twenty-four-hour drive away from Joondalup. Barry compensated me and another guy by paying us A$1800 a week. The work was simple enough when we got there. Rather than fitting air conditioning units we were insulating flat-pack housing, which had been assembled for the miners. It would have been easy enough to do were it not for the forty-degree heat, which stopped us working for several hours during the day. It was so hot that you'd burn your hands on the tools even if you wore gloves and we spent large parts of the day in the town's one tavern staying out of the sun. The living quarters round the back were spartan to say the least, with each room containing just a single bed and a wash hand basin. We were supposed to be there for five weeks but I stuck it out for two days. Barry was good enough to take me to a local airport to fly back to Perth but his parting shot left me in no doubt that I wouldn't be working for him again.

The main reason for chucking in the job was not the working conditions, which I could have coped with, but a telephone call I received on my second night. Heidi had come out with Mitchell and Jordan and had been living with me in Joondalup. At first everything had been fine and it was great to have some company. But she rapidly got bored of hanging around the house all day waiting for me to come home from work and we'd had some blazing rows. She called me when I was in Pannawonica and told me that she'd packed her bags and was catching a flight back to the UK. She would have had to have left at some point as she was only on a three month tourist visa. Yet I wasn't expecting her to just walk out. I wasn't expecting the note she left either in which she told me to stay out of her life and those of the kids. Her parting shot was a A$1,000 phone bill which arrived in the post a few days later after she worked out how to remove the block on international calls on the house phone.

I managed to find a job at another air conditioning firm in Perth but was beginning to get quite homesick. Much to my shame, I hadn't spoken to Dayna or Kevin since I'd left the UK nine months ago. I'd penned a letter during my first week in Australia, trying to explain why I'd left. It was the most difficult thing I'd ever written but I ended up chickening out and telling them that their mother and I no longer loved each other and I'd be able to tell them why when they were old enough to understand. I reasoned that they'd be better off being looked after by their mum rather than me, who didn't have an awful lot to give them. I'm embarrassed to admit it now, but I didn't even get in touch with them over Christmas or send them a card. At the time I'd convinced myself that it would be too upsetting to hear from me again. It was also my way of insulating myself against the pain I felt at having messed the whole thing up. I was the little boy again sitting on the stairs as my Dad walked out the door.

Christmas was made easier by the fact I'd persuaded Sue Hanson to come out to Australia and spend it with me. We got on well and enjoyed each other's company. But the homesickness returned when she had to go back to England in January. The football season wasn't far away and I had some decisions to make about my future. Helping Joondalup win promotion was the worst thing I could have done ironically, as they would start the new season in the Premier League. In order to take part in it players had to be resident in Australia and not on a one-year permit like me. Geordie was keen to keep me and organised various forms from the Australian Home Office, which ended up costing me A$400. While I was jumping through the hoops, I was also approached to play for Sorrento. They were now in the Premier League too and managed by Trevor Morgan, who had signed me when he was in charge of Birmingham.

The decision about who to sign for or whether to sign at all was taken out of my hands by the bureaucrats. They told me that if I wanted to take up residency I'd have to get letters from all my previous employers and put together a resumé of my career, including videos of me in action. They would issue me with another year's extension, but at the end of the process there would be no guarantee I'd be given leave to stay. There was no appeal process either, it was take it or leave it. Trevor and Geordie both wanted me to stay and apart from the home-sickness, I was enjoying much of my life in Australia. But then I walked into a Singapore Airline office on spec one day and discovered I could leave within seven days under the conditions of my return ticket. After a day to think about it, I booked my flight. Almost a year to the day after I left the UK forever, I was going home.

19

AN INSPECTOR CALLS

I arrived back in Britain as unprepared for life as when I'd left it. Carrying the same holdall and possessions I'd emigrated with a year previously, I wandered through customs in my light summer clothes and was frozen stiff by the February frost. I wasn't in it for long fortunately, as Sue had agreed to pick me up and take me back to her flat in the South Woodford area of London. I didn't really know what I was going to do with myself when I got there. But after a couple of days pottering about, her Dad offered me some work at his company.

The firm he ran unblocked people's drains and he'd been looking for an extra pair of hands for a while. My job was to clean out the pipes with a series of poles and if that didn't work, a high-powered hose. I'd played at a few dives during my career, but they were all paradise in comparison with some of the sights I witnessed when I opened those manhole covers. The stench was often unbearable. After spending just two days staring at the capital's crap, I decided I'd give my playing career one last try. I might not be Premier League material anymore, but I could still do a turn for somebody at non-league level. And I'd play at any old toilet if it meant I didn't have to stick my head down someone else's.

I printed up my CV and sent it off to a number of clubs in the south east, operating at Conference level or below. The first people to get back to me were Enfield Town. They were making heavy weather of it in the Isthmian League but I was quietly impressed with their Southbury Road Ground, which was just along the North Circular from Sue's flat. Manager George Borg was a really nice guy and sold the club to me as an ideal opportunity for both of us. I was about to sign on the dotted line when I got a call from Vauxhall Conference side Slough Town.

Manager Brian McDermott was also persuasive and he offered me a deal that ran until the end of the present season and another year after that. He could also find me £325 a week and a car as a signing-on fee. The fact that they played at a higher level was a major factor in my decision to join them. But I won't pretend that the money and the car didn't play a big part too. A couple of years previously, Jim Jefferies had offered me a similar amount at Hearts and there was no way I could accept. After being left almost penniless by the Child Support Agency and the divorce courts I was more than happy to take it now.

In a now familiar rerun of my experience in Joondalup, my company car turned out to be rather less than I'd hoped. I hadn't been expecting a Ferrari but, like its new owner, the battered 1.6 litre Ford Sierra that I was presented with had seen better days. It appeared to be taxed but I didn't ask any questions about an MOT or insurance. It got me up to my first match at Telford, however, when we took on the team several places above us in the table. I played in central midfield and was quietly impressed with both the pace and the level of skill on display. I tired towards the end but not before I'd helped us to our first victory in the league since mid-November.

The team was a mixture of old stagers like myself coming

down the leagues and promising youngsters hoping to travel in the other direction. The centre forwards Gary Brazil and Gary Abbott were good lads who knew their trade and we seemed plenty solid enough in midfield and at the back. I also caught glimpses in training of a talented teenager called Lloyd Owusu, who would go on to make a name for himself at Brentford and Sheffield Wednesday before injury ruled him out of playing for Ghana in the 2006 World Cup. But as I was to find out in the coming weeks, there wasn't an awful lot of strength in depth.

On the Wednesday after the Telford game we took on local rivals Wycombe Wanderers who edged a ding-dong affair 3-2 with the winner scored by Aaron Patton, who would go on to join Slough. We were then put in our place by Hayes who triumphed 3-1 at Wexham Park before three draws on the bounce against Southport, Bath and Dover. We only had three fixtures in April, which suited me as my knee was beginning to give me grief again. I'd be fine in the first half and feel raring to go after a rest at the interval. But halfway through the second period, it began to ache and I'd slow down considerably. Age was also beginning to catch up with me and I found it harder to get my breath after a run. We won one, drew one and lost one before closing the campaign with a 2-2 draw that would have been a 2-1 win but for a dodgy penalty decision. The team finished in sixteenth place, four places but only three points above relegation. It hadn't been the most glorious of seasons but we'd avoided the drop and I'd proved to myself that I could still play at a reasonable level.

At the end of May 1997 it was decided that it was high time that I got married again. I'd been living with Sue since mid-February and things were going pretty well. The only real source of tension was my trips to see Dayna and Kevin in Scotland and their infrequent visits to London. I think Sue may have been envious of the other family I had and it was difficult for her taking in someone else's children. She said she wanted children of her own in the near future and the best environment to bring them up in was a marriage. I didn't disagree with her, but I can't say I was any more enthusiastic about tying the knot than I had been on the previous two occasions. I'd had two marriages that had lasted months; I didn't see the third one being any different.

In a spooky repetition of my wedding to June, my knee played up again just before the big day. Last time it had been a blood clot, this time it just locked up as I got off the sofa. Sue was at work so I got a taxi to Whipps Cross Hospital in Leytonstone. It felt like someone had put a clamp on the knee and I was struggling to bend it. After a cursory look in the A&E department they told me to come back the following day, when a specialist would conduct a proper examination. After a couple of X-rays he carried out some keyhole surgery under local anaesthetic. The surgeon said I had several bits of bone and old cartilage floating around in my knee, which had made it swell up and refuse to bend. After half an hour of poking about he put an enormous bandage on it and I hobbled out of the hospital on crutches looking like Mr Bump out of the Mr Men. I was still wearing the bandage under my kilt when Sue and I did the deed on 31 May at Chigwell Register office. I had some friends down from Derby and her family came over from Ireland. My brother Mitchell performed the best man duties with 'third time lucky' jokes to the fore. After a reception at a nearby banqueting suite we went back to Sue's flat. Fortunately there was no repeat of June's threat to clean me out if I did the dirty on her. But there wouldn't have been any point as there wasn't an awful lot to clean out.

After a week honeymooning in Dublin and Belfast, I was raring to get back for pre-season training at Slough. But from the minute I pulled on my boots that July, I felt miles behind the others. I lagged behind on the long distance runs and was off the pace in the sprints. I could see the look in the eyes of the youngsters, ranging in varying degrees from pity to contempt. It was the same look I'd had when I was their age. I refused to believe that my legs had gone but with the knee swelling up after every training session it was clear they were on their way.

As I had done throughout my career when I was looking for guidance, I phoned up Gordon Guthrie at Derby and asked him what he thought I should do. He suggested I go up to the DRI and he booked me an appointment with Mr Cargill, who had performed the original operation back in November 1989. He gave me a local anaesthetic and had a root about in my knee with a keyhole camera. He then took off his gloves and with a little sigh delivered a short and sweet assessment: 'It's done Ted. I'm afraid you're finished.'

It wasn't the body blow I'd expected it to be. Some players say it's the worst day of their lives when they're told their career is over. But I'd been expecting the verdict for years now. Mr Cargill said I'd done amazingly well to get this far. When he'd first opened me up ten years ago he'd seriously wondered if I'd ever walk properly again, let alone play professional football. But after fourteen dark months on the sidelines I'd resurrected my career at Derby, before playing at Birmingham, Burnley, Joondalup and Slough. It wasn't half bad considering that the knee often felt and sounded like a bag of old washers.

As I clambered into the car in the DRI car park and made my way to the M1, I passed Derby's brand new Pride Park stadium, shimmering in the summer sunshine. It was a far cry from the old Baseball Ground where I'd played and signalled the dawning of a new era for both the club and the city. A new era was dawning for me too, one in which I would no longer be a professional footballer.

I'd last grafted for a living in a sawmill in Dumfries fifteen years ago. I wasn't sure what a thirty-five-year-old former footballer did if he didn't play football. The answer, as I discovered in the local free paper in South Woodford, was security work. There was a firm near the tube station who were looking for staff to work on a contract they had in London and Hertfordshire. I presented myself in a suit and tie and handed over my CV. Despite my lack of references and experience he took me on and talked me through what I'd be doing on my twelve-hour shift for £5 an hour. The job involved driving round a number of old hospitals in Waltham Abbey, St Albans and then down to Hammersmith, checking they were all secure. To make sure you weren't parked up in a lay-by or skiving off, you were given a data-strip gun, which recorded your presence at each site. I soon realised there wasn't an awful lot of checking that went on and it was a question of jumping out of the van, zapping the data strip and driving off to your next venue. It was mind-numbingly dull, but it paid a wage.

Many of the hospitals were deserted or in the process of being renovated, whilst others still had a full complement of patients. A lot of them were secure health units and contained some pretty dangerous inhabitants. I remember getting out of the van on one occasion to find a resident running round the grounds in a pair of pyjama bottoms. I could see in the moonlight that he was bare-chested and had nothing on his feet, but he didn't seem to notice the heavy frost. He was too busy dancing around an imaginary boxing ring, delivering jabs and upper cuts to a title challenger. For all he knew he was top of the bill at Madison Square Garden. The sweat was dripping off him as the crowd roared him on and the camera shutters clicked. For all I knew, I was his next opponent and he looked a little too handy for my liking.

A day or two later I checked out another place and noticed one of the windows was smashed. I phoned the office and they sent out another guy to help me investigate. We found the keys to the place and made our way inside, him with a crowbar and me with a heavy torch. In the first room we came to we found a stack of old Derby County programmes. More bizarre still was the fact that the top one on the pile had a picture of me on the cover, from when I made my home debut against Manchester United. Freaked out by our discovery, we made our way to another room at the back of the building. We pushed the door and it swung back straight away as if someone or something was behind it. I told my colleague that we should leave, but he pushed at the door again and was confronted by a ghostly figure clutching a syringe. He lunged at him as I turned on my heels and ran as fast as I could. When I realised he hadn't followed me, I came back up the stairs shaking like a leaf. It turned out that the guy was a former hospital porter, who was squatting in his old accommodation having been made homeless. He'd fallen on hard times and had become a junkie. I felt sorry for the guy after we sorted him out and gave him two weeks to find somewhere else to stay. But I told the boss after just over a fortnight that I'd had enough of the job. I needed the money but not so much that

I was prepared to have junkies charging at me with hypodermic needles.

I figured that my best chance of finding a job was to go back to Scotland and see if there was anything about in Junior Football. Sue and I had not been getting on and she was particularly unhappy about the amount of time I was away from home. With nothing to do in London I'd spend time up in Glasgow visiting Dayna and Kevin as well as looking in on old pals and family. I began going to watch my first club Glenafton again and fell in with the club's Chairman Jock Timpany. Jock was a local businessman who ran several companies when he wasn't watching Glens. One string to his bow was sportswear, which he used to flog to local teams at knock-down rates. He had a warehouse in New Cumnock but was looking to set up premises in the town, which he could use as a shop. I was interested in the idea and over a pint or two in the bar opposite the ground we cooked up a plan to set up a sports shop called McMinn Sports.

With the shop being the best opportunity to earn a living that I had, I told Sue that I would rent a place in Scotland and see her when I could. I don't think she was too bothered that we were drifting apart, having quickly discovered that my heart was not in our marriage. My heart was certainly in the new business however, and I traded in the old white Sierra I'd been given by Slough for a white van and rented a shop on the High Street. I'd known a few players who had sold sports gear during and after their playing days. Long before he became England manager, Steve McClaren used to sell kits and tracksuits to kids teams to top up his Derby County wages. And among others there was Frank Stapleton, who'd opened a few people's eyes to making a couple of quid with his suitcases full of sports gear. If they could do it, why couldn't I?

While I was busy setting up the shop and sourcing extra suppliers, Jock told me that Ayrshire side Kilwinning Rangers were looking for a new manager and suggested I went for it. They trained on Tuesday and Thursday nights and played on the Saturday. That suited me fine with the shop, so I sent in my CV. The chairman was another local businessman called Allan McLuckie, who'd earned a small fortune building up a technology firm called Fullarton Computer Industries in his native Irvine. Unlike the David Sullivans of this world, he had no desire to flaunt his wealth. Instead he preferred a pint with his old mates and went to watch his local team. He got me in for an interview and we got on like a house on fire, but I detected that he wanted someone with a little more managerial experience. I wasn't surprised therefore, when he gave the gig to a guy called Bobby Dickson.

Bobby had been working as a schoolteacher but had a wealth of knowledge at Junior level, having won the Scottish Cup five times with Auchinleck Talbot and Cumnock. I'd got down to the last three according to Alan and had just missed out. But after being told the bad news I received a phone call from Bobby asking me if I wanted to be his first-team coach. Former Kilmarnock player Jim Cockburn was going to be his assistant, but they needed someone who'd played at a good level to pass on some of their skills to the players. I was happy to help out and even happier when they promised me £50 a week for two training sessions. The arrangement worked well, with the two of them selecting the team and talking tactics on a Saturday and me putting them through their paces during the week. They were a responsive lot who were willing to learn and I struck up a good relationship with them straight away.

Things weren't going quite so well at McMinn Sports

unfortunately, where business wasn't exactly booming. We'd have days where we'd sell a couple of hundred pounds worth of sports gear and think we were getting somewhere. Far more frequently however, the shop would be deserted for hours on end and I'd be left twiddling my thumbs. We sometimes didn't sell anything at all. I suggested to Jock that we reduce the price on some of the gear in a bid to shift it. But we couldn't agree on profit margins and the whole business started to become hard work. I did my best to source cheaper and cheaper stock and would often drive to wholesalers as far away as Kidderminster and Bradford. I even began hawking kits round schools in Glasgow, using my name to try to make a sale.

We got the distinct impression that a lot of clothing was far from kosher and much of it could be described as falling off the back of a lorry. There were Lacoste T-shirts, Fila tracksuits and Timberland leisurewear that Stapelton would have been proud to call his own. We even began knocking out Armani and Versace T-shirts at ridiculously low prices. The real ones were selling for £80 or £90 in London and Edinburgh and we were shifting ours for a tenner. We were prepared to turn a blind eye and ask very few questions to make a few quid. 'You get what you pay for' became the company motto.

The chickens came home to roost just before Christmas 1998 when we were paid a visit by trading standards. They got a tip-off from a guy we'd supplied, who got himself out of trouble by telling them that all the stuff came from McMinn Sports. We had a number of runners called bagmen, who would buy stock from us at a certain price and then sell it in pubs and clubs at a profit. We sold the gear under the strict condition that they never revealed to anyone where they got it.

This guy broke rank when confronted by men from the council

and blabbed our details. In fairness to him he phoned us up to tell us they were on their way and we had five frantic minutes to get rid of as much stuff as we could. After running around like the Keystone Cops we got most of it loaded into the van, which Jock drove away as they pulled up at the front of the shop. Bright red in the face and with sweat on my brow, I then tried to pass the time of day with them as they inspected the bare shelves of the shop like members of the Gestapo. One of the few items of clothing left were some tracksuit trousers, which we'd bought in good faith believing them to be genuine. But our efforts to pull the wool over their eyes backfired when they analysed the cotton content and reported back a couple of weeks later that it didn't match the care label. They had reason to believe they were fake.

We took the £50 fine and the warning that followed in our stride and vowed to keep our noses clean in future. The fine amounted to one week's wages at Kilwinning and with the way things were going we were hoping we might get a good bonus for our performances. It was clear when I took over coaching responsibilities that we had the basis of a good team. Stuart Robertson was solid in goal, there was experience in defence and midfield and goals galore from Norman Montgomerie, Alan McTurk and Gerry Peline up front. We tasted success early in the season when we beat Auchinleck Talbot 2-1 to win the Ayrshire League Cup on October 5th. Talbot were leading 1-0 at the interval, but contrived to have three men sent off in the second half and McTurk scored the winner in extra time. Five days later we played our first game in the Scottish Junior Cup, earning a draw at Port Glasgow before beating them 4-0 at our Abbey Park ground in the replay. We then stuffed Strathspey Thistle 7-0 in the second round,

Troon 3-2 in the third round, Whitburn 1-0 in the fourth round and Stoneywood 3-0 in the fifth round. In between the last game and our sixth round meeting with Auchinleck Talbot we beat Annbank United 13-0, equalling a record set by the club in 1901. A crowd of 3,500 watched us concede a goal against the Talbot in the first minute and then have McTurk sent off. But we clawed our way back into it when Jim Duffy scored a header from a free kick ten minutes before halftime. Against all expectation, we won the replay 1-0 in front of the STV cameras and booked a place in the semi-finals at St Mirren's Love Street ground against Arthurlie.

Disaster struck before I could get there when I was left in charge of the team for our visit to Largs Thistle in the league. Bobby was away but had picked the team before he left and given me instructions. As the game progressed, it became clear that our right midfielder Jimmy Duffy was having a stinker. I was annoyed by his performance and hauled him off. He hadn't put a decent shift in like the rest of the team. As he came towards the bench he asked me why I'd taken him off and in the heat of the moment I told him it was because he was a 'lazy bastard'. He replied that I was a useless so and so who didn't know what the fuck I was doing. Jimmy's outburst was caught by all the subs on the bench and a good few people in the crowd. I was still angry after the match and told Allan McLuckie that I was resigning. He tried to persuade me to stay but I argued that I couldn't have players talking to me like that. Had I let him get away with it, the others would have known I was a soft touch.

As I drove home to my flat in Maybole that evening I knew I'd made a mistake. I was enjoying it at Kilwinning and it was great to be at a successful club, who were on the verge of winning things. But I couldn't have the players treating me with contempt. I'd never spoken to a manager like that during my career and didn't expect it now. Had I ignored Jimmy's comments I would have looked weak and easy to undermine. We could easily have resolved the issue if common sense had prevailed. But despite Jimmy phoning up to apologise and Bobby trying to persuade me to stay, I cut my nose off to spite my face and walked out.

It was a crying shame. The Buffs went on to become the most successful team in the history of Junior football that season, winning the West of Scotland Cup, the Ayrshire District Cup and Ayrshire Cup. The only one they lost was the North Ayrshire Cup when they went out to Kilbirnie Ladeside in the semi-final. Between May and June the club played an incredible twenty games in forty-nine days and lost only one league game all season. The big one was the Scottish Junior Cup, which the club hadn't won since 1909.

They reached the final against Kelty Hearts by beating Arthurlie 1-0. Despite leaving the club I went back to see them contest the final at Firhill. The atmosphere was incredible inside the ground, with over 6,000 making their way up to Glasgow from Ayrshire. Gerry Peline scrambled the ball into the back of Hearts' net in the third minute and the team managed to hang on for the rest of the ninety minutes to lift the trophy. People were very complimentary to me at the game and said that my coaching had been the real reason for the club's success. But I thought that did a grave disservice to Bobby, who had done a fantastic job in managing them. Sadly he couldn't repeat his success the following season and was unceremoniously fired.

A week after walking out on Kilwinning I pulled the plug on McMinn Sports too. Jock and I were disagreeing on too many issues and business had fallen off a cliff. I was also concerned about getting into trouble with the police for selling dodgy gear so I just walked out. Like the Australian one before it, my Scottish adventure had come to a swift and unexpected conclusion. I returned to London like a bedraggled Dick Whittington, minus the cat. Sue felt sorry for me and took me in again, pledging to give our marriage one last try. I promised to look for work and applied to a number of local clubs including Leyton to see if they needed an extra pair of hands on their coaching staff. None replied and I began to get depressed about my prospects as an unemployable ex-footballer. Seeing my kids became a source of tension again with Sue desperate to have her own. With two that I saw and two others that I didn't, I had no desire to have any more and told her so.

The emotional high-water mark was reached, as it often is, at Christmas. I wanted to spend it with Dayna and Kevin and she wanted to spend it with her family. With no compromise reached we spent it alone in the flat instead, with party hats and cheap champagne serving as the fig leaf to our failing marriage. This continued for a couple of days with the atmosphere getting worse and worse. By the morning of the 28 December I'd had enough and told her I was going out for a paper. When I returned to the flat an hour later there were two holdalls containing my clothes on the landing. She'd locked herself in and, by the tone of the conversation we had through the letterbox, had no intention of coming out. There was no way I was getting in either and I was told to sling my hook.

I had £60 in my wallet and some loose change in my pocket. Walking out into the chilly December air again, I didn't have much of a clue where to go. I knew very few people in London having never really settled in and what mates I had were all in Derby. I went to a cab rank near the station, woke a guy who was sleeping off his Christmas dinner and asked him how far north I could get with the money I had. After giving me a funny look and doing a bit of haggling he agreed to take me to Toddington Services on the M1 near Luton. We pulled out of South Woodford as Mud's 'Lonely This Christmas' came on the radio and I couldn't help but smile at the irony. The cabbie dumped me at Toddington, relieved me of my money and wished me a Happy New Year before speeding back to London.

As the drizzle began to descend, I rang a friend in Derby who kindly agreed to pick me up. I also phoned my old friend Marian Taylor at the club and she got me a ticket for that afternoon's match against Middlesbrough. The Rams won 2-1 in front of a full house thanks to goals from Dean Sturridge and Jonathan Hunt. But with no house to go to myself I was as miserable as the visiting Boro fans, who had a long trip back to the north east. Christ, even Mary and Joseph had a stable.

20

KINGS OF THE KASSAM

For one reason or another I've never mixed in the same circles as Joan Collins. She's probably heard of Dumfries, but I'd be surprised if she could find it on a map. I'd be even more surprised if she could find her way to Palmerston, Ibrox, the Baseball Ground or Turf Moor. But in marrying a number of people we really shouldn't have married, the two of us have plenty in common. Joan is now on her fifth husband and I'm on my fourth wife. She may yet make it a double hat-trick, but I've certainly no plans to make any further adjustments to the scoreboard. In finding Marian, I netted the winner a long time ago.

I spent the night after the 'Boro game curled up on her couch, fortified by endless cups of coffee. She'd driven me back to her house in the Oakwood area of Derby after I told her I had nowhere to stay. On the way we talked about Derby's victory that afternoon and anything other than my parlous position. But once the kettle had boiled, the main matter in hand was discussed in full. There were some harsh words, some sympathetic ones and plenty of tears in between. But we quickly reached the conclusion that I needed to sort my life out and I needed to do it pretty quickly. As the evening wore on our true feelings towards one another also came out.

Marian had always had a soft spot for me and I was very fond of her. She also knew all the ins and outs of my failed marriages, so there was nothing to hide. She was the one who picked up the pieces; who replied to the solicitor's letters and made sure my bills were paid. I'd been in relationships when she hadn't and on the rare occasions I was single, she'd been shacked up. But despite the fact she was seeing someone else at the time, we reached another conclusion that night; that it was high time we got together.

Stability was one thing, employment was another and I needed a job. I still nurtured ambitions to work within football and felt I had a lot to offer the game. But the days of making a seamless transition from player to manager were fading fast. Clubs were now looking for coaching certificates as well as past performances on the park. I decided to do my UEFA B licence and enrolled on a fast-track course at Aston Villa's training ground. It was run by Villa legend Dennis Mortimer, who'd captained the club to their European Cup triumph in 1982. He was a jovial Scouser who'd coached some of the top managers and I learnt a lot from him in a short space of time. Andy Townsend, who was then seeing out his playing days at Middlesbrough, and centre half David Linighan were also put through their paces and everyone rubbed along nicely. It was merely a question of repeating the drills you were shown, whilst they assessed how you communicated your ideas. Having never been short of something to say, it all came pretty easily to me.

Putting my new skills into practice proved somewhat tougher. But I kept my nose to the ground and applied for any positions that became vacant. Local sides Ilkeston Town and Belper Town were both looking for bosses and I sent in my CV, confident that I'd be in with a shout. I got down to the last three at Ilkeston but was pipped at the post by former Grimsby Town centre forward Keith Alexander. Lack of experience was given as the reason for my rejection, as it had been at Kilwinning. Chairman Paul Millership was honest enough to tell me that playing top-flight football was one thing, but managing at non-league level was quite another. I needed a better working knowledge of the scene. Despite pledging to work for nothing on a trial basis until the end of the season Belper turned me down too. Things were proving harder than I'd imagined.

My big break finally arrived when a job at Derby County's academy came up. Academy director John Peacock was looking for someone to help run the U15's team and his assistant Steve Taylor had put my name forward. Steve had cleaned my boots as an apprentice when I was at the Baseball Ground and I was now grateful that the boot was on the other foot. John was a highly respected coach and by the time he left Derby the club had fourteen youth internationals and three under-21 players on their books. He is now head of coaching at the FA and runs their U17's side. Darren Robinson, who went on to coach at Coventry, ran the U15's side and I fitted in quite nicely as his assistant. Darren was a great one for meetings and spent hour after hour planning our strategic approach. In truth, I didn't know what he was on about for the most part. But fortunately I managed to say yes at the right time on more occasions than not.

My strength was in dealing with kids and getting the best out of them. I empathised with them, having struggled to break into professional football myself. The hardest thing was knowing that the vast majority of them weren't going to make it. Unlike the academy scholars today, who are already driving around in fancy cars, all our lot had was ambition. In most cases it wouldn't be enough. Our job was not to turn out ready-made professionals but to spot the ones who had the potential to make it as a professional. There were a lot of talented players who gave their all at our training facilities at Repton School. But the criteria were very strict and inevitably most fell by the wayside. It's hard telling a youngster with a head full of dreams that he's not good enough, but a football club can be a harsh environment and there's a fine line between success and failure. Of the crop that we produced in my time there, only goalkeeper Lee Camp and centre forward Izale McLeod were eventually taken on.

After just a few months at the academy during the summer and autumn of 1999, I got a call from my old pal Mark Wright. He'd just taken his first step on the management ladder after being appointed at Vauxhall Conference side Southport. He hadn't moved from the area since his Liverpool days and the job was ideal for him. What suited him less was Paul Lodge, the assistant he'd inherited from his predecessor Paul Futcher. Wrighty didn't rate him and told Chairman Charlie Clapham that he wanted to bring in his own man. That man was me. We'd always said during our playing days at Derby that whoever went into management first would take the other with them. I felt guilty about leaving the academy, who'd helped me get back on my feet. But this was too good an opportunity to miss.

Southport had lost four on the bounce and were languishing in eighteenth place when we took over ahead of the home match against Northwich Victoria on 18 December. After ninety minutes we were down to twentieth following a solitary goal from Northwich midfielder Val Owen. Christmas wasn't coming early that year on the Wirrall. But we stopped the rot soon afterwards with five consecutive draws, three in the league and two in the FA Trophy, that saw us through on away goals against Altrincham. Our first win came against Hednesford at Haig Avenue, before three more draws followed in the league. We seemed to be saving our wins for the cup, seeing off both Wakefield and Emley & Woking in February. Robert Pell scored in both matches, but couldn't stop us finishing the month with two more reversals in the league.

Wrighty's answer to defeats was the old-fashioned hairdryer treatment. In the heat of the moment players would be called everything from a pig to a dog and threats were made to both their careers and lives. He didn't mean it, of course, he just hated losing as much as he did when he was a player. My job was to pick up the pieces and put an arm round the shoulders of the players he'd just savaged. Five minutes after he'd stormed off I'd have them laughing and joking again. It was classic good cop, bad cop stuff but it seemed to work.

For all his bluff and bluster, Wrighty put an awful lot of time into preparation and tactics. He worked very hard to bring a professional attitude to the club and concentrated on getting the minor details right. For an evening game I'd be told to get to his house for lunchtime so that we'd have enough time to cook up a plan of attack. His wife Sarah would bring us count-less cups of coffee as he then took me through flip-chart page after flip-chart page, highlighting formations, set pieces and predicted points totals. As I had at Derby's academy meetings, I developed an ability to nod in the right places.

We slipped out of the FA Trophy in March following a quarter-final replay to eventual winners Kingstonian. But five straight victories in the league took us up to twelfth. Striker Ian Arnold would hit fourteen Conference goals by the end of the season earning us points and him plaudits. Centre half Phil Bolland was the main man however, and the real reason why a point at Stevenage on the final day of the season gave the club its highest finish since 1996. His classy displays earned him both the players' and supporters' player of the year awards and reminded many of a young Mark Wright. It was clear he and I had inherited the basis of a reasonable side. But we wanted to kick on and were determined to get the club back into the league for the first time since they'd been voted out in 1978. It was clear we needed to invest.

Charlie Clapham was largely sympathetic and I'm sure he shared our ambitions. But at our regular meetings he began to wear the look of a father who knows his daughter's demands to join the pony club are going to be expensive. His reticence didn't stop us signing old warhorses Shaun Teale, David Linighan and Mike Marsh ahead of the 2000/01 season. Former Aston Villa man Teale, whose family was from the area, had reached the end of the road in the professional game after a distinguished career but wasn't yet ready to be put out to grass. Marsh had played with Wrighty at Liverpool and turned into a fantastic signing after arriving from Kidderminster. They'd been promoted to the league under Jan Molby, but Marsh was unable to play in the league. When he had been at Southend, his contract had been cancelled before it expired due to the poor state of his knees. Under the terms of the insurance payout, this meant that he was entitled to play at Conference level or below but could no longer play in the league. Their loss was most certainly our gain.

By Christmas we had cemented third place in the league and were well in the hunt for promotion. Unlike the high-earners Yeovil and Rushden, who filled the two places above us, we were still semi-pro. Wrighty had a budget of £2,500, which covered our wages and those of the eighteen players. Many of the lads were travelling large distances on match day and for training during the week. Ian Arnold commuted from Carlisle and long-serving goalkeeper Steve Dickinson was one of a number who came across from Bradford. We wanted to introduce stopovers in hotels for long-distance away games and occasionally got our way. But the benefits it brought to the players had to be balanced against the deficit in the budget, and as often as not the latter won. We had talented players on our books and had the potential to be a league club. A young Lee Trundle excited the crowd when we could get him to turn up – he was a notoriously poor timekeeper! – and Tunisian Dino Maamria added a touch of glamour. But the squad would need to be strengthened and Wrighty thought it was imperative that we went full-time.

Despite repeated appeals, Charlie thought otherwise. It was him that would have to stump up the cash or attract investment and he didn't think it was worth the gamble. The club was on a relatively even keel and with average crowds of around 1,300 I could see his point. Reaching for the stars was one thing, but ending up in the gutter if we fell was another. Wrighty disagreed and became increasingly frustrated at what he saw as a lack of ambition. Following a 1-1 draw with strugglers Forest Green Rovers in mid-February he vented his spleen to the media, claiming the result had all but ended our chance of promotion. He felt the big-money backers at rival clubs were polarising the league and felt let down by his own benefactor. He thought going full-time and the boost in personnel that would bring us would make the difference next season. But by the last day of the season, the assurances hadn't come. We lost

1-0 at home to Dagenham and Redbridge, who finished eight points ahead of us. As the players did their lap of honour to thank the supporters, he handed in his notice.

Wrighty's resignation was news to me and so was my own, which he tendered on my behalf at the same time. I'd probably have walked out with him had he consulted me as I shared some of his frustrations. But it would have been nice to be given some prior warning! What I didn't know was that he had other irons in the fire. On the Sunday after the game he drove down to London to meet Oxford United chairman Firoz Kassam. He was looking to replace David Kemp, who'd fallen foul of supporter unrest a couple of weeks earlier. Kassam, who'd been born in Tanzania to Indian parents, was building an impressive new stadium after buying the club for £1 and inheriting its £13 million debt. He'd made his fortune as a slum hotelier in London after starting off life running a fish and chip shop. Despite some people's doubts about him, Wrighty was impressed. So was Kassam and a deal was done. He'd been linked with the job the previous October, only for Southport to deny Oxford permission to speak to him. This time it was for real and at thirty-seven and thirty-eight respectively, we'd been handed the keys to our first league club.

I'm surprised Wrighty didn't have us in camouflage gear when he faced the press for the first time on 9 May. His tough-talking message was combative to say the least. We weren't going to tolerate indiscipline and we expected 100 per cent from the players 100 per cent of the time. Despite the fact they'd played their last game of the season, they were going to be recalled for an impromptu boot camp to assess their abilities. 'In any successful managerial partnership,' he went on, 'you have a good guy and a bad guy and, unfortunately for the players, I'm the bad guy.' The good guy, who thought he'd stumbled onto the set of a war movie, was me. But at least former boss Jim Smith was impressed. The Bald Eagle told the *Oxford Mail* that Wrighty was a 'superb appointment' and just the man to lead Oxford back up through the leagues.

Before we could do so, there were a lot of personnel changes to be made around the club. Wrighty was understandably keen to be his own boss and quickly dispensed with the services of football advisor and former gaffer Denis Smith, who ironically had recommended him to Kassam. He also brought defenders Phil Bolland and Scott Guyett from our old club Southport, as well as goalkeeper Ian McCaldon from Livingston and midfielders Dave Savage and Martin Thomas from Northampton and Swansea. We wanted a big-name signing to inspire the fans and enquired about Wrighty's former Liverpool teammate Neil Ruddock, who had just been released by Crystal Palace. Unfortunately Razor had let himself go a bit. He was the size of a small bungalow, which was no good to a new management team still laying the foundations. Instead we spent £150,000 on Barnet's right wing back Sam Stockley. To our eternal shame we bought him blind having never once seen him play. He'd been earning rave reviews from respected sources but we were taking a hell of a chance and it never really paid off.

That money had helped build an impressive 12,500 capacity stadium, which supporters were eager to fill. But it was also paying for the club's high earners, who were blocking our recruitment of fresh faces. The likes of Andy Scott, Phil Gray and Joey Beauchamp were all on long-term contracts and earning up to £1,500 a week. After deciding we no longer wanted them we tried to get rid, but clubs were reluctant to match their salaries. They didn't want to take a cut either and when Kassam refused to pay them off, we were stuck with them. Before the season even started, storm clouds began to gather. Things weren't helped by the fact that Wrighty's marriage was going through a sticky patch. On occasions he'd leave me to take charge of training and dash back up to Cheshire. The occasions usually coincided with a visit by the chairman, who became sceptical about the number of times his new manager was 'looking at a player' at 11 o'clock in the morning.

Despite or because of the fact we took the players away to a navy camp near Portsmouth, pre-season was pretty dreadful. We looked woefully short of quality, particularly up front. The opening fixture against Rochdale, who'd just missed out on a play-off place the previous season, was going to be tough. And so it proved when we lost 2-1 in front of nearly 8,000 expectant fans. We then drew 0-0 at Swansea, went out of the League Cup in unfortunate fashion against Gillingham and succumbed again to Shrewsbury. We had the best ground in the division and had contrived to lose our first three games there.

We finally got off the mark with a 2-0 Monday night win at Halifax. Scott and Gray both scored, before the former got himself sent off for two bookable offences. We then got the rub of the green against newly-promoted Rushden & Diamonds in a 3-2 win. The game was settled when referee Joe Ross sent off one of their players for a professional foul, which was no more than a shoulder-to-shoulder tackle. Afterwards, Wrighty felt sorry for our opponents and said he would consider any plans for the game to look at a 'third umpire'. His sympathy with officialdom, and Joe Ross in particular, wouldn't last for long.

The cracks really began to show with our 2-0 defeat at home to Macclesfield Town on 18 September. We were outfought and outplayed and managed just one shot on target in the ninety minutes. The supporters booed us off the park. We tried to win them back by signing centre forward Paul Moody from Millwall a few days later and he scored on his debut in a 2-0 win over Southend. Wrighty also made an audacious bid to convince our old pal Dean Saunders to come out of retirement to play for his old club. But he was happy coaching the forwards at Blackburn and had no desire to be kicked off the park in the lowest reaches of the league. It was an increasingly unhappy changing room. Two camps were forming; one with the new players we'd signed and one with the old players, who weren't keen on Wrighty's tactics or selection policy. Following the victory over Southend we failed to win any of our next five outings.

Things got even worse when we entertained Brian Law's Scunthorpe on 20 October. Both sides were concerned when Joe Ross was put in charge of the clash. I had previous with Ross after he'd sent me from the dugout at Telford when I was at Southport. I'd confronted him about it at halftime and had to be dragged away by Wrighty. I thought he was a shocking referee but he also got my goat driving round in a flash Mercedes with a personalised number plate. He booked Scott Guyett against Scunthorpe, which took him to five yellows and an automatic ban. But in the last five minutes he then sent off Paul Moody and Phil Bolland. Moody was said to have raised his hands to Scunthorpe's Peter Beagrie whilst a well-timed tackle from Bolly was judged to be recklessly late. Wrighty hit the roof and gave Ross both barrels from the touchline. Inevitably, he was given his marching orders too, but not before he'd given the ref another piece of his mind.

The steam was still coming out of Wrighty's ears at the post-match press conference. He admitted to reporters that he deserved to be sent off for the comments he'd made to 'that man'. But he went on to say that he didn't think he was fit to referee a kid's match. The remarks made a number of the newspapers the following day, as the spotlight was shone on the club's poor disciplinary record. It was only the middle of October and we'd already had eight men sent off, including one who was out on loan. Wrighty had become the ninth sinner and joined me in facing a touchline ban. I'd received my marching orders at Exeter following a fracas on the touchline with their manager Noel Blake. The bans came through on November 6th. I'd been fined a small amount and told to sit in the stand for two matches, whilst Wrighty was fined £1,750 and banned for four matches. He was charged under section E1 and E2 of the Football Association rules, which forbade the use of 'indecent, abusive and insulting language towards a match official.'

Wrighty didn't have a leg to stand on in truth, and was happy to take the rap. The problem was that the FA said the bans would run concurrently, meaning he and I would both be absent for the games against Leyton Orient and Cheltenham. We lined up reserve-team manager Mark Ford as a stand-in and appealed against the decision. We also appealed against the sendings off of Moody and Bolland during the Scunthorpe game. They saw sense on the touchline bans and also overturned Ross's decisions on the players. We were delighted with the result and pledged to keep our noses clean for the rest of the season, thinking the matter was now at an end.

Just when we thought we'd ridden out the storm, lightning struck on Sunday 18 November. The *Sunday People* newspaper carried an interview with Joe Ross claiming the FA was sweeping the bust-up under the carpet. Not only had he been abused, he claimed, he'd been racially abused. Now I don't know if

Wrighty called him a 'black bastard' or not, but I do know he didn't say it when I was in earshot. He wasn't in earshot of Brian Laws or the fourth official either, and both were standing next to me on the touchline as the incident unfolded. The paper made a big deal of Wrighty being a former England captain and sensationalised the story. It struck me that this was Ross's revenge for the FA chalking off his dismissals, as he must have felt undermined by his bosses. His timing was fantastic however; October 20th had been National Racial Awareness Day.

Wrighty took legal advice and was told to keep his mouth shut, but not before he vehemently denied the allegations in the *Oxford Mail* newspaper. Firoz Kassam had until now kept his counsel too. Yet the day after Wrighty's piece in the *Mail*, he told the paper he would sort the situation out. As well as the Scunthorpe incident he meant matters on the pitch, which had gone from bad to worse with our 3-0 defeat at Leyton Orient. The small band of Oxford fans who made the trip to the East End had sung 'stand up if you've had enough' and the ever-populist Kassam claimed he'd been tempted to join them. The following day, Thursday 22 November, Kassam suspended Wrighty on full pay. In a statement the club stressed it had everything to do with the events of October 20th and nothing to do with the fact we were twenty-first in the league and had been knocked out of both cup competitions in the first round. But hey, how convenient?

Wrighty asked me to come with him to the showdown talks with Kassam. I wouldn't be allowed in the office, but he positioned his BMW opposite the window so that I'd be able to see in from the passenger seat. Before he left the car he took a couple of deep breaths and told me: 'I've got to stay calm on this one Ted. Keep the head.' Less than five minutes after going into the office he was banging his folder on Kassam's desk and wagging his finger at him like Basil Fawlty. He then wrenched open the door and slammed it shut, before entering again momentarily for another bout of finger wagging. When he arrived back at the car a few minutes later he didn't seem to appreciate my comment that everything seemed to have gone according to plan. His only reply was: 'The chairman wants to see you.'

Kassam told me I was in charge of the first team until such times as Wrighty's position was made clear. I was to take training in the morning and then look after the game against Cheltenham at the weekend. I told Wrighty, who was as reluctant to hand over the reins as a jockey on a sure thing. Before he left to go back to Cheshire he picked the team, insisting that I stick with the 3-4-3 formation that hadn't been working. I was in no position to argue.

I did kick up a fuss, however, when the goalposts were moved the following morning. I was just trying out the big leather chair in the manager's office when there was a knock at the door. It was Ian Atkins, who'd been parachuted in overnight as our new director of football, and his agent. The latter asked me if I'd have a problem working with him and I told them straight out that I would. I'd been told that I was in charge and responsible for team selection. But here I was meeting my new boss. I began to feel that he and Kassam had hatched a plan to manoeuvre me out the door.

I drove straight to training and was confronted by the players, who were eager to know what was going on. I explained it to them as we did our warm-up and watched for their reaction. It was as mixed as I had expected, with some disappointed and some secretly pleased. There was nothing secret about it for the smiling Andy Scott, who had mysteriously declared himself fit after weeks on the treatment table.

'You'll be happy then Andy,' I said.

'Fucking delighted,' he replied.

I took a step towards him, thinking I'd spark him out and then something stopped me. I wasn't convinced I had enough supporters in the ranks and didn't know how many I'd be taking on. Phil Bolland later told me he'd have loved it if I'd thumped him and said he was right behind me. But I was less hot-headed than I used to be and concluded that discretion was the better part of valour.

By the time I got back to the stadium Wrighty had resigned. He had no desire to rake over the coals again and couldn't be bothered with the disciplinary process. Both of us thought that our poor form in the league would be held against him. The Ross debacle was just the excuse they needed and a cheap way of getting rid of him. I phoned Arthur Cox for some advice and he told me to stay put. But the prospect of working with Ian Atkins wasn't appealing. I sat on the bench as we thumped Cheltenham 3-0 on the Saturday.

Mick Ford, who was desperate to keep his job, was running round like a blue-arsed fly shouting 'yes boss', 'no boss' to Atkins. I didn't even take the warm-up and got straight in my car and drove home afterwards. I went in to see the club secretary on the Monday morning and said I'd be happy to take a six-month pay-off as I had eighteen months left on my contract. The chairman thought otherwise yet eventually offered me £5,000. It was half of what I'd asked for but he had me over a barrel. Barely six months after their coronation, the first kings of the Kassam had been dethroned.

21

SHOCK JOCK

Leaving Oxford was probably a blessing in disguise for both parties. We hadn't exactly been setting the heather on fire. Our record, which read played twenty-two, won four, lost eleven and drawn seven, was pretty bloody average in fact. People criticised our tactics and in particular the 3-4-3 formation Wrighty was so keen on. But the main problem we had was that we didn't have the players to play it. They were skilful enough – it's just that half the team weren't trying and we couldn't ship them out because nobody wanted to pay their wages.

On a personal front, I was also getting fed up with living in rented accommodation down there and seeing less and less of Marian. I would have liked a better pay-off, but at least I got one. The laugh of it was that I paid the cheque into the bank and it bounced. Kassam had decided to stop it because he wanted to make sure we hadn't trashed our flat, which was in the club's name. I don't know what he was expecting to find, as we weren't exactly students away from home for the first time. It was typical of a man who'd made his money at the lower end of the property market, I suppose.

I eventually got a cheque through two or three weeks later

and decided I'd take Marian on holiday. Wrighty told me not to go as it might prevent us getting another job if I was away. He'd already put the feelers out and was hoping to land something soon. But I needed a break and couldn't be bothered playing the waiting game. Marian deserved a break too having hardly seen me over the last few months. Three days later I got a call as I was dozing by the pool on a sunlounger in Tenerife. Unsurprisingly it was Wrighty. He'd got the Chester City gig and wondered if I fancied another crack at the Conference. It was ideal for him as it was just ten minutes down the road from his house. It was another long commute for me and I was in two minds whether to take it or not. But after spending several weeks watching *Channel Four Racing* and pottering about in the garden, I was bored to tears. The deadly duo was back in business.

The club was in a bit of a state when we turned up. They'd been relegated from the league after sixty-nine years and had finished eighth in their first season in the Conference. Liverpool boxing promoter Steve Vaughan had taken over from American owner Terry Smith and was keen to make his mark. He sacked manager Graham Barrow in the summer and replaced him with youth-team boss Gordon Hill. Hill then left in October to make way for former Tranmere player Steve Mungall, who himself lasted just three months. It was clear Hollyoaks was not the only soap opera set in Chester. Wrighty was keen to get stuck in however, and ordered me to come straight up on my return from holiday. Marian and I landed at East Midlands Airport just after midnight on Friday 11 January and I was drinking coffee in his kitchen by 6 a.m. the following day. He was as excited as a kid on Christmas morning.

Sadly Santa couldn't bring us a home win in our first game

in charge. Wrighty had been introduced to the crowd in the mid-week as they lost 2-1 to Northwich Victoria. Afterwards he went into hard-man mode and was critical of the team in the *Chester Evening Leader* newspaper. The shape-up-or-ship-out stuff was getting a bit tiresome by now, but it was clear big changes were needed. We got a draw as we took on Dr Martens west side Stourport Swifts in the FA Trophy and managed to beat them at their place in the replay. But it was pretty dismal stuff. Chester had won just six matches all season and were languishing second from bottom, having played more games than their relegation rivals. Wrighty tried to bring in a number of new faces before our next league game against Barnet, but was only successful in recruiting Phil Bolland. He'd served us so well at Southport and Oxford and jumped at the chance. It did the trick and we beat Barnet 1-0 going on five, for only our second league win in nine outings. Brian McGorry, who we'd also had at Southport, was drafted into midfield and we then thumped Telford 3-0 at Bucks Head.

We didn't then lose in our next eight league and cup games, until my old nemesis Nigel Clough and his Burton Albion side put us out of the FA Trophy in the sixth round. With Wrighty and I in one dugout and Nigel and his assistant Gary Crosby in the other, it was like our East-Midlands derby days all over again. But whilst both management teams were desperate to get one over on the old enemy during the ninety minutes, there was no ill will at the end. We were all a little too long in the tooth for a repeat of any of the old nonsense.

The season had its ups and downs and it looked like we might be in a relegation dogfight after a series of bad results around Easter. But we did enough to eventually finish four-teen, ten points clear of relegation, much to the relief of all concerned. It was the same old struggle to make ends meet that we'd been used to during our two previous spells in management. Every day we fought to improve the team and winkle a few more quid out of the chairman. Steve did his best to wheel and deal for us as we got rid of the dead wood and brought in replacements. And at least he recognised the importance of being full-time. But money was tight, particularly when the club had to pay off former manager Kevin Ratcliffe. Steve was a typical self-made man and could be abrasive. A number of directors came and went as a result of it. But I have to say I got on well with him throughout my time there. The issue I had was with his manager, who was beginning to rub me up the wrong way.

Part of the problem was the commute, which was driving me mad. It was also taking its toll on my battered Volkswagen Jetta. The car began to protest at the number of miles I was asking it to do and things began to go wrong. First up was the gearbox, which eventually only worked in second and fourth after much manhandling. The windscreen wipers then gave up the ghost after a night game and I spent the final thirty miles of my journey pulling them back and forth with a piece of string. What was more annoying was the fact that a local garage had given us a couple of brand new Hyundais. Wrighty told me that mine was a pool car and wasn't allowed out of the Chester area in a bid to get me to stay up there even longer than I already was. He was getting stressed out about almost every aspect of the club and demanded I stuck around until all hours of the day and night. He also got fed up with me clowning around at training and didn't think I took the job seriously enough. He was having difficulties at home again. His estranged wife Sarah accused him of harassment at one point before the charges were later dropped. It was clear something had to give.

The low point in our relationship came when I was approached by Gresley Rovers to become their manager. I didn't mention it because I hadn't decided if I wanted the job. I was certainly keen to work closer to home and the fact they were based in Derbyshire was ideal. But it was a drop down the leagues and the money was certain to be a lot less than we were on at Chester. Wrighty found out I'd been for an interview and angrily accused me of being disloyal. He also said I didn't have the balls to be a manager and would always be a number two. It was an arrogant and unnecessary thing to say, but I knew deep down that he was right. I didn't have and still don't have the ruthless streak you need to be a boss and I don't think I could be bothered with the hassle. I reluctantly turned the job down. But I realised that I was coming to the end of the road with him. He wanted me in Chester all the time and, understandably, Marian wanted me back at home. I helped him make some pre-season signings and we scoped out the coming campaign. But my heart wasn't in it and before a ball was kicked I handed in my notice.

After several years of commuting up and down the motorway, first to Birmingham and then Burnley as a player and then Southport, Oxford and Chester as a manager, I'd had enough. I didn't fall out with Wrighty about it but he was disappointed that I'd decided to pack it in. I still consider him to be a great pal despite the fact we don't speak quite as often as we did.

I was back to where I was when I quit playing, looking for a job outside football. The first thing that came up was working for the Post Office at East Midlands Airport. It was part-time, which made a change from the long hours at Chester. All we had to do was load various bags of letters and parcels onto planes as they made their way round the country. After a few months the twenty-hour-a-week shifts, which lasted from 10 p.m. to 1 a.m., began to get me down and I started looking for something else.

Fortunately there were some jobs going at the main sorting office near Derby station on Midland Road. The job was a doddle and involved picking up packages at various Post offices outside Derby and bringing them into the sorting office. I'd start at Horsley in the morning and work my way in through Allestree, Little Eaton and Oakwood and then on to Mansfield Road, Kedleston Road and various places in between. It was certainly different to managing a football team in the Conference but I loved pottering about in my little red van. I was also following a well-trodden path for former Derby players. No less a legend than Kevin Hector had also become a postie after his career. If it was good enough for the 'King', it was good enough for me.

It was whilst I was doing Postman Pat impressions that I got a call from BBC Radio Derby wondering if I'd like to do some work for them. The sports editor Colin Gibson was looking for cover when his usual presenters couldn't do a game on a Saturday or the phone-in for the fans on a Monday night. I'd always got on with Colin during my playing days and was happy to help, despite the fact I had next to no broadcasting experience.

I forget the first game I did as it passed in a flash and can't have been the most exciting. The main presenter was a guy called Graham Richards who'd become a legend with the fans after joining the station in 1977. His knowledge of the game and Derby County in particular was encyclopaedic and he made life easy for me. He'd rabbit away in his passionate and excitable style for a few minutes and then occasionally remember to ask me for a comment. It all came very easily to me. I also enjoyed doing the supporters' phone-in as it renewed the great rapport I had with them and brought back memories of chatting to the lads on the pop side.

After a couple of goes at it, I remember telling Marian that I'd love to work on the commentaries on a full-time basis. But former Derby footballer and Derbyshire cricketer Ian Hall was the usual summariser and had been for a number of years. Marian had more pressing concerns as at around the same time I'd finally agreed to marry her. I hadn't really thought of tying the knot again, having got myself into a tangle on so many previous occasions. I'd also used up practically every solicitor in Derby sorting out the wreckage and I feared they'd try to throw me in prison if I ever stepped foot in a church or register office again. But after finally sorting out my divorce with Sue, we came to the simple conclusion that it would be a really nice thing to do. Unlike my first three attempts I didn't feel under any pressure to go through with it. I'd had the chance to live with Marian, unlike the other three, and we very rarely argued. There was no sense of foreboding and I knew there'd be no threats as I carried her over the threshold. I was forty-one years old, had made my mistakes and was happy to finally settle down. For the first time, I'd found someone I really wanted to spend the rest of my life with.

The wedding was at Derby Register Office, in the city's council chambers. Fortunately it had recently moved from the site where I'd married June several years previously, and by now there were no photographers clamouring to take our picture. My pal John Timmins, who'd taken me to Heathrow when it all turned sour at Burnley, was my best man and the presence of the three men who'd previously performed that duty served as a reminder that it was about time I got it right. The reception was in one of the function rooms at Pride Park, where Marian was still working as Club Secretary. The day flew by in a bit of a blur but I remember the two of us being very happy that we'd finally found the right person. Whether Marian was quite so happy on our honeymoon in Antigua remains open to some debate. I spent most of it playing football on the beach with the locals and even became the first Scotsman since Mike Denness to develop a taste for cricket. Mind you, with the amount of rum we put away we could have been playing anything.

Before the wedding, four pals and I went on a stag trip to Tenerife. During one of the more sober moments I noticed I'd missed a call from Colin Gibson at Radio Derby. I phoned him back and he told me they were looking for a full-time summariser following the retirement of Ian Hall. I jumped at the chance and went in to see him as soon as I got back. Graham Richards had also called it a day and had been replaced by a talented young journalist called Ross Fletcher, after the station had briefly flirted with a particularly useless Australian called Charles Collins.

Ross was a great guy and we became firm friends as we found our feet in broadcasting and navigated our way around the country. It was the 2004/05 season and fellow Scot George Burley was in charge of the Rams. He'd kept them in the Championship by a point the year before and we weren't expecting big things. But despite losing four out of their first six games, they did unexpectedly well. Silky Spaniard Iñigo Idiakez provided the ammunition and gangly Polish forward Gregorz Rasiak fired in the goals. Ian Taylor enjoyed an Indian summer in midfield and Tommy Smith with his wing wizardry was a man after my own heart. Away trips proved particularly fruitful for them, as they equalled the record twelve wins on the road, set during my playing days.

I tried to tell it like it was on the radio. There was no point hiding things from the fans or spinning a positive line. If Derby played badly I said so and singled out the players who were worst of all. Luckily they didn't play badly too often and there wasn't too much to be critical about. Their fourth place finish was a fantastic achievement in the circumstances and a lot of credit has to go to Burley. Sadly they ran out of steam and were unlucky with injuries in the play-off semi-final against Preston, managed by former Rangers man Billy Davies. I got on well with Burley who realised that we had a job to do and tried to give a balanced view of proceedings. The only criticism my comments attracted was when I was accused of having a go at German winger Marco Reich. He was a talented player who, unlike Tommy Smith, didn't make the most of his skills. Some took my criticism as me having it in for him. But I wonder if they'd have leapt to his defence if they'd known that one of the reasons for his lethargy on the field might have been his nicotine addiction.

Like the fans I was disappointed to see Burley leave Pride Park in the summer of 2005. He seemed to get the most out of the players and had done remarkably well in turning the club from relegation fodder into promotion candidate. If interference by Director of Football Murdo Mackay was the real reason for him leaving I have great sympathy, having baulked at the idea of a similar relationship with Ian Atkins.

I had a great deal of respect for his successor Phil Brown, who I knew from my playing days. Many believed he was the power behind the throne at Bolton Wanderers and optimism was high. I genuinely believed he would do well for the Rams and was excited by his appointment. But his failure to convert draws into wins had the club going backwards after the success of the previous season. He was hamstrung by a lack of investment in the club by the so-called 'Three Amigos' who were in charge, and the number of loan signings he was forced to make suggested there was a lack of commitment to the club. I still think he could go on to become a successful manager and I'm pleased he's done so well at Hull City. Sadly he was just the right guy at the wrong time for Derby.

Terry Westley, who took over from Brown in the New Year, was a really nice guy and had done a good job at the club's academy. He did well to keep them up in the end with crucial wins over Burnley, Crystal Palace and Millwall. But I was surprised he got a bit chippy when I idly suggested after one match how many more points the club would need to survive. In typical football fashion he preferred to take it one game at a time and said he didn't make predictions about points totals. Yet after securing a draw on one occasion he sarcastically told Colin Gibson during a pitch-side interview that they were one point closer to 'Ted McMinn's target'.

I didn't take it personally and had no problem with him picking up on something I'd said. But there were voices within Radio Derby who felt slightly uneasy that the manager was reacting to perceived criticism from one of their employees. They believed it was our job to provide uncritical commentary on events and were fearful of rocking the boat. What the fans liked about me, I thought, was that I had no truck with such political correctness. I was paid to have an opinion. If the pen-pushers were worried about that, it was nothing in comparison with what was just around the corner with Billy Davies.

Despite playing with Davies for a short time at Rangers, I didn't really know him. He'd been in the reserves for the most part and changed in the away dressing room at Ibrox during training. But as with so many professionals who'd had an average playing career, he was determined to prove himself as a coach. He'd built up a reputation as one of the coming managers in the game and had taken Preston to the play-offs in the past two seasons. I thought he was a good appointment and was optimistic that he'd be a success. Derby was his first big club, however, and I thought he would need time to settle. I said as much in my new column in the match programme, following criticism on internet message boards after the team won just one of their opening six league fixtures. A couple of hotheads were already calling for him to be sacked. I acknowledged this but said that if the club got rid of Davies now, they would end up going through six managers a season.

To my complete surprise, Davies interpreted the piece as an attack on him and went ballistic. I presume he told the Chairman Peter Gadsby that he wasn't happy, because he later had a go at Marian. I'm also told that he then tried to have me removed from the programme but was eventually persuaded to calm down. Gadsby told the club's PR man Jim Fearn, who ghosted the column for me, to tone it down. Jim phoned to tell me that further 'criticism' of the manager wouldn't be tolerated. He realised that I hadn't intended to have a go at Davies, but was fearful of the new atmosphere at the club, in which dissent wasn't tolerated. We had to be positive about Davies and the team's prospects for the rest of the season, if I was to continue picking up my £50 cheque for the column. I didn't give a toss about the £50 and told Jim that there was no point doing it if I had to pretend everything was rosy in the garden. He persuaded me to continue for the time being, but not before I told him about my concerns for the thin-skinned man at the helm, who was showing worrying signs of being a control freak. It was like living in the Soviet Union.

Sadly Glasnost hadn't yet set in at Radio Derby either. They were worried about the row continuing and I got the impression they wanted me to keep my head down. I did so until Craig Fagan arrived at the club from Hull City. I couldn't work out whether he was a forward or a midfielder and said I wasn't sure what he brought to the party. Despite signing in January 2007, Rams fans had to wait until the first week in April to see his first league goal for the club, which came in a 1-1 draw at Leicester City. He was interviewed on Radio Derby afterwards and pretended to forget who I was. 'That'll shut what's-his-name up, er, McMinn is it?' was his witty retort. If ever the phrase 'one swallow doesn't make a summer' was more applicable then I'd like to see it.

I could be being paranoid, but the Fagan incident suggested to me that Davies was telling the players what I was saying. If he used it to motivate them then fair enough as we've all benefited from wanting to prove someone wrong. But if Fagan was a case in point, he wasn't doing a very good job. His scoring record was even worse than mine. I hadn't liked criticism as a player – and Graham Richards used to give me pelters if I had a bad game – but you accepted it from punters who'd paid for the privilege or professional commentators who were paid to give their opinions. It just made me more determined to have a better game the following week. Davies, who appeared to be getting more paranoid by the day, couldn't seem to take it, as he proved most spectacularly before the club's play-off final against West Brom in May 2007.

I'd been phoned out of the blue by Scott McDermott on the *Sunday Mirror* in Glasgow, who was writing a preview piece ahead of the game. I said Davies had yet to win anything and that history never remembered the losers. I'd lost in the play-offs myself and sincerely hoped, after two failed attempts, that it would be third time lucky for him. True to form, Davies took it as another slight and again complained to the chairman. This was again communicated to Marian, who found herself as an unfortunate piggy in the middle. As a result she passed on my mobile number to people concerned. I don't know if they ever got it, but if they did they were never man enough to ring me and discuss what I'd said.

Derby won the lucrative game 1-0 thanks to a Stephen Pearson goal and the scenes at Wembley were brilliant. I was so pleased to see the club back in the Premier League and delighted for the fans, who'd had to put up with so much. Davies saw it differently unfortunately. He used his post-match interview with Colin Gibson to sarcastically thank me for the inspiration the *Sunday Mirror* article had given him and the team. There was no mention of the magnificent travelling support or the exciting prospect of taking a fantastic football club back to where they belonged, just a ridiculous rant from a bitter man. It was to get worse the following day, when he spoiled the play-off party by telling the media that there was no guarantee he would be in the job for the first game of the following season. Like a pint-sized philosophy student he pontificated in the papers: 'nothing is guaranteed other than one day we will all pass away.'

Derby spent the summer making sure Davies's every whim

was catered for. The cast of *Ben Hur* arrived to help him in his pursuit of Premier-League survival. I was very much looking forward to the new season, but asked Radio Derby if I could have some more money. I'd originally started on £65 a game, home or away, and got an extra £20 for doing the football phone-in. That increased to £85 a game during my second season, yet I felt I deserved a bit more. I'd recently done a short piece for the BBC in Scotland and been paid £150 for an hour's work. Unlike the other journalists working on the show I didn't get any expenses other than my hotel room for away trips. That meant I had to pay for my own meals and drinks and quite often take time off work on the Friday if it was a long trip. On a number of occasions I actually lost money doing the commentary, which wasn't much fun in the cold light of day. But Radio Derby claimed there was no more money and that I'd have to make do with what I had.

Before the start of the season the station had its routine meeting with the club to renew their contract. News editor John Atkins was there among other staff from Radio Derby, with Chief Executive Trevor Birch and Peter Gadsby representing Derby. At some point during the meeting the club asked who was going to do the commentaries and were told it was Ross Fletcher and I. There was an uneasy silence across the table before Gadsby said they would be listening carefully to what I had to say. He didn't explicitly ask for me to be fired or put pressure on the station to change their team. But when I heard what he'd said, I got the impression that he wasn't happy that I would still be the summariser. Marian was also getting grief at Pride Park, with Billy initially moving her up to the Moor Farm training complex and then back to Pride Park. He also refused to speak to her, getting his PA Jeanette Brennan to pass on messages – even, on occasions, when Marian was in the same room. It was just getting ridiculous. I did the friendly matches at the start of 2007/08 and the first game against Portsmouth and then quit. The club didn't want me and were putting pressure on my wife and the station was paying a pittance. What was the point?

I was particularly disappointed with Peter Gadsby's role in the whole affair. I'd known him for years and still appreciate the friendship and kindness he's shown over the years to both Marian and me. He also did a terrific job for Derby, bailing the club out and putting them back on an even keel. But I felt that he and many other members of the senior management in place at the time lost the plot during Billy Davies's short reign. In getting them promoted in the first year of a three-year plan, Davies did a terrific job and it is doubtful whether any manager could subsequently have kept them in the top flight in their first season back. But the clamour to keep him happy at all costs that summer, exacerbated by his constant need to be loved, bred an unhealthy atmosphere and skewed the focus of the club. It's easy to be clever with hindsight and I understand the deep concern that they'd lose a talented manager if he didn't get his own way. But I'm afraid that Gadsby, like too many other people at Derby, became sheep rather than Rams.

22

FOOTING THE BILL

Aches and pains go with the territory when you're a footballer. Well they certainly did in my career. During your playing days they can be treated by the best physiotherapists and doctors. Afterwards you accept that they're the price you pay for being paid to play sport for a living. I developed a pain in my right foot on the middle Friday of July 2005 and thought very little of it. I'd been doing some work with my friend Clive Thompson replacing broken tiles at the David Lloyd Leisure Centre in Nottingham. We worked through the night and after a couple of hours' kip, arranged to meet up at midday for a game of golf at Horsley Lodge, a course about five miles outside Derby. We finished the round and I retreated to the bar with a dull ache on the top of the foot. I put it down to gout, which I had suffered with for many years. The doctors had got it under control, but I appeared to be having a relapse.

Marian and I went to a party at Derby's Polish Club that evening. After standing around for twenty minutes my foot was killing me and I was desperate to go home and take my shoe off. I swallowed some gout tablets and went straight to bed, but slept fitfully as even the weight of the duvet caused me pain. In the morning I could barely get out of bed and had to crawl to the bathroom. After finally doing so, I ransacked the bathroom cabinet and began popping painkillers and any pills with my name on them that looked like they might help. The cocktail of drugs merely served to make me sick and give me diarrhoea.

I was due to commentate on Derby's pre-season match against Birmingham City that afternoon but had to phone in sick. By the Sunday morning I was no better and Marian phoned for an emergency doctor. He concluded that I was having a particularly strong gout attack and left me with some steroids. I couldn't help but notice that they were the same as the ones I'd been taking and wondered if they'd do any good. By Monday morning the answer was no. The only place I could get relief from the pain was in a hot bath. I'd stopped eating and could only keep down the smallest sips of water. On the Tuesday morning, Marian rang Les Redlaff, Derby County's team doctor, and he came out to our flat in Aston-on-Trent straight away. He took one look at my face and told me I was dehydrated. He took another look at my foot, which by now was red and swollen, and said there was no way I had gout.

Dr Redlaff told me he was going to phone for an ambulance but I refused. I had a swollen foot and dodgy guts but I wasn't a basket case yet. Instead I hobbled out of the flat and went down the four flights of stairs one by one on my backside. I was pouring with sweat by the time I got to the bottom and regretted my decision. Marian drove me to the Derbyshire Royal Infirmary and I gladly accepted the offer of a wheelchair. It was no time to be a hero. They didn't really know what to do with me in Accident and Emergency so I was kept in overnight for tests.

The first doctor who saw me concluded that I had diabetes

and stuck me on a drip. Tests proved otherwise and so they took a number of X-rays of my foot. I was asked if I could remember any cuts that I suffered that could have let in an infection. Marian and I had recently been away to Corfu to celebrate our first anniversary. During a walk we'd gone through some swampy ground and I wondered if I'd been bitten by something. I'd also nicked my hands when I was cuttings tiles for Clive and scratched my hand on a gorse bush playing golf, watching in disgust as a horsefly landed on it when I was retrieving my ball. I'd also burst a blister on my ankle after wearing a new pair of golf shoes. But none of the explanations seemed conclusive to the doctors.

Tuesday turned into Wednesday and Wednesday into Thursday as one white coat after another sucked the end of his pen and sent me for more tests. On the Friday morning I had a full MRI scan and joked with the operator that it felt like a dry-run for a cremation. There were more gags later when a junior doctor came in and quipped that they could do amazing things with artificial limbs these days. I'd have laughed more were it not for the fact that I was still in a lot of pain. By now my foot was badly blistered and swollen and had turned an ugly black and yellow colour. I felt like sticking a needle in and popping whatever it was. After dinner that evening a group of doctors suddenly swarmed round the bed and told me I had an infection in my foot caused by a bacteria called Staphylococcus Aureus. It meant nothing to me, but I sat up and paid attention when they told me they were going to operate at midnight.

I began to worry that it might be something important if they couldn't wait until the morning. But I convinced myself that it would be a simple job of removing the infection and letting me out with a big bandage wrapped round my foot. I went up to theatre and had a general anaesthetic, thinking as I always did that the slow drift into sleep would be a perfect way to die. But I wasn't ready to meet my maker yet and woke some hours later sick as a dog. That morning the Surgeon John Rowles came round and explained what he'd done. He'd opened up my foot and done his best to remove the poison. But as soon as he got rid of it, it came back and he'd have to go in again on Sunday. This time he would put a pump in to drain off the source of the infection. Hopefully they would then get a better idea of how the bug was attacking my foot. By now I was slowly being gripped by a fear that something more serious was at work.

I woke up groggily on a new ward on Sunday night, with my foot throbbing under its dressing. Mr Rowles came round the following morning and looked grave behind his droopy moustache. He hadn't been able to put the pump in or carry out the work he wanted to, so he was going to operate for a third time. It was pencilled in for Tuesday morning and we both hoped it would be third time lucky. In the meantime dozens of visitors began arriving to wish me all the best and I became faintly embarrassed to greet them. There were people in the ward beside me with much more serious complaints, but here I was with a minor infection in my foot and an endless procession of well-wishers.

I went down to theatre on the Tuesday and was further embarrassed to find I was now being recognised. They meant well, but I became a bit fed up with people wanting to swap football anecdotes as I waited for surgery. I wished they would just knock me out. When they finally did, I awoke feeling like I'd been in surgery for ages. Marian confirmed that I'd been away for several hours as I lay in bed staring at my foot, hoping it was now cured. Mr Rowles dropped in an hour or two later and asked me if I could feel my toes when he tickled them. I couldn't feel a thing but lied that I could. It was no wonder when he told me he'd had to remove the bones at the top of my second, third and fourth toes. They'd flaked away like pealing paint as he scraped at the infection.

As soon as he arrived he was gone. Marian and I were shocked by what he'd told us and hadn't had time to ask any questions. We both wanted to know how the operation would affect my walking and if things would now go back to normal. In the absence of answers we told ourselves things must be okay. With any luck I'd be allowed out in the morning. That proved not to be the case when a nurse called Tom Crowley came to see me the following afternoon. I'd had a number of problems with the cannula needles in the back of my hand, which were used to take blood for tests. I had to have several replacements as the veins in the back of my hand protested and I was beginning to feel like a pincushion. Tom, who'd become quite friendly with me during my stay, told me I had to have a peripherally inserted central catheter line put in.

I was beginning to wonder what the hell he was on about when he brought out a long thin tube and told me he was going to put it up my arm. It seemed an appalling and painful idea, and it dawned on me that I wouldn't be getting out anytime soon. Tom, who knew of my fear of needles, was very good about it and spent an age explaining how it was going to work. I eventually let him get on with it and looked away. But after it travelled two or three inches up the vein in my arm I inadvertently tensed up and it shot back out. So too did a large spurt of blood that covered his plastic bib and my white bedclothes. With the patience of a saint he tried again as I tried my hardest not to panic.

We were in the middle of this hide-the-spaghetti game when Mr Rowles and a team of doctors burst onto the ward like gunslingers in a Wild West saloon. He greeted me and in a cheerful voice said: 'We're going to amputate tomorrow.' The PICC line shot out of my arm, drenching poor old Tom with my blood again. Marian burst into tears and ran out into the corridor. She was sat with her head in her hands when my mates Clive Thompson and Mark Jennison arrived for afternoon visiting some moments later. They saw Marian and quickly glanced into the ward to see my bed covered in blood and surrounded by doctors. 'Oh Marian, I'm so sorry,' said Clive. 'When did he die?'

As Marian fought back the tears and explained that I was still very much alive, I tried to find out how much Mr Rowles was intending to cut off. He was understandably reluctant to make any promises, as he wasn't going to know how far the infection had spread until he operated. But before he left I pleaded with him to save as much of my foot and leg as he could. Once Marian had calmed down I did my best to persuade her that I was going to be okay. She reluctantly left at 9 p.m. to go home to bed and I was left with my thoughts as I stared out of the window at the lights of Derby. I didn't sleep a wink that night and spent a good portion of it weeping and feeling sorry for myself. Why was this happening to me?

I wondered how I'd caught the infection and racked my brains for an answer. Was it any of the cuts I'd had or had I been bitten by something. The docs told me that the bones were frighteningly brittle in my toes. I thought back to September 1986 when I broke my foot in the Skol Cup semi-final against

Dundee United. I'd then taken several injections before the Aberdeen game to make sure I was fit enough to play in the final. I hadn't heard of anyone else having a similar reaction. But was this my body's idea of revenge?

The past came to meet me the following morning, when Alex Cargill popped in to see me. He'd carried out all of my knee operations and reassured me that I was now in good hands. Dayna and Kevin also came down from Scotland and we were getting used to the idea of life without my right foot when the porter came to take me down to the slaughterhouse. I saw the same old faces on what I hoped was my fourth and final visit and wondered at the hard work and dedication of our NHS staff. They never seemed to be off duty. Fortunately, for them and for me, they could put the PICC line in when I was knocked out this time. I lay on a bed in a room waiting in the queue for what felt like a lifetime. When it was finally my turn I drifted off to sleep not knowing what I'd wake up to find. A small part of me hoped I never would.

The pain I had when I came round made me wish I was still under the anaesthetic. Marian was sitting at my bedside. But after catching her eye momentarily, the first thing I looked at was my foot. Remarkably much of it seemed to still be there. The toes had gone, but the size of the bandage indicated that a good chunk of the foot remained. Nurses who came round to dress the wound confirmed that it was. When they removed the bandages for the first time it looked like a particularly horrible samosa. I felt sick when I saw it and said to myself that it would always be covered up. Mr Rowles had cut off my toes but kept the sole of my foot and stitched it back over the stump. The counsellors who followed the nurses suggested I might want to consider having the leg removed just below the knee. They were confident that they'd got rid of all of the infection but ironically, walking would be made easier the more they took off. Doctors would be able to fit me with an artificial limb if I had more removed, but they didn't have anything to attach it to in its present form. They were very persuasive but I told Marian that there was no way I was having another operation. I just couldn't face going under the knife again and vowed to get on with it.

Getting out was easier said than done. They wanted to keep me in for another week to check the infection didn't return. They also wanted to make sure Marian and I were capable of changing my drip, which would stay with me for a couple of weeks to come. After a few days a porter brought up a brand-new wheelchair and parked it by my bed. The nurses also gave me a pair of crutches, which I was a dab hand at using after all the injuries I'd sustained as a player. But they insisted that my leg would heal quicker if it was kept upright in the chair. I hated the bloody thing and saw it as a constant reminder of my new disability. But in a bid to get out I persevered and passed the wheelchair ability test they set me. I also weaned myself off the forty pills a day I was taking and just over a week after my operation I left the DRI, hoping to God nobody would ever see me.

They might never have done had I been able to get up the four flights of stairs to my flat and hide. I quickly dispatched the wheelchair to the garage before spending the best part of half an hour puffing and blowing up the steps. It was okay once I was up, but the prospect of repeating it twice a day to get my dressing changed at the DRI wasn't appealing. There was also the small matter of a life I had to lead. I couldn't sit in the flat for the rest of my days so it was clear that we were going to have to move. My friend Matt Morgan came to our rescue with a cottage he had to rent in Weston-on-Trent. The village lies south of Derby and is near my old stomping ground at Swarkestone. It still had upstairs bedrooms, but one flight of stairs was certainly better than four and we were grateful to be given the opportunity to make a new start. I was also encouraged by the large fish pond just outside the front door, which seemed like an ideal spot to while away the hours as I made my recovery.

I'd hobble over to the pond of a morning and cast a rod into its tranquil waters, occasionally pulling out the odd carp. Marian would come home in the evenings and friends would stop by and take me to the pub. Were it not for the constant pain I was suffering it wouldn't have been too bad. Much of it was self-imposed. Despite the advice of the doctors, I was treading on my heel as I walked and the wound was taking longer to heal than it should. My Achilles tendon was also becoming painfully stretched as I hobbled around like a lame horse. As the autumn approached I began to worry that I'd slip on leaves on the decking near the pond, which became greasy after a shower of rain. And the final straw came one evening when I got out of bed to go to the toilet, forgot about my leg and fell over. I used to do that when I was half-pissed, but I was now doing it because I had half a foot.

I looked into the water the following day and thought about chucking myself in. If I could just sink beneath the surface all of this would go away. I stopped myself from doing so, but burst into tears in my despair. What was the point of going on if my life was as bad as this? It was never going to get any better, so why should I bother? I couldn't even put a shoe on it. After an hour or two in the doldrums I pulled myself together and remembered all those Jock Wallace team talks at Rangers and Seville. He'd told me about the fire in my belly and the need for what he always described as 'character'. The cry, as he now reminded me from beyond the grave, was No Surrender.

I had to wait five weeks before the operation, but there was now no chance of me changing my mind. I told a few pals including Iain King at the *Scottish Sun* that I was going under the knife again and the papers picked up on the story. The *Derby Evening Telegraph* had also wanted me to keep them in touch with events and I did an interview with them one Saturday. I'd booked an appointment with Mr Rowles on the following Monday to tell him that it was full steam ahead. But he already knew my decision having read it in the *Telegraph* when he went to pick up his Chinese takeaway on the Saturday night. He assured me that I was doing the right thing and booked me in for 5 October. Mick Maguire, the Deputy Chief Executive of the PFA was kind enough to phone and tell me that they'd be happy to pay for it if I went private. But Mr Rowles said he would perform the same operation for free under the NHS. This way I would have more time to think about how I was going to cope and prepare for life afterwards.

My biggest fear as a winger had been going past a fullback and his clumsy lunge breaking my leg. Now I was volunteering to have it sawn off. I had visions of my three ex-wives sitting round taking turns on a Ted-shaped voodoo doll. They were sticking a pin in my foot for all the times I'd hurt them and other people in my life. And who could blame them. I was now being taught the ultimate lesson as they chopped it off. But I didn't want to be on crutches, or in a wheelchair, for the rest of my life. I was sick of being reliant on other people to do the simplest things. If I made a cup of coffee in the kitchen I had to drink it in there because I'd spill half of it getting it through to the living room. Poor old Marian was ferrying me around everywhere and was forced to be at my beck and call. If I could be fitted with an artificial limb, life would be easier and I would get back at least some of my independence. The doctors told me I may even hit a golf ball again, which came as great news after I'd convinced myself that I'd played my last round.

I was playing a golf game on my PSP in hospital on the morning of 5 October when Mr Rowles came round to see me. He was a different man from the one who'd startled us with the news he was going to amputate back in August. Instead, he put me at ease with a few jokes and a bit of light-hearted banter. It was a good job as I hadn't slept a wink the night before and was a nervous wreck. I'd had visions of him coming at me with a saw and watched in horror as he hacked at my leg. I wanted to know how he was going to do it and how he intended to round off the stump. Was there some piece of kit that Black & Decker produced to do the job? For Marian's sake as much as my own I refrained from asking. I was number three on the list that morning and as I was wheeled away there were plenty of tears. But there was no turning back now.

I woke up later on as Ted McMinn, disabled person. The truth was I'd acquired the disability when I had the first operation, but somehow this felt more final. The limb had now been removed to within four inches of my knee. I was in a lot of pain and pushed the button on the self-administered morphine drip for all it was worth. The thought of looking at what was left of my leg had filled me with fear, but I got used to it pretty quickly. The nurses were happy with it too and within two days they let me out. My initial concern about getting back into circulation was how people would react to me when they saw my stump. I was taught not to stare at people when I was a child but knew that others weren't always so kind. The ice was broken when I went into the pub on the Sunday afternoon after the operation. My friend Morgie greeted me like I'd never been away, saying 'hello peg leg' at the top of his voice. The pub fell silent for a moment, waiting to see how I'd react. But when I laughed, they did too and I knew my friends and family were going to help me through it.

The hard work and dedication of the staff at the DRI's amputee unit and the Pulvertaft Hand Clinic was incredible, and one of the main reasons why I got back into the swing of things so quickly. Just a few days after the surgery they got me in to start doing physiotherapy and to prepare me mentally and physically for life as an amputee. Before long they put me in my first artificial limb, which was a prelude to getting my own. The device, which was a normal prosthetic leg with a rubber cushion at the top that held the stump in place, was known as a Personal Adaptive Mobility Aid – or PAM Aid for short. I still had the stitches in when I first put it on and it hurt like hell when the rubber gripped the wound. But I was determined to start walking again as soon as I could. I stumbled about between parallel bars for a while until I got the confidence to walk on crutches. It was then a question of walking unaided, bending to pick things up and performing a number of manoeuvrability tests. It was hard work but I could see I was making progress quickly and I was encouraged that a semblance of normality wasn't far away.

Unfortunately I received a setback a couple of weeks later when I was invited to an event at Derbyshire's County Cricket Ground, designed to help disabled people lead an independent life. The organisers, LivAbility UK, had read about my plight in the papers and hoped that I'd be able to share my experiences with others in a similar boat. I had no objections and went along with Marian in my wheelchair, glad to be of some use. But as soon as I got there, I hated it. Being in the chair meant folk had to look down on me if they were standing up and some became unintentionally patronising. As stupid as it sounds, I also felt uncomfortable being surrounded by people with disabilities and didn't feel I had very much in common with them at all. The organiser was a pleasant, well-meaning woman called Glenys Crooks. But, much to her surprise, I turned down her invitation to say a few words. The usual protocol would have been to thank people for inviting me there, yet by doing so it felt like I'd be thanking them for making me disabled. There was also a strong possibility that I'd have broken down and I didn't want anyone to see me in tears. After an embarrassing silence, I posed for a few pictures, feeling more uncomfortable than I'd ever felt in my life.

Marian and I talked about my feelings that night when I finally escaped. The exhibition confirmed in my mind that I was going to be disabled for the rest of my life and the realisation really upset me. But I felt guilty about my self-pity and told myself that there had been people there who were a lot worse off than me. The stalls at the exhibition had not been without their benefits either. Whilst passing one I was heartened to discover that I could have a car converted so that I could drive again, something that had never occurred to me. The prospect handed me back my independence and convinced me that I might not always have to rely on other people. As I lay in bed that night I realised that there was no point wallowing in self-pity. If I let this thing eat me up it would. Instead I should concentrate on what was good in my life and what I had to be thankful about. I should draw on the pain and use it as inspiration to help not just myself, but others too. So many people had done so much for me, not just in recent months but also throughout my life. It was now time to put a bit back.

23

THOUGH THE STREETS BE BROAD OR NARROW

The first thing people notice when they file through the Ibrox trophy room is the sheer scale of the club's achievements. All four walls are covered in paintings, pennants and pictures and the cabinets are stuffed full of gleaming medals, silver trophies and crystal vases. The second thing they notice is an old racing bike, which appears to have been abandoned under a portrait of the club's legendary manager Bill Struth. The unique gift was presented to Rangers by the French side Saint Etienne when the clubs met in the European Cup in September 1957. The bike, coupled with an interest in that summer's Tour de France, prompted my old teammate Dave McKinnon to call me out of the blue in December 2005. He wondered if I fancied doing a bike ride to raise money for amputee charities, as a way of saying thank you for the help I'd received. I hadn't yet been fitted with my artificial leg but the idea intrigued me, even when he suggested we cycle all the way from Glasgow to Derby. It sounded like incredibly hard work and I wondered if I was up to the challenge either physically or mentally. But after mulling it over for a day or two, I sent Dave a text message saying 'Let's do it'. Struth, who himself had part of a leg amputated in 1952, would have been proud of us.

At around the time we were formulating the plan for what would eventually be rather grandly called 'Ted's incredible journey', I got another call. It was from Derby's Chief Executive Jeremy Keith. He invited me in to Pride Park and told me that I could have the stadium to myself on a day during the closed season if I wanted to organise a benefit game. It was a generous offer and I was very grateful for their assistance, particularly as I'd slated him on the radio. Keith said I would have to organise my own teams – a Derby side and their opponents. My first thought was the current Rangers team, knowing they would attract a huge following to the game. But a quick call to their marketing manager and former player Sandy Jardine revealed that they were booked up in friendly matches for over eighteen months. Before he rang off, Sandy told me that the next best thing would be to get the legendary Rangers 'Nine-in-a-Row' side, who had dominated Scottish football during the previous decade. The team was organised by former player John 'Bomber' Brown, who was only too happy to help. He couldn't promise who exactly would be there or how fit they'd be, but we set the date for 1 May 2006.

My own fitness levels were in serious need of improvement if I was to get through my endurance test. A Derby company called Moore Large & Co generously agreed to supply us with the bikes and they arrived in the first week in January. I was concerned about my balance and it was decided that I'd be better off on a tandem with my mate Clive Thompson at the front. Clive's sister Kim was going to ride on the trip too alongside my friends Paul Wightman, Aidie Fearn, Rob Collington, Dave McKinnon, Marian and her son Gavin. I'd done next to no exercise since the operation and puffed a bit when we went out on our first practice run. But we did around twenty miles and weren't too knackered when we got in. In the weeks that followed we built up the mileage and slowly increased our fitness. We went out in all weathers, keeping our goal in mind at all times. I decided that I would raise money for the amputee unit at the DRI but also wanted a Scottish charity. The Murray Foundation set up by Rangers Chairman David Murray, who lost both his legs in a car accident as a young man, fitted the bill perfectly.

In our spare moments we planned the week-long journey from Ibrox to Pride Park, which we'd pencilled in to begin on Saturday 8 April. I'd been up and down that road a thousand times during my life and hated every inch of it. The thought of doing it on a bike staring at Clive's arse was no more appealing, so in the last few weeks of training I switched to my own bike. It wasn't much different and I didn't have too many problems with balance. But there was the odd occasion during training that I forgot my artificial leg was in a bike clip and keeled over. Luckily my pride was the only thing that was ever hurt and like a child learning to ride I was able to get back on and start again. By the end I got up to around thirty or forty miles a day and was confident I could do it.

Twelve of us assembled outside Ibrox on the Saturday morning, six months to the day after my operation. Nine of us would be riding and we had a bike for everyone, the tandem in case it was needed, two vans, an overnight bag each, several puncture repair kits, maps and our three support drivers, Simon Twigg, Eddie McLellan and Graham Jones. The only thing we'd forgotten was my spare leg. We'd hoped to leave Ibrox at around 10 a.m. but by the time we'd had our photos taken and I'd signed dozens of autographs for the fans who'd turned up it was nearer 11 a.m. Clive led us off and seemed to know where he was going until we realised he was taking us the wrong way down a one way street. We got the odd catcall from Celtic supporters, but most people wished us well and we were constantly tooted by passing cars. After four hours and forty-one miles we rolled into Abington in Lanarkshire, which was to be our first stop en route. None of us was the worse for the experience other than being a little saddle-sore and walking like John Wayne. But to nobody's surprise the first beer in the bar that night didn't touch the sides.

We had an extra ten miles to do the following day when we headed out of Abington for Gretna on the border with England. Along the way we passed through Lockerbie, where Dave McKinnon solemnly pointed out to the English boys the site of the air disaster. He was so gripped with his history lesson that he wobbled off his bike into a ditch, as we tried not to laugh. The weather stayed fair for us and we were blessed by not having to ride into too many headwinds. I'd been able to do more training than the rest and was finding it relatively easy. The only problem I had was not being able to feel the pedal. My stump also felt like I was wearing a pair of shoes that were two or three sizes too small. After a time it became numb like I was walking barefoot in the snow. But it was just like doing pre-season training all over again and I relished the challenge.

As the rain began to fall we upped the ante and put in a sixty-mile shift between Gretna and Kendal in the Lake District. All of us were lost in our own little world of wetness when we were passed by a police car on the road between Carlisle and Penrith. It doubled back and the officer stopped us to ask if we'd lost any kit. We thought they meant puncture repair kits at first until they told us they'd picked up some kids who'd been stealing from a service station. Their car had two large boxes containing the Rangers jerseys, shorts and socks that Bomber Brown had given us to take down to Derby. After a forty-minute wait at the side of the road we breathed a sigh of relief when our support van finally came back to confirm the stuff was missing. There was further heavy breathing when we then endured the steepest climb of the journey, all 1,400 feet up Shap Fell, as day four took in the forty-four miles between Kendal and Preston. I lagged behind the others as I couldn't stand up in my saddle. But I gritted my teeth and made it over the top in my own time.

Our fifth day saw us trundling between Preston and Stockport, where I kept my head down after my experiences with their fans playing for Burnley. On the sixth day we arrived in Derbyshire, ticking off the forty miles to Ashbourne. For once there was someone worse off than myself in our group. The previous morning, van driver Eddie had stumbled in the car park of a Sainsbury's supermarket after we'd popped in for a fry-up. It turned out that he'd fractured his foot and we were concerned that he should get to a hospital. But in summing up the spirit of the whole trip he refused to abandon his post.

I had a nasty cut on my stump but nothing was going to sidetrack me either as we headed out of Ashbourne for the final fifteen miles. Riding down the A52 we got beep after beep from the passing cars, which grew to a cacophony as we headed into the city. The goodwill was unbelievable. With just a mile to go, Dave's pedal fell off outside the Crown Court and he was forced to roll into Pride Park using just his crank. There was a great reception when we finally arrived, exhausted but elated.

We'd travelled over 300 miles and raised over £15,000 for our two charities. Nobody had dropped out and we'd all managed it together. I'd also conquered my own demons and proved to myself that I could overcome my adversity.

With the testimonial game just a fortnight away we had no time to rest on our laurels. Most of the hard work had been done by my committee, which was chaired by my old friend Colin Tunnicliffe. Tunners had played cricket for Derbyshire before becoming their commercial director and then joining Derby County. We also brought in my accountant Bill Williams, Alex Grant from BMI, Toby Sills from Derby's Disabled Supporters Association, the club's Director of Operations Paul Clouting and the *Scottish Sun*'s chief football correspondent Iain King, who'd kept the pot boiling with a series of articles north of the border. The only time we disagreed was when they asked me how many tickets we needed to send up to Rangers. I thought about it for a moment and concluded that we'd have to provide at least 10,000. Derby were averaging around 23,000 at the time and there were a few stifled guffaws from the English contingent when I suggested the figure. But their laughs turned to amazement when a 12,000 strong army of supporters began arriving in town days before the game.

I was nervous that none of the players would take it seriously and it wouldn't be competitive or a very good spectacle for the fans. But my fears were laid to rest when the two managers began assembling their sides. Walter Smith and Archie Knox had agreed to look after the 'Nine in a Row' team and Arthur Cox was in charge of the Derby County Legends. Arthur took it deadly seriously and drew up plans to put out the best side he could. To my astonishment he said he wanted my old enemy Stuart Pearce to be his captain, along with fellow

Nottingham Forest player Nigel Clough in midfield. I didn't believe either would want to play given the tempestuous relationship I'd had with them during my playing days. But without a moment's hesitation both agreed. Seeing them in Derby kits and in particular Stuart Pearce kissing the Derby badge when he scored was one of the most remarkable sights on a remarkable day.

Pearce and Clough weren't the only big names on display. Igor Stimac and Stefano Eranio both flew in to play and my old teammates Tommy Johnson, Dean Saunders, Gary Micklewhite and Paul Goddard all agreed to take part. For the older fans there was Roy McFarland, Roger Davies and Kevin Hector from the championship-winning sides of the 1970s. The Rangers team boasted great players too, including Andy Goram, Chris Woods, Nigel Spackman, Ray Wilkins, Gordon Durie, Stuart McCall and Mark Hateley. Paul Gascoigne and Chris Waddle also came along despite not being able to play through injury. Walter was short of players on the day due to call-offs and went into the home changing rooms to see if he could pinch anybody. He was given short shrift by Arthur when asked for his skipper Pearce and emerged with my old apprentice Steve Taylor and my son Kevin, who'd begged me to play and had been stripped from midday. Wrighty had said to Arthur he only wanted to play for half an hour, but was told in no uncertain terms that he'd play for as long as he was required. It was going to be competitive all right.

I'd arrived at the ground at 8 a.m. that morning, driving past the hotels on Pride Park draped in Union Jacks. Thousands of Rangers supporters were beginning to mass in the city centre too, where they were doing their best to drink the bars dry. I began meeting corporate clients and doing interviews soon after and before I knew it kick-off was approaching. I felt incredibly emotional when Kevin and Dayna led the teams out and declined an invite to say a few words in case I broke down. Kevin later came on as a substitute and forced a good save out of Lee Camp in the Derby goal. It was a proud moment for me as well as his grandparents Tom and Isabelle, who were watching from the stand. The whole experience was humbling and the response from the supporters was mind-blowing. Here were two clubs looking after one of their own and I felt privileged to have represented both. It was unbelievable to see the Derby fans in white shirts and the Rangers fans in blue ones, both with Tin Man and number seven on the back. And it all seemed a millions miles away from the darkest days of my life.

The game was a half decent spectacle too, when it finally kicked off fifteen minutes late. Dave McKinnon forced a corner early on and Gordon Durie stooped to head it in. But Dave's weak header out some minutes later set up Nigel Clough to put the Rams level. Stuart Pearce then scored after Dean Saunders beat the offside trap and Bobby Davison showed how he poached so many goals in his career. But the 'Nine-in-a-Row' boys weren't to be beaten and a goal from Ally McCoist and another from Jukebox made sure both sets of fans went home happy. The Rangers support in particular sang their hearts out throughout the game, with their Derby coun-terparts in awe of the atmosphere they created. One of the highlights for them was linesman Bill Ramsay's decision to exchange his yellow flag for a giant union jack. As Iain King summed it up in the piece he filed for the *Scottish Sun*, this truly was The Beautiful Game.

I later chewed over the day's events with a McChicken Sandwich in the McDonald's restaurant on Pride Park. Dayna and Kevin had persuaded me to pop in after finally dragging me away from the ground. I hadn't wanted to leave but was absolutely exhausted. It had been an unbelievable day and I felt lucky to have been the focus of its attention. Due to the lack of segregation, the crowd of 33,475 remains the biggest the stadium has ever held. Fans had journeyed from the four corners of the United Kingdom to turn out for little old me. The website set up to support the game later revealed that they'd also flown in from as far afield as Russia, Algeria, Argentina, Australia, Germany, Spain, Sweden, Norway and the United States just to be there. I will never be able to repay the kindness they showed or that shown by the thousands who visited me in hospital or sent me get well cards. If I had inadvertently touched their lives during my career, they certainly did the same for me in my hour of need.

People's generosity in buying tickets and souvenirs also provided me with some financial security and I'm very grateful for that. Since the operation my ability to work has been greatly restricted. Health and Safety won't allow me in a factory and I would be a danger to myself as well as others on a building site. Had I some qualifications to my name I might be better off. But when others were studying for exams, I was out kicking a ball. My dedication to that task gave me a great career and in looking back on it I'm proud of my achievements in three of the top leagues in Europe. People often ask if I wish I'd played football nowadays and been exposed to the untold riches washing around the game. It's true that even if I'd started ten years later I would probably have been made for life with salaries and signing-on fees, let alone commercial agreements and the extras. But I honestly believe that if you're in it for the money, you're in the wrong game.

THE TIN MAN

I couldn't have cared less for money when I joined my home-town team Queen of the South. And it certainly wasn't my motivation when I moved on to Rangers, Seville or Derby County. Circumstances meant that financial considerations had to be taken into account when the time came to sign for Birmingham and Burnley. But I went there because I wanted to play football too. I hope people enjoyed watching me at these clubs as much as I enjoyed playing for them. The fact that I was lucky enough to be selected in Queen of the South's all-time XI and in a book on 100 Rangers Greats, was picked in Derby County and Burnley's top three cult heroes and managed to get my name on Seville's centenary shirt – not once but twice – suggests that they did. They might have got a bit more out of me as well, had I not picked up so many injuries or endured such a rollercoaster of a personal life. If I had my time again I'd have spent less time in hospitals and certainly treated one or two people a little better. But I've done my best and tried to be honest throughout. If the Tin Man in the *Wizard of Oz* didn't have a heart, I'd like to think this one has.